The Soul of Economies

THE SOUL OF ECONOMIES

Spiritual Evolution Goes to the Marketplace

Denise Breton
and
Christopher Largent

IDEA HOUSE PUBLISHING COMPANY
Wilmington, Delaware, USA

THE SOUL OF ECONOMIES
Spiritual Evolution Goes to the Marketplace

An Idea House Book

For information, contact:

Idea House Publishing Company

Editorial address: SAN: 297-228X
2019 Delaware Avenue, Wilmington, DE 19806
(302) 571-9570   FAX: (302) 571-9615

Ordering address: SAN: 630-3463
c/o Maxway Data Corporation
225 West 34th Street, New York, NY 10122
(212) 947-6100   (800) 447-8862   FAX: (212) 563-5703

First edition

ISBN 0-9626238-1-4   Cloth: Library Binding and Cover
ISBN 0-9626238-2-2   Paperback
Library of Congress Catalog Card Number: 90-81854
Permanent (acid-free), high-quality recycled paper

 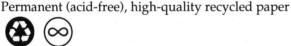

Cover and text design by Claudia Ballou of Peyton Associates
Printed and bound in the United States of America by
BookCrafters of Chelsea, Michigan

The coin on the cover is a Syracuse dekadrachm from early in the fifth century B.C., sculpted by Kimon, a noted Greek sculptor.

I do not believe the spiritual law works on a field of its own. On the contrary, it expresses itself only through the ordinary activities of life. It thus affects the economic, the social, and the political fields.

Mohandas K. Gandhi

Contents

Foreword

In the 1970s, worried, even terrified, by the oil-energy crisis, humankind gave many poignant expressions of the need for a world view of economic survival, symbolized most graphically and articulately perhaps by the Club of Rome.

But the crisis passed, at least temporarily, and the 1980s saw a huge resurgence of economic lavishness. Now, just in time, we may hope, Denise Breton and Christopher Largent remind us that the crisis of the global economy was not something that passed with the seeming end of the oil shortage of the '70s but something broader and deeper, which neither the communist nor the capitalist system has even begun to address in a serious global perspective. It is significant that the authors of this study both have a background in philosophy.

Indeed, not since Will and Ariel Durant has a team of philosophers been able to articulate to a broad reading public the practical meaning of philosophical concepts and their application to real life situations, in this case, the economic problems of our real world. Here is what we hope will be the first of several volumes, emulating the Durants, by this new husband-wife team as they endeavor to put the whole field of economics into a framework that addresses the human condition in a world perspective.

This comes at a most opportune time, as we emerge from nearly a half century of cold war between capitalist and communist blocs. The authors insist that it is time and that there is opportunity to move from "billiard-ball" to whole-seeking methods in the economic sphere. Thus, instead of self-centered capitalism and materialistic communism, we may in the 1990s be able to map a whole (and wholesome) approach to economic development.

And it is entirely possible, even probable, that we may discover that scarcity of and conflict for economic resources are not inevitable, but only seem so because of the "billiard-ball assumptions" that have limited our vision up to now (pp. 138–9). Utilizing the teachings of the world's various religions, the authors show how each of them has revelations—albeit imperfectly understood—as to what an appropriate course for improving economic conditions on a global scale, ultimately meaning our global survival, might be.

The idea that knowledge stemming from insight, genius, even revelation is always imperfect is central to the authors' analysis. Such knowledge, rather than giving perfect answers, leads toward solutions that may be worked out. But that solutions can be found, given broad enough perspective, is implicit.

The result is that we have here a much broader perspective on the world's economies than either Wall Street or the Kremlin could produce.

F. Hilary Conroy
Professor of History, University of Pennsylvania

France H. Conroy
Professor of Philosophy, Burlington College

Preface

We're not economists. Only the smallest fraction of the earth's population is. Nonetheless, like every other soul on earth, we participate in economies and wrestle daily with economic concerns. Our premise is that, since everyone is involved with economies, everyone takes part in shaping them. Together, "we the people" direct their course.

In turn, economies reflect their creators. They mirror not just our needs but more our aspirations and values: questions of philosophy and religion.

Trained in comparative religion and philosophy, we treat economies from these perspectives. That is, we don't delve into micro- or macroeconomic theory, nor do we give investment advice or stock tips. Instead, we examine the roots of economies in the deeper questions of life. The bottom line here relates not to numbers but to ideas. In other words, the philosophical yardstick measures neither private assets nor the public GNP but the practicality of the philosophies we live by.

Unfortunately, when experts get near economies, we don't hear much about religious and philosophical issues. At most, they tie the sticky-fingers epidemic to greed, one of the seven deadly sins, but that's about it. Listening to them, we end up shaking our heads at how corrupt we've become, without thinking more deeply about causes and alternatives.

Yet the deeper issues are timely. The very fact that we're finally fed up with corruption everywhere, after decades of letting it go, means that we ourselves are changing. That we see scandals on Wall Street or Main Street has a bright side. We realize where corrupt world views lead, and we no longer find their worlds acceptable. We're ready to tackle the deeper issues: What are our philosophies? Where do they take us? And can we go somewhere else?

The more we look at our philosophies, the more we change them. As they change, we change, and with us, our economies. Gandhi, for instance, insisted on wedding inward *and* outward growth. As he put it, only the evolution of "Soul-Force" can bring peace, equity, and justice to the worlds of "brute force."[1] If he was right, then evolving our philosophies isn't armchair intellectualizing; it holds the mind and life of our future.

How does this book contribute to the job Gandhi described?

First, we'd like to take the religions and philosophies of the world more into the marketplace, so that their insights can help us where we need help. Scholars have done a tremendous job translating the sacred texts that discuss "Soul-Force" and its evolution. But the fruits of their labors often remain cut off from everyday affairs. We do academic or spiritual things, and then we do life. The different spheres don't talk, even though each has much to give the other.

Second, according to religions and philosophies, we all have a role in shaping economies. Economies aren't out there happening to us. They are us. Not that each of us is to blame for all the economic messes. How could we be? No one of us makes all the decisions. Rather, we're simply not helpless before economies. We can do something about them.

Third, doing something about economies starts with our minds. Changing *doing* without first changing *thinking* doesn't get us very far. We think the doing has changed, when really it's the same old theme played over again. Real change starts with our philosophies. We evolve how we conceive of reality and ourselves. As it turns out, evolving our philosophies affects more than our heads. Both we and our economies end up transformed.

Fourth, to evolve our philosophies, we need the philosophical tools to do it:

- The *first chapter* contrasts two different ways of making tools: a billiard-ball method with a whole-seeking method.

- The *second chapter* shows how these two different methods give rise to two contrasting models of economies.

- The *third chapter* looks at what makes up practical philosophies—the tools that form them.

- The *fourth* and *fifth chapters* discuss the dynamics of spiritual growth—how we go forward and what keeps us going.

- The *last four chapters* show how the philosophical tools of Chapter 3 evolve our everyday philosophies on a spiritual basis—and keep them evolving. To do this, we've enlisted the help of some of the most basic teachings in Western religion: the Bible's days of creation, Commandments, Beatitudes, and Lord's Prayer.

In short, the book isn't about answers, mainly because we don't know the answers to modern economic problems. Nor do we know which philosophies are right for which people at which stage of development. The book does, however, explore *methods*. If we can get our hands on reliable methods for evolving our philosophies, then we can each work out the answers we need as we go.

Chapter 1

The Crises that Came To Dinner

🔳🔳🔳🔳🔳🔳🔳

I. Whose economy is it anyway?

Whether we're watching television or chatting with friends, we hear about crises. Virgin coasts go black with oil, while the ozone layer shrinks. Tax money goes to arms profiteers and drug runners, as the infrastructures of our cities crumble. Banks reel under bad loans, while entire countries contemplate bankruptcy.

The crises aren't distant rumors. They've moved into our homes like nuisance visitors who won't leave. The only advantage to having them around is that we've discovered what makes them tick: money, or to put it properly, economics—not the academic discipline but the everyday way we arrange who gets what.

Crime—from inner city to organized to white collar—is a thoroughly economic creature. Even so-called crimes of passion—shooting the stray lover or spouse—often have economic roots.[1]

Poverty and homelessness are equally economic. The gap between rich and poor—that less than one per cent of the population controls more than half the nation's wealth, or that the maximum wage is roughly 18,000 times the minimum wage—is economic for sure.

Drugs, which visited ancient Persia and Mesopotamia long before they came to New York and L.A., are every bit economic. Today's drug empire makes the political empires of the past seem paltry by comparison.

Pollution, a newcomer in modern proportions, occurs for economic reasons and is tolerated for the same. How can we afford to clean it up? We went deeply into debt just to create it.

War, a real old-timer, is ragingly economic. As Socrates put it over two millennia ago, "All wars are undertaken for the acquisition of wealth."[2] In *The Rise and Fall of the Great Powers,* historian Paul Kennedy argues a modern version, namely, that defense systems are necessary for the protection of wealth.[3] Somehow money is always lurking behind conflicts.

Political corruption smells economic. Power may corrupt, but it needs cash to make it stick.

Personal, corporate, national, and international debts are up-front economic—and the hardest to get out of the house. Interest compounds faster than we can count and certainly faster than we can pay.

With all these visitors intruding, family life suffers. We can't afford the time to raise the kids, much less to relax and enjoy the life we've worked so hard to establish.

The good news is that we know what brought the visitors through the door. The bad news is that they might be here to stay. So far, the best minds, intentions, and institutions haven't budged them.

But the bad news overlooks one point: it's our house. We have a say about who lives with us.

Driven by distraction

Not that the intruders pay much attention to our complaining. They have a long list of excuses why they can't go—a list rehearsed nightly on the news. Uncontrollable, economic forces are at work. Blind laws of economics, like the blind forces of volcanos or hurricanes, created the crises and prevent their resolution.

But the blind-laws view ignores the bottom line: the economic story is about us. We own the house. "We the people" make up economies. For better or worse, economies don't function apart from our decisions, since without us they don't exist.

After all, economies aren't like rock formations, tornados, or gnats. They're no more determined by blind, faceless forces than architects are determined by gravity. We create economies to be the way they are, just as architects create buildings to look the way they do. If we don't like the way our economies come out, we can make them work differently.

Which is why we have economies in the first place. We create them to *work for us*—to feed, clothe, house, and educate us. We build them to channel creativity, to exchange goods and services, and to advance knowledge.

What happens then? How did we get stuck with the crises that came to dinner, since we certainly didn't invite them?

A famous Hindu image—the metaphor of the chariot and the charioteer[4]—suggests how the crises sneaked in. In the original metaphor, the chariot represents the body, the horses represent the senses, and the charioteer the mind. If the charioteer falls asleep, the horses run away with the chariot. If we let our minds go to sleep, the metaphor says, we allow the senses to take over. Material desires run our lives.

But it doesn't have to be this way. As soon as the driver wakes up, the horses go wherever he steers them. Our minds can guide the senses and keep them out of trouble. The more awake we are, the more we're able to manage the physical side of life wisely.

The message for economies isn't hard to figure out. Economies become the chariot, economic desires the horses, and we the charioteer. Ideally, we steer our economic desires so that our economies go where we wish.

The trouble is, that's not happening. Why not? It can't be because we're asleep. Clearly, no one gets much sleep in modern economies. We do, however, get sidetracked by the rat race. Raising a family or managing a business keeps us running. We're awake but distracted.

Unfortunately, distractions can be as dangerous as sleep. Working to keep ahead, we stop steering our economic desires, which gives them a chance to start steering us. The horses take over, carrying the chariot and the charioteer (us) to places we never meant to go. Economic fears and motives call the shots. After a while, we feel helpless to change our course.

Which is precisely what has happened. While we were busy getting busier, the horses—ours or someone else's—ran us into one crisis after another. Ivan Boesky's name hit the headlines because he let his insider-trading team run out of control. Defense contractors apparently have herds that no one stops, as do hospitals and insurance companies. Those in charge of national and international debts could have said "Whoa!" several trillion dollars ago.

Fortunately, horses running away with chariots tend to give charioteers a bumpy ride—at least bumpy enough to get their full attention. Crises have the same effect. Whether jolts come from a sharp decrease in the oxygen supply or a sharp decrease on the stock exchange, they focus the mind. Jolts remind us that we have a say in making economies what they are. We wake up to find that the reins are in our hands.

In a mess, it's no good blaming the horses (economic desires), the chariot (the economy) or even the charioteer (ourselves). The chariot goes where the horses take it. The horses go where the driver lets them, while we (the driver) do the best we can with barely half an eye on the road. Blame is irrelevant. We don't need scapegoats; we need to get back on track—to show the nuisance visitors the door.

II. Looking for big maps

Recognizing that the crises are economic and that economies are ours to change puts us back in the driver's seat, this time with our eyes open. But what then? Where do we go with the chariot?

To set a good course, we need maps. Maps show us where we are, good places to go, and safe roads that take us there.

Economic theories, explained on televison by experts using toy houses and play money, provide one set of maps. The theories document the course that economies take. When interest rates go up, economists tell us what happens next. When markets go down, economic theories explain why. Economic maps describe the specifics of the terrain. They're useful for negotiating the chariot's short, immediate course.

But we need more. Presumably, we drive the horses and chariot not just for the fun of it but in order to go somewhere—to achieve something. But what? And which direction takes us there?

More than supply-and-demand maps, we need maps about the big questions—maps that sort out our basic conceptions of ourselves and what's ultimately real. Who are we, and what are we doing here? How we answer these questions sets the aims that our economies then serve. If we're here to make as much money as possible, we act one way. If we're here to develop our minds and souls, we act differently and get different results.

Both religion and philosophy design maps around questions of meaning and direction. They sketch big maps that relate us to what's beyond us (an economy, a universe, God), so that we can find our way.

Drawing on these disciplines, we adapt their maps to our needs. We develop philosophies for everything we do: for running governments, businesses, and schools, raising children, and generally getting along with each other. The maps of religion and philosophy orient us not only in eternity but also day to day. They provide the head tools we need to keep us on track.

If the philosophies are good, we get around just fine. The chariot goes where we intend. When we face challenges, the maps show us how to meet them.

If, however, the maps guide us badly, we run smack into reality's order; things go wrong not just here and there but all over. Following a bad map can have the same effect as falling asleep at the reins. We wind up in the ditch.

Wherever the maps lead us, though, they set our course through the territory. Whether philosophies guide us well or badly, they shape how we confront reality.

Marketplace maps

Since we confront reality every day in the marketplace, we use philosophies there as well. Different maps take us through different economic landscapes. For instance, a subjectivist philosophy ("reality is whatever I think it is") leads to subjectivist economic attitudes: "Money can be made by whatever means suit me." Similarly, a materialist philosophy ("reality is the world of material things") leads to materialist economic attitudes: "All that counts are material possessions; the real is the hoardable."

Whatever philosophies we use, our economies reflect them. When materialist philosophies shape the actions of millions of people, as they have for most of this century, economies show it. Standards, quality, and competence plummet.

Not that we've all become more lazy or irascible. It's just that materialist maps exclude higher values. It makes no sense, they claim, to exert time, effort, or expense on maintaining standards, if money can be made by ignoring them. The intangibles don't register. They don't count.

Unfortunately, the results aren't intangible. There's nothing intangible about waiting in long lines, being ill-treated and tricked by salespeople, or having brand new products break down or even explode in our faces. Bad service, inadequately tested products, and unsafe, cheaply made equipment are tangible. Consumers notice and competitors notice—often from the opposite side of the globe. We don't need more cases of Thalidomide babies or exploding gas tanks to be convinced that intangibles count. It's our knowledge (or ignorance) of intangibles that determines how we manage the tangibles.

Economies, then, aren't just us. They're our maps in action. With every exchange of goods and services goes an underlying, invisible exchange of philosophies. Through the symbols of everyday economic life, we act out exactly what we think about ourselves, human nature, the world, and ultimately, reality or God. For a change, our money is buying more than we thought.

But there's a catch. As we go about our business in economies, we're philosophical nudists. Whether we know it or not, we're parading our philosophies up front. Even when we cover our philosophies with rhetoric, our actions expose us, revealing to everyone precisely the kinds of maps we follow. Economies work like mirrors. When we look into them, we see more than ourselves: we see the philosophies we live by.

Which is encouraging. If blind laws—an economic survival of the fittest, for example—ruled economies, we'd be powerless to change them. If uncontrollable forces were the charioteers, we'd never have a say about where our chariots go.

But if economies are our shared creation, children of our philosophies, then we can do something about them. If our economies are good, we can encourage them to grow. If they're bad, we can correct them, starting with a long look at our maps.

Right now, economies are being quite bad. Even if markets go through the roof, they're prospering at our expense—at the expense of our air, earth, and water, our health and well-being, our hopes for world peace, and our rights to choose work freely and to be paid fairly for it. Economies don't limit their tantrums to investors' port-folios. They throw fits everywhere.

The question is, what philosophies make economies behave like spoiled children? What maps take us into the surreal world in which the two biggest industries are illegal drugs and weapons? What maps tell industries they can prosper by destroying our planet? We might expect such economies in Bedlam or maybe the Twilight Zone, but what are they doing in our living rooms?

Maps that chart shifting interest rates or fluctuations in the money supply can't help us negotiate this terrain.

Economists' charts weren't drawn to do this. The maps we need to examine are philosophical. Economist Zach Willey looked beyond economics to philosophy in an interview with *Time Magazine:* "We've had 100 years of development and the environment's been kicked around pretty badly. We're trying to figure out a philosophy to rehabilitate things over the next 100 years."[5]

In other words, we need maps that are bigger than charting who sold what to whom for how much. We have plenty of maps of individual trees. We need some maps of the forest.

III. Making big maps: billiard-ball vs. whole-seeking methods

Basically, there are two ways of forming philosophies—two approaches to map-making. The first focuses on specifics, on bits and pieces. We figure out which tree is which, and why willows don't behave like oaks. If we're in the tree business, these maps are useful.

But there's a limit to their usefulness. However valuable the maps are to arborists, they're not so great when applied to big questions. Mapping forests isn't their forte. We get lost using them if we think it is.

The second approach, by contrast, investigates forests; it seeks the whole. Not that any map can pin down the whole, whether it be the whole economy, the whole earth, or the whole of reality. Maps can, though, give us a rough idea; they can approximate the whole. They can sketch the big picture, however imperfect their sketch may be.

Billiard-ball maps

The first map-making method is atomistic. It forms philosophies by narrowing our view of reality, until we see only a world of things, bits and pieces. If we can't know everything about everything, at least we can focus on a few single things that we have a better chance of knowing everything about.

The trouble is, since atomistic methods see only a world of separate things, relationships don't turn up on the maps. Nothing rules the bits but blind chance. Atoms just bounce off each other randomly. Super-micro to super-macro billiard balls become the stuff of the universe—the only real stuff.

Not that billiard-ball maps are limited to atoms and stars. They apply to us as well. According to atomistic maps, we're all bits in the void, and life is one long series of chance encounters with other bits. We bounce off each other for a lifetime and then disappear. Cynics love this stuff, as do telescientists.

In the interim, we survive as best we can. If, as our maps tell us, we're isolated billiard balls, we have a problem with security. We don't feel safe. What if another billiard-ball tries to knock us out? Self-defense becomes top priority.

The best way to defend our billiard-selves, the maps suggest, is to control people and events before they control us. After all, dominating thingish worlds brings thingish rewards—power and wealth. With these, we make sure we're the predators and not the prey.

To show what it's like to live by billiard-ball philosophies, psychologist Charles T. Tart has devised a mock credo—a modern version of the Apostles' Creed:

> I believe in the material universe as the only and ultimate reality, a universe controlled by fixed, physical laws and blind chance.
>
> I affirm that the universe has no creator, no objective purpose, and no objective meaning or destiny.

I maintain that all ideas about God or gods, supernatural beings, prophets and saviors, or other nonphysical beings or forces are superstitions and delusions.

Life and consciousness are totally identical to physical processes, and arise from chance interactions of blind, physical forces. Like the rest of life, my life and consciousness have no objective purpose, meaning, or destiny.

I believe that all judgments, values, and moralities, whether my own or others', are subjective, arising solely from biological determinants, personal history, and chance. Free will is an illusion.

Therefore the most rational values I can personally live by must be based on the knowledge that for me what pleases me is Good, what pains me is Bad.

Those who please me or help me avoid pain are my friends; those who pain me or keep me from my pleasure are my enemies. Rationality requires that friends and enemies be used in ways that maximize my pleasure and minimize my pain. . . .

Virtue for me is getting what I want without being caught and punished by others.

I maintain that the death of the body is the death of the mind. There is no afterlife, and all hope for such is nonsense.[6]

Tart adds:

In my workshops I often have people go through an experiential exercise where I ask them to stand with their hands over their hearts and recite [the creed] as if it were a pledge of allegiance. This is a perspective you'll find in almost any science book, and I wrote it up as a deliberate parody of the Apostles' Creed.

By and large, it depresses the hell out of people, especially when they realize that they believe a lot of it, and that these beliefs are culturally reinforced.[7]

Billiard-ball economies

Played on the stage of economies, billiard-ball methods create a drama that's even more depressing. Economies exist to satisfy our wants. In the Hindu metaphor, the horses run the show.

What's wrong with wants running things is that they don't stay fixed. They have a way of multiplying. Satisfying little desires gives us a taste for something bigger. The chariot race is on, making Ben Hur's contest look tame by comparison.

If we're in the race, we need values that help us win it. For instance, we can't be timid. We can't worry about those we beat, or how we beat them. Winning the race demands tough values. As Tart's credo says, whatever puts us ahead is good; whatever frustrates our wants is bad. As bits in the void, our only duty is to minimize personal loss and to maximize personal gain.

What this entails for other bits—people, society, the earth, the future, even the rest of the economy—isn't a concern, unless of course it costs us as well. The wider consequences of actions as well as the character of actions themselves don't enter into the equations. To come out on top, we have to play the game no matter what the cost. That's how the "real world" works.

But the "real worlds" these values create aren't the kinds of worlds we want to live in. In fact, billiard-ball ethics produce, in law professor Peter Riga's terms, new though better dressed barbarians:

> We are graduating, for all practical purposes, a bunch of legal and financial barbarians. It is no longer the barbarian that wears a leopard skin suit and goes about with a big club. The barbarian is someone who is untutored in the philosophy and ethics of what he does and the dimension of the work he does that affects people.

Consequently these barbarians wear Brooks Brothers suits and write with a ballpoint pen, but they are barbarians nonetheless, because they don't take into account or consideration what these things do to real people.[8]

If barbarians kept to themselves, they'd simply annoy each other. Unfortunately, fulfilling unlimited desires demands wealth and power—tons of it. Someone must be stolen from; someone must be dominated.

To survive the new barbarian invasions, self-defense isn't enough. If our competitors are out to take everything we have, then we need to stop them before they even think of making a move. Billiard-ball philosophies turn economies into battlegrounds. The more we have, the more we need to secure ourselves from those who have less. We don't use the chariot as a vehicle to go somewhere but as a place to hide while we plan our next raid.

In short, billiard-ball philosophies create what 17th-century philosopher Thomas Hobbes feared: a society reduced to a war of each against all, everyone struggling for either gain or self-preservation in a predatory world. Darwinism rules the marketplace—a view of economies championed not by Charles Darwin but by 19th-century sociologist Herbert Spencer, who authored the charming phrase, "survival of the fittest."

Billiard-ball souls

But the violence done by the billiard-ball outlook isn't limited to outward worlds. It hurts inward realms as well. Philosopher Thomas I. White offers a case very like the aspiring broker in the movie *Wall Street*. Suppose, White says, that an intelligent, idealistic young man gets a job at a firm where he runs into the billiard-ball ethic:

"Look, kid, if you want to make it big, you play hard ball. You've got to be aggressive but politically savvy.

You've got to use people, and you'll have to step on
people now and then to get ahead of them. Show no
mercy. Be ruthless. . . . You've got talent and promise, but
you're going to have to do some stuff your mother might
not be too happy about. But then she didn't get to be a
vice-president by thirty-five, did she? I'm just telling you
the rules of the game. This is business, not Sunday
School."[9]

Suppose further, White continues, that the young man
gradually conforms to this ethic:

He gets to be very good at it himself, and he rises
quickly in the company. What do you think he'll feel?
Probably considerable pride at his accomplishments and
abilities. And what about his initial reservations? I suspect
he'll dismiss them as childish, idealistic, and naive, won-
dering why he ever seriously thought that way. . . ."The
only people who cry 'Foul!' are those who lose," he says to
himself. He sees nothing wrong with what he does. His
opponents just look at it from the wrong perspective.[10]

But, as White asks,

Is his appraisal accurate? No. Is he stronger? No.
Did he "overcome his weaknesses?" No. What really
happened? He's been corrupted! His initial reservations
were accurate, but his actions since then did two things—
they blinded and weakened him. . . . He's grown weaker,
not stronger.[11]

White's story is a modern telling of an ancient truth.
Spiritual teachings are unanimous in treating billiard-ball
maps as enemies of the soul. But their reason is more than
moral. As cartographers of life, billiard-ball philosophies
don't work.

Billiard balls aren't alone

Ultimately, billiard-ball philosophies don't fail just
because they create conflict (who gets the most? which

billiard ball dominates?), though that's a good reason, too. They fail because they're not true to reality. Billiard-ball maps cut out pieces of life and line them up in front of our noses, until we can't see the totality from which they came. As a result, their maps don't give us the whole picture.

Yet the whole picture is what we need to understand how things work and to manage our lives well. According to one of Einstein's favorite epigrams, the field generates the object, not vice versa. That is, whole systems give rise to specific things, not the other way around. To know the things, we need to know the whole from which they came.

Which makes sense. Alone and isolated, billiard-ball "things" have no meaning, not even existence. Eastern teachings point out that there's really "no-thing" there. Philosophies that focus on *things* miss the *relations* and *whole contexts* that make those "things" possible. They depict stuffed squirrels under glass domes, miles from the forest that gave the squirrels life. Without a context, a thing is really nothing.

This logic also applies to the thing we call a self or ego. If we talk to Buddhists, they tell us that a self has no existence. It has no "own being." We don't exist as things in isolation. The separate ego is just a map that we fall into the habit of using, but it doesn't represent who we really are. Ego-maps layer us with ego-perceptions that make us feel cut off and isolated. They make us think we're off on our own, when in fact we're embedded in reality's total order. We're made up of fields within fields, which ultimately nest within the whole.

If we think about it, that's just common sense. Egos aren't the centers they seem. To live in the physical world, we have to adapt ourselves to physical laws; they don't adapt to our egos. We can't arrange the laws of nature or physiology according to personal preference or ideology.

Regardless of wealth or position, we can't ignore gravity, the ecosystem, or lunch.

In society as well, no ego occupies the center, though there's plenty of competition for the spot. We get started in families and then move on to societies. Both are dynamic structures. In them, we accomplish more working together than if we spend our efforts vying for control. In any case, we're not keen on being dominated. Those who push to dominate get more resentment than respect.

That's also the way things work in the professions and disciplines. The field itself—music, physics, history or literature—remains central. No matter who we are, if what we claim isn't true to a discipline, no one pays much attention. True, we're amused by ego-flexing from time to time. It keeps the conversation going at cocktail parties. But it makes gossip, not history.

In life, reality itself remains at the center. The whole establishes a dynamic system of being, which gives rise to the order of things. Reality's total order operates like the principles of ecology, which make the earth function as one integrated system. The forest works according to these principles and exists because of them. As do squirrels. To deny dependence on this order, a macho squirrel would have to deny the very grounds (as well as the treetops) of his existence.

Spiritual traditions assume the same about ultimate reality: the whole manifests an order that unifies physical, conscious, moral, and spiritual life. In fact, according to spiritual teachings, reality's whole order gives us life. Everything we do is bound up with it, because we can't get outside the whole. Its order permeates everything we do, whether we realize it or not.

Billiard-ball philosophies, by contrast, ignore reality's order and cut us off from it. If we follow thingish maps, we become oblivious to the whole contexts on which we depend. In particular, we ignore the intangibles that keep us from strangling each other—intangibles such as mutual respect, integrity, honesty, and a shared quest for Truth and the Good. In the end, billiard-ball maps exclude too much of what we need to know, if we want to manage human life well.

Yet managing is what economies are all about.

Whole-seeking maps

Which raises the second map-making method: instead of centering philosophies on things or egos, we can pattern them on whole systems. This, as Einstein reasoned, is the more practical approach. It makes sense, he argued, to assume that reality operates as a unified system—as one coherent whole—whether we have the theories adequate to explain it that way or not. Why?

(a) As the name suggests, a whole-seeking approach looks for maps of forests. It opens us to reality as it is wholly, not just in bits and pieces. It looks beyond this or that tree. Whole-seeking maps point to the realities that transcend us, so that our philosophies confront the wider contexts (the whole forests) in which we exist.

For example, whole-seeking maps in physics—from ancient Indian and Chinese concepts to modern theories—postulate that the universe consists of unified patterns of energy or light. The thing-perspective is really a limited view of these whole fields. According to the maps, we're more light-beings or energy-flows than hard and fast physical bodies. (Scotty, beam us up?)

In the fields of energy, patterns interrelate. Dissecting the patterns into isolated bits doesn't give us the best map, because it isn't how things work. Our patterns move in relation to other patterns. Our lives interact with the lives of other people, of whole communities and nations, as well as with the life of the earth. Like the squirrel in the forest, we function in a network. We're not alone.

(b) To show us how to work in harmony with these contexts, whole-seeking maps draw in the intangibles. They explore how ideas and qualities unify the networks into systems. By understanding systems of ideas, we're able to interact with them more constructively. Seeing how the intangibles work, we see how to work with them.

Even on physical levels, ideas of order, balance, and harmony shape processes ranging from the earth's eco-system to the creatures living in it. The forest's ecological order and balance, for instance, give the squirrel a chance. If nuts grew capriciously or if winter came unpredictably, the squirrel couldn't cope. The intangibles (whether we call them ideas or laws of nature) transform a jumble of bits into a working unity—one that sustains life.

It's true for us, too. Ideas and values empower us to understand whole systems and to work within them more harmoniously. Given the same set of circumstances, two people react quite differently depending on the ideas and values—the intangibles—each lives by. Their philosophies put them in different worlds.

Psychiatrist Viktor Frankl saw the power of intan-gibles during his experience in four Nazi concentration camps. As he recounted in his book, *Man's Search for Meaning*,[12] those prisoners who maintained the richness of their intellectual and spiritual lives survived better than those who didn't, even though many of the survivors were physically weaker than the others in the camp. The intan-gibles sustained them, in spite of the terrible physical and psychological conditions around them. They were able to go on, even to share their rations and to encourage others, because the prison's order wasn't for them the final order.

(c) Ultimately, a whole-seeking approach tackles the biggest question: it develops maps for understanding God, reality as the whole. Seeking God spurs us to go beyond map-imposed limits. We adjust our individual maps more closely to what's ultimately real. Twentieth-century philosopher Brand Blanshard identifies this as the essence of religion:

> Religion is an attempt to adjust one's nature as a whole to ultimate reality. In a sense all human life is that. But whereas the larger part of such life consists of an adjustment to what is immediately around us, religion seeks to go behind the appearance of things to what is self-subsistent, to something which, intellectually and causally, will explain everything else.[13]

Such notions aren't limited to theologians and philosophers. Nobel-prize-winning physicist Werner Heisenberg (1901–1976) talked about the whole-seeking approach similarly. In a discussion with fellow physicist Wolfgang Pauli, he described the method as a striving to find our relatedness to a central order. The clearer we are about the central order, the easier it is for us to put the many partial orders into perspective and not to be misled by them. Heisenberg wrote:

> The problem of values is nothing but the problem of our acts, goals, and morals. It concerns the compass by which we must steer our ship if we are to set a true course through life. The compass itself has been given different names by various religions and philosophies: happiness, the will of God, the meaning of life—to mention just a few. . . . All such formulations try to express *man's relatedness to a central order.*
>
> Admittedly, the subjective realm of an individual, no less than a nation, may sometimes be in a state of confusion. Demons can be let loose and do a great deal of

mischief, or, to put it more scientifically, partial orders that have split away from the central order, or do not fit into it, may have taken over.

But in the final analysis, the central order, or the "one" as it used to be called and with which we commune in the language of religion, must win out. And when people search for values, they are probably searching for the kind of actions that are in harmony with the central order, and as such are free of the confusions springing from divided, partial orders.[14]

Heisenberg would be the last to say that one map ever captures the central order or explains it once and for all. The confusions that plague subjective realms (what's in our heads) are always a problem. That's true even when we study nature. Our maps about physical systems change as we learn more.

When it comes to ultimate reality, maps continually develop. Gregory of Nyssa (335–394 A.D.), third of the three great Cappadocian Fathers, expressed what teachings East and West affirm:

Even if one has said about [Divinity Itself] all one can, yet one has said nothing worthy of It. For the mind cannot reach that which IS; even if we continue to think ever more sublime thoughts about It, yet no word can express what is meant.[15]

Final answers—maps to end all maps—aren't what a whole-seeking approach offers. The approach does, however, point us in constructive directions. By reminding us of the limits of our maps—that reality is more than any map can symbolize—a whole-seeking approach puts us on a quest to understand the big picture. We use maps to discern the harmony of reality, without locking ourselves into one map or another.

IV. Why buy the whole-seeking approach?

In the end, we want maps that work. We want maps that show us the lay of the land, so that we can find our way around. Spiritual teachings claim that whole-seeking methods give us better maps than billiard-ball methods do. Their maps work better, because they cover more of what we need to know. To support their claim, the teachings cite many examples of how whole-seeking maps have transformed people, cultures, and economies.

According to Riane Eisler's *The Chalice and the Blade*, for instance, the Neolithic cultures flourishing between 7000 and 4000 B.C. were goddess-oriented, meaning that their central, spiritual image was the feminine principle of wholeness and unity as the source of life.

On Eisler's reading of the archaeological evidence, this whole-seeking premise gave rise to cultures that were egalitarian, peaceful, and without extremes of wealth. They operated on a partnership model—mutual benefit rather than one side exploiting another. Only when the Kurgan invasions began (4000–2500 B.C.), bringing with them a violent, patriarchal, dominator philosophy, did the system of universal peace and prosperity break down.[16]

But even after the patriarchal, dominator model took over, whole-seekers came along to challenge the system and to restrain its billiard-ball, dominator excesses.

Zarathustra (660–583 B.C.), who may well be the great-grandfather of Western monotheism, radically reformed ancient Persia within his own lifetime. Greedy priests and nobles had all but ruined the economy by demanding costly sacrifices of farmers and by selling the people hallucinogens.

Zarathustra broke the stranglehold of these ruthlessly powerful few by appealing to each person's innate ability to understand reality and to be guided by it. The people responded. The culture, including the economy, turned around. On the power of Zarathustra's teaching, Persia went from an impoverished community to a world leader within a few centuries.[17]

Of course, there's Joseph in the Bible, who applied a whole-seeking approach to managing everything from his own trials to Pharaoh's economy. By doing so, he rescued not only himself and his family from famine but the whole of Egypt as well. (Genesis 37–50)

The great Indian King Asoka (270–230 B.C.) converted to Buddhism and transformed India from a war economy to an economy devoted to serving "the welfare of the people"—a novel approach then as now. All actions, he said, must be based on Dharma. "Dharma" is a broad term in both Hinduism and Buddhism that refers to cosmic law. It represents the dynamic spiritual order that stems from the whole and infuses all right action.

In his edicts, King Asoka wrote, "There is no gift that can equal the gift of Dharma, the establishment of human relations on Dharma, the distribution of wealth through Dharma, or kinship in Dharma."[18] For Asoka, Dharma is how the whole comes home to human affairs. Seeing the whole is the gift that the whole gives us, because it's the means by which we can manage our affairs in peace, prosperity, and harmony.

Muhammad (570–632 A.D.) became the Prophet precisely for his dedication to applying whole-seeking methods to social and economic reform. Wherever Islam went, concepts of economic equality and justice followed—concepts Muhammad himself used in running the city of Yathrib, now known as Medina. One of the five pillars of Islam is to provide for the poor—not to make them depend on charity, but to help them become active again in the community. Islamic scholar Fazlur Rahman explains the link between a vision of the whole and a whole-governed way of life:

> The Prophet seems to insist: One God—one humanity.[19]
>
> Muhammad's monotheism was, from the very beginning, linked up with a humanism and a sense of social and economic justice whose intensity is no less than the intensity of the monotheistic idea.[20]

The *Qur'an* underscores the link in Sura 107: "Have you seen someone who rejects religion? That is the person who pushes the orphan aside and does not promote feeding the needy."[21] Muhammad's whole-seeking methods worked. Early Muslim economies thrived, enough to revive classical Greek and Roman learning and to advance philosophy and the sciences.

In eleventh- and twelfth-century Europe, the Benedictine, Cluniac, and Cistercian monastic reforms contributed greatly to re-establishing economic prosperity after the barbarian invasions. The Gothic cathedrals that sprang up all over France, Spain, England, and Germany are monuments not only to the spiritual but also to the economic achievements of the reforms. The spires were built on the concrete practicality of Christian, monastic ideals.[22]

Closer to home, William Penn (1644–1718), one of the leading lights of the Friends, came to America to establish a community governed by whole-seeking methods—a community he called a "holy experiment." He grounded the experiment on fundamental, immutable laws: "To live honestly, not to hurt another, and to give every one their right." These laws, he wrote, "are the cornerstones of human structure, the basis of reasonable societies, without which all would run into heaps and confusion."[23] In his view, no economy can last long without them.

But beyond all the historical examples of how the whole-seeking approach works, spiritual teachings appeal to what's successful every day. Families, for instance, work best when their relations are built on higher values. Treating families like mutual exploitation societies doesn't make happy homes. It just keeps lawyers, therapists, and realtors busy.

The same applies to how we manage relations with friends and associates. Billiard-ball methods create divisions that lead to conflicts. In no time, it's us against them—who gets the better of whom. By contrast, whole-seeking methods strengthen relationships by nurturing growth on all sides. Friendships and businesses become mutual-support systems that foster everyone's creativity.

Why should the methods that work in economies, the teachings argue, be any different from those that build good relations in every other aspect of life?

The real problem with whole-seeking maps isn't that they don't work but that they work far too well. They create so much prosperity that others notice. Thieves move in for some easy pickings. If the thieves don't change their philosophy, wars follow, which even the best economies find hard to survive. Wars make money only if they're held somewhere else. No economist ever recommends hosting one.

Henry Carey, whose economic theories greatly influenced Abraham Lincoln, made this argument in *The Past, the Present, and the Future.* Carey used the example of farmers who settle in an area to do honest work, but who become so productive that plunderers move in to steal their earnings. The robbers do this first by force but later by taxes, fees, and rents. In the end, everything the farmers generate by honest, whole-seeking methods is in danger of being consumed by billiard-ball methods.[24]

If whole-seeking methods work so well, though, why do billiard-ball methods dominate our economies? Why do we think that the "real world" is a billiard-ball world? It's a question of philosophy. We're sold the no–philosophy philosophy of economies, namely, that philosophies don't have a say when it comes to economies. Billiard ballism is just the way economies are. But is it so?

Making Maps

The methods we use for—	Billiard-ball methods	Whole-seeking methods
mapping reality:	We map things that bounce off each other randomly.	We map systems within larger systems that work within the whole.
mapping ourselves:	We're isolated bits in the void and have to look out for number one.	We're open and evolving systems, developing our individual at-one-ment with the whole.
mapping values:	Good is whatever gets us what we want; bad is whatever stands in our way.	Good is whatever reveals the whole and brings us into harmony with it; bad is whatever makes us feel cut off and isolated.
mapping economies:	Economies are a war: a Hobbesian, Darwinian struggle for survival.	Economies work best when they're run according to whole-seeking methods—when they're based on economic justice or "Dharma" in the marketplace.

Chapter 2

Who's Driving the Chariot?

🔲🔲🔲🔲🔲🔲🔲

I. Is greed good?

The line goes something like this: economies don't have anything to do with religion or philosophy, because they're just self-interest in action. Selfish passions run the show. We don't go to economies for wisdom but for profit—at least to pay the bills. When we get near economies, we don't think. We just want.

Which is great: wants keep economies going. In the real world, "greed is good"—a line in the movie *Wall Street* taken from a speech that Ivan Boesky gave at a university graduation. According to the Boesky-view, without the perpetual motion of greed, economies would stagnate. In other words, without wants pushing us, we'd just sit on our tails.

Yet there's a hitch. Greed starts the race to buy up the available billiard balls—the real-life game of Monopoly. Driven by greed, we turn economies into wars for acquisitions. The result? As in the board game, a few win by sending the bill to everyone else. Rents go up, as do taxes, fees, and costs. Economies managed like Monopoly boards eat away at the middle of economic society, until only the poles remain: the super-privileged and the super-poor.

According to economists, though, this isn't a formula for prosperity. From economic analyst Ravi Batra and sociologist Pitirim Sorokin to journalist Christopher Wood, New York correspondent for *The Economist*, the consensus is that a Monopoly approach to economies doesn't work.[1] Greed let loose polarizes economies and destabilizes them. It brings on depressions. If we reverse polarizing trends, we can avoid the worst. If not, we're in trouble.

Through the clamor of "greed is good," then, we hear a different story: greed strangles economies. Selfishness let loose wrecks free exchange.

Which is it? Is greed good for economies, or a danger to them? Back to the chariot analogy: should the horses run wild, or should we drivers steer them?

Expecting economists to answer this question is asking too much, because the question involves more than what supply-demand curves can chart. It's not even a question for economic theory. Greed can take over any system, and it doesn't matter whether the system is capitalist, communist, or socialist.

In the end, how we deal with greed goes beyond economic theories. It even goes beyond moral issues. The issue is philosophical. Is Boesky's message to the graduating students correct? Does his philosophy—his map—describe economic reality? If it does, then it won't cut any ice to say that we shouldn't be greedy on moral grounds. What works carries the day.

Selfishness vs. "enlightened self-interest"

Adam Smith didn't think Boesky-maps work at all. However much they may describe a certain side of human nature, they don't get at the heart of economies. Not that Smith wasn't keenly aware of greed in economies. Writing first as a moral philosopher, Smith wrestled with the question of what regulates the passions, greed in particular. He figured something must check greed; otherwise he didn't see how civilization could have survived. Only after tackling the philosophical question in his first book did he publish the second, *The Wealth of Nations*, the work that inaugurated modern economics. (The date of its publication is easy to remember: 1776.)

Given his background in moral philosophy as well as his experiences in 18th-century Scotland, Smith knew how destructive selfish ambitions can be. Letting greed take over economies wasn't an option. He had seen "selfish merchants" do this, and he knew it didn't work. But he was practical as well. The passions can't be controlled by superficial means. One group telling another what desires they should or shouldn't have, he argued, won't work. Wagging fingers alone can't hold greed in check.

Instead of denying the passions, Smith sought to yoke them to constructive goals. Specifically, his "invisible hand" operated on each individual's self-interest, which, *if sufficiently enlightened*, can't be separated from the interests of the entire economy, that is, the collective good.

Smith appealed to something philosophical, namely, to our ability to think out the consequences of our actions long-term and large-scale. The more we understand economies as whole systems on which we ourselves depend, the less we're likely to act in ways that weaken them. Our enlightened awareness of how economies work and of our place in them shapes our interests.

Enlightened self-interest and selfishness aren't, therefore, synonymous. As Smith understood them, they're opposites. Enlightened self-interest builds economies. Selfishness destroys them, which is what Smith believed monopolistic merchants were doing to Britain. *The Wealth of Nations* documents many historical disasters which

Smith traced to the avarice of powerful merchants. "Say yes to greed" wasn't his choice.

Instead, he sought to enlighten self-interest out of its selfishness by exposing the dangers inherent in letting wants run loose. For economies to develop, he argued, individuals can't prosper at the expense of systems, nor can systems thrive at the expense of individuals. Both do well, or both suffer.

Not that Adam Smith had all the solutions. But he put his finger on the problem: economic health can't be separated from the aspirations of individuals, and these aspirations must go beyond selfish gain.

Greed in the making

Why, then, do Smith's interpreters so often turn him on his head, as if he were a champion for money-grubbing? Why do greed and selfishness command such a following in spite of all Smith's warnings? Not because we're necessarily that greedy, but because we believe—as Smith's interpreters claim—that these responses reflect the realities of economic life. In the end, we think either that greed can't be restrained, or that without it economies would fizzle. The root is philosophical: we take greed and selfishness to be what economies are all about.

In a recent interview, a member of an organized-crime family rued the violent methods he claimed he had to use. However unfortunate it may be, he said, extortion, bribery, and murder reflect economic reality. The price of not conforming to this reality is financial oblivion: a lifetime of drudgery and counting pennies.

His response isn't as perverted as it sounds. Philosophically speaking, it simply pushes textbook notions of economies to their logical extremes. Not that economic textbooks endorse crime. But they depict economies as governed by scarcity. In the worlds that follow from this premise, unlimited desires compete for finite resources, gain to one person entails loss to another, and greater powers swallow lesser ones—all for the purpose of maximizing profits.

If we take this view of economies seriously, why aren't the mobster's methods—or Boesky's—the formula for success? Goodness goes to saints; good business to those who follow the gospel of greed. Economic realities, not moral or spiritual values, select those persons most fitted to succeed.

In other words, reducing economic reality to a herd of horses running after one bucket of oats narrows our economic options. Either we adopt desperate methods, as the mobster did, or we slip to the bottom of the economic ladder. Horse sense says that we either eat or starve. We either play Monopoly, or we're out of the game.

The only thing that keeps this description of economies from collapsing into utter chaos are the institutions and mores of society. But mere conventions crumble under such fierce economic drives. When we're pressed by circumstances or fear, the mobster's methods seem worth a try. How else can we survive?

The question is, do economies work this way? Is the mobster's or even the textbooks' view the best characterization of economic reality?

II. Rethinking economies: How do they really work?

To start with, *economy* refers to how we *manage our household*, which is also its original Greek meaning *("oiko-nomia")*. Economies are our ways of handling the basic needs of human life: food, housing, clothing, transportation, education, not to mention cable TV, PCs, and VCRs.

Economies develop systems for meeting these needs. Each person contributes to the system, which then makes these contributions available to everyone else. The more efficient the system, the more time we have to develop other-than-economic talents.

As well-managed systems, economies run smoothly. They become virtually invisible in supplying goods and services and then moving them to those who need them. When crises arise, economies handle them. More importantly, well-managed economies prevent economic crises. Economies become flawless servants to something greater, namely, us and our lives. We know we can depend on them to manage the household for us, so we can get on with our real life's work, whether it happens to make money or not.

A sure sign of bad management is when we don't have time to think of anything but household problems. Every relationship takes on an economic hue. Meeting basic demands becomes a life-consuming activity, until we have no time or energy left for anything else.

Moreover, any disturbance can spell disaster. Losing a job or contracting an illness can wipe us out and put us on the streets. One or two major banks or corporations going bankrupt can trigger a collapse of the financial system. Third-world countries defaulting on loans can bring down the world economy.

Nor can we depend on economies to be there for us when we need help. What taxes don't take, rent, food, interest, and insurance costs eat up. If we climb out of a hole, it's often in spite of the system, not because of it.

But this isn't invisible management; it's front-and-center breakdown. The horses are running off with the chariots, leaving us drivers hostages to events. When economies don't help us and only burden us, their reason for existing disappears. Why have them? We'd be better off fending for ourselves.

Turning things around—mastering economies instead of letting them master us—means rethinking what economies are all about. It means evolving our philosophy of economies, which starts with re-examining our premises. What *assumptions* do we use to manage our households?

1. Which premise should we use: scarcity or creativity?

To manage things, we first take stock of what we have. Early 19th-century economists, especially Thomas Malthus and David Ricardo, emphasized what we don't have. Because the earth is limited, they insisted, its resources must also be limited. We humans, though, have unlimited desires, especially as we multiply our populations into the future. No matter how much we have, they claimed, we always want more. Our hunger for billiard balls won't be filled. As a result, there's never enough. Resources are always running out.

To Malthus and Ricardo, the "economic realities" of scarcity and overpopulation seemed so terrifying that wars, famines, and plagues began to sound like natural saviors, delivering the human race from its own short-sightedness. If these are saviors, though, there's not much left to be saved from. One Malthusian economist can ruin your whole day.

The limits of our knowledge. The premise behind 19th-century fears—persisting right up to today—is that economies are closed systems, bound by fixed quantities of material goods. No matter how large economies become, they remain closed, thus limited. Their territory is fixed, which means there's only a fixed quantity of resources available to us.

But that's a strange premise. Economies involve not just resources but our management of them. Economist and sociologist Kenneth Boulding, for example, bases economies on "know-how": knowing how to produce and exchange goods and services. On this premise, economies have to do less with procuring things and more with restructuring and combining them.

Assuming that scarcity of resources limits economies is like assuming that chemical elements limit chemistry, foods limit cooking, or notes limit music. The key lies not in what we have but in what we do with it, as any good tart (cherry or apple, of course) can prove.

Discoveries in chemistry, for instance, aren't made by collecting the largest number of elements. The best meals aren't those with the greatest quantities of food. Nor are the best symphonies those with the most notes. The value of each lies in their ingenious arrangement.

So, too, in economies: arrangement introduces order. Order multiplies the ways we use resources and so functions as an anti-scarcity factor. With order, we can do more with less—not by skimping but by being creative.

Without order, we don't have access to resources at all. Oil was plentiful to the Comanches and Apaches, even a nuisance when it contaminated the water supply. But they didn't use it. The ordered arrangement was lacking. An oil burner in the tepee didn't sound like a good idea. Wood is so much easier to carry. As a result, neither the scarcity nor the abundance of oil was a factor in the Indians' economy.

Similarly, we're surrounded by abundant energy sources: sun and wind, as well as the earth's heat, motion, and magnetism. We could even be living on a huge geo-battery. But all the energy sources imaginable aren't of any use to us if we haven't developed the know-how to tap them. Or, if someone has, it's not available. After all, where there's no meter, there's no profit.

What we call scarcity, then, actually refers to our own limits—limits either of human knowledge or of its application. Scarcity isn't an absolute fact but a changing indicator of what we know and of what we're doing with our knowledge. Of course natural resources are finite, but that's not the issue. Economies thrive or fail on our responses to what we have—on how we manage resources.

If, for instance, two people are stranded in the wilderness, the one who knows how to forage will find food in abundance, while the other may starve. To the one who can manage what's there, resources abound. To the one who lacks that knowledge, they're scarce.

In the end, scarcity doesn't describe reality but our perception of reality. If we accept closed-system premises, we regard scarcity as an iron law. But the so-called law describes us, not what's out there. We create scarcity from the limits of our knowledge and the narrow uses of our creativity. No matter how much scarcity makes us feel trapped in limits, the walls binding us are our own.

Economies or a war? Whether we reason from scarcity or anti-scarcity makes a huge difference. If scarcity governs economies, then we have to grab as much of the pie as possible or die off. By ignoring knowledge and creativity, the premise of scarcity reduces our role in economies to that of animals: can we gather enough nuts for the winter, or will the other squirrels take them all? Limited resources and unlimited desires meet as opposing forces in economies, making conflict inevitable. The war of each against all begins, giving power to those who grab the most.

But if economies challenge us to manage creatively what we have, then economies can develop away from scarcity. True, a struggle ensues, but not against others in a win-lose battle. The struggle is against ourselves—against the limits we impose on creativity by harboring too narrow a vision.

The source of prosperity. If economies thrive on know-how, neither scarcity nor abundance determines economic health. Prosperity lies elsewhere. Writer-entrepreneur Paul Hawken illustrates this in his book, *Growing A Business:*

> The major problem affecting businesses, large and small, is a lack of *imagination*, not capital. A ready supply of too much money in start-ups tends to replace creativity. Companies with money buy solutions by buying consultants, lawyers, clever accountants, publicity agents, marketing studies, and on and on. Companies without money dream and imagine. . . . Small businesses, at least entrepreneurial ones, are formed in order to address problems that money alone cannot solve.[2]

Scarcity of capital forces entrepreneurs to overcome obstacles in ways essential to success—through knowledge and creativity. By contrast, as business consultant Tom Peters observes, businesses flounder when they become "fat and flabby."

The same logic applies to national economies. The more resources a nation has, the more it may drift into complacence. Abundant resources become cheap, leading to mismanagement and waste. No matter how badly the nation uses its resources, sheer abundance can bail it out. By contrast, countries without rich material resources are forced to survive by their wits. They have no choice but to be creative.

But even a richly endowed economy reaches its limits. The abundance dwindles. Sooner or later the nation has to develop real economic sinews: knowledge, imagination, flexibility, and ingenuity, as well as diligence, integrity, skill, and self-discipline. Fairness wouldn't hurt, either. These qualities, not fixed amounts of things, build economic strength.

In short, the premise that scarcity rules economies is an emperor without clothes. It's a myth. True, the perception of scarcity is useful for driving up prices, just as the perception of jackpots is useful for spreading lotto-fever. The fear of scarcity makes money for those who control the market when everyone else panics.

But economies don't exist for the purpose of driving up prices or garnering profits. They exist to serve the needs of humanity. In this activity, scarcity, just like risk, poses economic challenges, but it says nothing about how economies meet those challenges. That's for us to decide.

These two different starting-points reflect two different views of what we *assume* economies are all about. They also reflect the two different methods of map-making described in Chapter 1:

Rethinking economies	Billiard-ball maps	Whole-seeking maps
	Economies are all about	
1. Assumptions	scarcity: unlimited desires competing for limited resources.	know-how and creativity: managing creatively what we have and using order to offset scarcity.

2. The basics of economic systems

According to which premise we choose, we define the fundamentals of economic life. Our economic premises and assumptions—whether of scarcity or of anti-scarcity— give rise to basic economic *strategies.*

Scarcity-based economies build strategies around the possession of material goods, which traditional economic theories categorize into land, labor, and capital. What counts is how much real estate we own, how much money we have, and how many hours we work. We're back to counting billiard balls. Economic strategies involve trading our countables to increase our net value.

The ideal for many, though attained by few, is to own enough land and capital so that we don't have to sell our labor. In other words, we work to buy back our time from economic society, so that economic worries no longer dictate our choices.

With inflation and the insecurity of modern economies, however, the price of economic freedom goes up, and the period of indenture increases. Philosopher John Locke's insistence that people possess their own labor becomes an illusion. Instead, we lease our labor from the economy with an option to buy, though we never seem to collect enough assets to complete the purchase. The economy turns into a company town like those of the early 20th century, in which the company—in this case, the economy—owns us, and all we do is get "another day older and deeper in debt."

The danger with this strategy is that it tends economies toward feudalism. By making freedom cost more, scarcity-economies reduce societies to two classes: the few in power and the many who are economically disenfranchised. Both groups go to their graves burdened by money. Both shortchange themselves because of the economic model.

For example, since the decisions of both rich and poor are limited by fears about scarcity, their talents in other areas go untapped. How many Leonardos, Mozarts, or

Einsteins have come and gone undeveloped, because money matters took precedence in their lives? The poor don't have time for frills such as education, while the privileged often push aside their talents in order to acquire wealth. They get hooked on getting more, long after their needs are met. In scarcity-based economies, money-concerns make it hard for people to pursue their life's calling. Individual gifts go to waste.

Applying capitalist or socialist terms to such economies doesn't make them less feudal or less wasteful of human talents. In fact, scarcity-based economies develop precisely the economic imbalances that both Adam Smith and Karl Marx railed against.

Unfortunately, Smith and Marx didn't challenge the scarcity-premise but focused on different ways of distributing goods. In practice, however, distribution strategies haven't prevented the economic poles from widening, since they don't challenge the premise that causes the gap. The root assumption that scarcity rules economies remained unquestioned.

Economies based on creativity and knowledge. If, in contrast to scarcity, economies build on creativity and know-how, they focus less on things and more on how we manage things. Our economic roles shift from possessors to stewards, from consumers to managers. Fixed quantities of things no longer dictate our actions. "Energy and materials are limiting factors," Boulding writes, "not creative or formative factors."[3] The "limiting factors" pose economic challenges; the "creative or formative factors" meet those challenges.

Because we can be creative whether we own things or not, ownership isn't the primary concern. Not that we should stop owning what we need to live and work. Historically, as private ownership became possible for more people, it increased economic independence from kings, states, aristocracies, and plutocracies.

But the strategy of owning as much as possible misses the economic mark. The game of Monopoly isn't a model of how economies work but an analysis of how they fail. The Depression of the '30s inspired Monopoly's creator to invent the game to show where inflated ownerships lead. Monopoly ends when one player dominates the board, having caused the rest to go bankrupt. No further exchange can occur when all but one player is broke. The more economies resemble Monopoly, the closer they are to a breakdown. No more game.

By contrast, successful economies keep exchange going, enhancing it wherever possible. The more players participate, the more diverse the system. The stronger and better all the players are, the more each has to offer. Exchange increases. The whole system is enriched.

By establishing a system of exchange, economies link problems with solutions, needs with know-how. What counts isn't so much the things available—the fixed stock of billiard balls—but the *process* of creativity and the *flow* of knowledge. How does the process work?

a) What's common to all. In the first place, know-how gives everyone equal access to an economy's main source of wealth. We can all cultivate knowledge and work with it creatively. The system in turn protects what each of us has to offer and then explores ways to enhance this primary resource.

For instance, knowledge-based economies depend on education. Education becomes top priority, even if it means paying people to go to school, as many companies are now doing. What's more, education isn't limited to business, math, and the sciences. Creativity blossoms the more we rediscover our home in the realm of ideas. Ideas spark our imagination. They also give us reasons to care—beyond the reason to make money.

Not that making money is wrong; it's just inadequate to meet today's economic challenges. The money-reason hasn't, for instance, made top executives care about the environment, the quality of life, or the welfare of future generations. Yet these factors are central to good household management.

Fortunately, there are disciplines that inspire creativity and caring on wider levels. Religion, philosophy, literature, history, and the arts touch us where balance sheets can't. By enlarging our minds, these disciplines enlarge our worlds, making us enduringly rich, as Viktor Frankl discovered even in concentration camps. The happy by-product is that they also extend our economies' resources. The more we explore our potential on intellectual and spiritual levels, the more insight and creativity we bring to how we manage our households.

Today, with the information explosion, the possibilities for developing knowledge and creativity are virtually unlimited. As Vartan Gregorian, former head of the New York City Library, now President of Brown University, recalled in a recent interview, information doubles every five years.[4] Clearly, scarcity of information isn't our problem. What's scarce is our ability to digest all the information, to make sense of it, and to apply it wisely.

With the information age, then, creativity and knowledge provide a basis for economic equality. Knowledge is our common inheritance. There's plenty of it, and it's becoming increasingly accessible to us all.

b) What's different. But complete equality is achieved only when all differences disappear, which is neither possible nor desirable. Each of us cannot know all there is to know in exactly the same way. Neither would we want to.

Economic systems thrive on a diversity of interests and talents, otherwise there would be no reason for exchange.

Which is precisely what we have. Each of us cultivates knowledge differently. No two of us have identical ways of digesting the information available. Even if we did, two people can use the same knowledge quite differently. As Plato noted in the *Republic,* each person focuses the totality of knowledge in a unique way; each citizen expresses the whole republic through unique skills and talents. Or, as in the philosopher G. W. Leibniz's theory of monads, each person develops an individualized view of the whole—a distinct window on the world.

Diversity is great for economies. The more diverse a system, the more possibilities it includes for developing new levels of order. Diverse economies generate more ways of getting around scarcity. If we have electricity, for example, we don't have to cut down trees for fuel. The new order makes the scarcity of forests no longer an issue, at least not for staying warm. Of course, it's still an issue if we'd like to breathe or to avoid frying the planet.

By increasing order, diverse systems become more flexible. They include more options for responding to stress. If one method doesn't work, we have a back-up, and more back-ups behind that. By increasing an economy's power to overcome scarcity, diversity increases an economy's chances of survival.

Investors are well aware of the uses of diversity. If we spread our risk by putting money in different places, we're less vulnerable if any one of them fails. Our whole future doesn't depend on the success of one venture.

Communities also know something about diversity. A one-company town can become a ghost town overnight if the main employer pulls out. The more businesses a community nurtures, the more stable and secure its economy.

Diversity, therefore, constitutes the second fundamental factor of knowledge-based economies. The diversity that individuals bring to economies gives economies their strength and durability.

The effect of the first two factors—knowledge and diversity—is that economies free everyone to be creative. The fact that we each don't have to grow our own food, for example, frees us to put our energies elsewhere according to our abilities and interests. By developing our talents, we can offer something to the system that's uniquely ours.

c) Systems of exchange. But it's no fun developing individual talents without ways to exchange them. We want to share our abilities as well as to draw on the abilities of others. There's "a propensity in human nature to exchange," Adam Smith wrote, a "disposition to barter."[5]

Exchange brings economies alive. What's the use of diversity if we can't move it around? Economies exist precisely to provide an efficient system through which knowledge can flow. What bees do for flowers, economies do for us. They cross-pollinate our creative abilities, so that something new is always cropping up.

All this cross-pollinating makes economic exchange synergetic. Through exchange, diversity increases diversity. Knowledge, skill, and creativity feed each other to yield possibilities greater than what individuals alone could produce. By exchanging ideas as well as goods and services, economies jump to new levels of prosperity.

By contrast, hoarding, the opposite of exchange, chokes economies. Hoarding works on the fort-premise: acquiring as much as possible provides an illusion of security apart from the system. Even though the system might collapse, at least our private fort will stand.

But the fort-strategy works against economies. The more we hoard, the less exchange occurs and the weaker the entire system becomes. Nor does the strategy achieve the security imagined. If the system fails, the fort hasn't much future either.

Healthy economies establish security as a function of the whole system. If the system is diverse and exchange ongoing, then the economy is both flexible enough to weather storms and rich enough to provide opportunities for everyone. Security lies in the integral system of exchange, not in fragmenting the system with forts.

d) Mutual benefit. Why should we enter into economic exchange? Because it benefits us to do so. But the benefit isn't one-sided. Exchange depends on mutual benefit, a concept that Adam Smith adapted from Plato. Either both sides gain, or there's no exchange. No one freely enters into a relation in which all the benefit goes to the other party.

For this reason, win-win is the only practical and realistic economic strategy. In fact, it's what we do all the time. Day to day, we don't demand benefits from others without offering benefits in return. The concept of reciprocity goes to the bone. If others get more than we do, we feel cheated. If we get more than they do, we worry that they feel cheated, in which case we'd lose the chance to do business with them in the future. In the end, we strive for a balance. We want fairness—mutual benefit.[6]

When reciprocity prevails, economies are better off. Mutual benefit increases prosperity on all sides. It builds trust. If we're not afraid of being ripped off, we do business freely. Trust makes exchange flow, so that the entire system becomes more secure.

The opposite strategy (win-lose) encourages subtle and blatant forms of stealing, plenty of which are legal. Win-lose strategies follow from the premise of scarcity. After all, given limited resources, we can't all win. Some people and nations must simply go without (as long as it's not us).

But win-lose strategies don't build economies. Who agrees to such an arrangement? Once burned, who subjects themselves to it again? Who does business with someone who's out to bilk us? We'll do it only if we're forced to—if we have no other choice.

Because win-lose strategies aren't a form of mutually beneficial exchange, they aren't intrinsic to economies. Nor are they practical. Quite the reverse. They foster practices that endanger economies. Without contributing anything in return, win-lose strategies siphon off the prosperity that win-win economies produce without contributing anything in return. They drain economies, until we reach the end of the game.

The tricks for siphoning are everywhere, though none of them counts as truly economic. Making money on other people's ignorance, for instance, isn't exchange. Profiting from contrived scarcity isn't exchange. Speculating on currencies isn't exchange. Controlling markets isn't exchange. Driving up interest rates isn't exchange, nor is driving out the competition or lowering the quality of products and services while increasing the prices.

When win-lose practices dominate an economy, we stop trusting both the economy and each other. We all suffer. When exchange isn't for mutual benefit, we stop exchanging. The game ends.

But the loss to the economy is even greater. Win-lose strategies give us an excuse to abandon our creativity. We lose sight of our powers as givers and only develop our roles as takers. The economy loses more than what's siphoned out of it. Once again, individual knowledge and talents go to waste.

Two systems: which one? The premises of scarcity on one hand and of creativity on the other set up two contrasting economic systems.

From the *scarcity premise,* strategies develop that, first, make limited material resources the starting-point.

Second, what passes for diversity are different uses of labor, which depend on how land and capital are distributed—who owns what. Instead of developing individual talents (which diversity does), mere division of labor traps us in dead-end jobs, determined by our place in the economic hierarchy. Creativity isn't nurtured but squelched; diversity isn't increased but diminished.

Third, we manipulate the division of land, labor, and capital to own as much as possible. Acquiring is the name of the game, since hoarding secures our private interests.

Fourth, to increase our ownership of limited resources, we struggle to win out over others. Our gain is another's loss, and vice versa. The system makes us feel and act like thieves, whether we want to or not. It brings out the lowest passions in us and rewards them.

But does this model really work? In his critique of it, the third-century philosopher Porphyry wrote:

> In the light of unlimited desires, even the greatest wealth is but poverty. . . . No fool is satisfied with what he possesses; he rather mourns what he has not. . . . Many have attained wealth, and yet not found release from their troubles but have exchanged them for greater ones. Wherefore philosophers say that nothing is so necessary as to know thoroughly what is unnecessary. . . . [Otherwise] while the pile of wealth is growing bigger, life is growing wretched.[7]

Fortunately, there are other models for economies and other strategies for acting in them. From the *premises of knowledge and creativity,* a system develops that, first, includes everyone. Creativity belongs to us all. It comes with being human (we know this from comparing children with chimps). Moreover, the knowledge we need to be creative is universally available. And it isn't scarce. As a resource, it's unlimited in its potential for growth.

Second, diversity increases as we work creatively. The more we diversify our talents, the stronger our economies grow, which frees us to diversify our talents further.

Third, we interact with the economy not to maximize ownership but to exchange the best we have for the best others have. To keep exchange going, we bring it our best.

Fourth, we do this so that all may benefit. Either we all win, or we all lose. To paraphrase John Donne, every loss to a person or nation diminishes us, while every gain increases us. It's great prose because it reveals a great truth. It's how economies work as systems—something more than billiard balls knocking each other out.

Rethinking economies	*Billiard-ball maps*	*Whole-seeking maps*
2. Strategies	*We interact with economies by*	
	maximizing owner-ship of things:	developing systems of exchange:
	a) land, labor, and capital	a) what's common: knowledge and creativity
	b) what's different: who owns what or whom	b) what's different: how we develop and use knowledge
	c) hoarding	c) exchanging differences
	d) one-sided gain (win-lose).	d) mutual benefit (win-win).

3. Regulating economies:
making the invisible hand visible

What regulates economies in practice, for better or worse? Adam Smith referred to an "invisible hand" that regulates free markets. But what is this mysterious hand?

Because "we the people" make economies, whatever regulates us also regulates them. Governments aren't the regulators (despite regulations), because they're run by people as well. Rather, economies reflect us. We make them with our day-to-day *responses*. The question of regulation begins, therefore, with who and what we are.

a) The spectrum of human nature. We're not saints. But we're not total scum, either. Our scum-side just makes more sensational headlines. Neither rosy optimism nor dark cynicism captures human nature. Optimism can be naive and invites disillusionment; cynicism sees only darkness and shuts out hope. Moreover, the two poles—optimism and cynicism—are related. The first invites the second, as Socrates explained in the *Phaedo:*

> Misanthropy is induced by believing in somebody quite uncritically. You assume that a person is absolutely truthful and sincere and reliable, and a little later you find that he is shoddy and irresponsible. Then the same thing happens again. After repeated disappointments at the hands of the very people who might be supposed to be your nearest and most intimate friends, constant irritation ends by making you dislike everybody and suppose that there is no sincerity to be found anywhere. Have you ever noticed this happening? . . .
>
> Isn't it obvious that such a person is trying to form human relationships without any critical understanding of human nature? Otherwise he would surely recognize the truth: there are not many very good or very bad people, but the great majority are something between the two.[8]

Economies include plenty of soured friends, insofar as we form economic relationships "without any critical understanding of human nature." We go into economies hoping for the best but sooner or later encounter the worst. Disillusioned, we assume everyone is rotten, so why should we act differently? As a result, we adopt the very responses that caused our disillusionment. Then we pass these responses along to our children, making them disillusioned as well.

But the uncritical generalization that lies at the root of our disillusionment—namely, that everyone behaves badly when it comes to economies—simply isn't so. As Socrates said, human nature covers a spectrum of qualities. We're creatures in transition, moving from one pole to the other.

At the *dark end,* we harbor fears that make us suffer and cause us to inflict suffering on others. Buddhists and Hindus describe the dark pole as rooted in ignorance. This ignorance isn't just personal, though its effects are felt by persons. It's an impersonal lack of understanding about the real nature of things. What we take ourselves to be isn't who we really are, they say, and what we take others to be isn't really them. We don't know ourselves, and we don't know reality. This deep, philosophical ignorance gets us in a mess.

According to Buddhist and Hindu thinkers, the mess starts with desires. Because of ignorance, we bind ourselves to wants and define ourselves through them. The more wants we can fulfill, the more powerful a person we are. Wanting more and being able to get more makes us somebody.

But wants aren't kind. They lure us into a state of insatiable thirst. Driven by them, we look for things in the wrong places or struggle to get things we don't really want. In the horse-and-chariot metaphor, our desires, the horses, become our masters. Yet under their tutelage, we behave like donkeys.

At the *light end*, we find not the chariot's driver but its owner, the one overseeing the entire activity. In Hindu terms, we find the Atman, the true, spiritual self. The true self doesn't *want*; it *is*. The Atman is one with Brahman (God, the whole) and draws its being from this source. Reflecting the whole, the true self embodies wisdom and understanding. It has all it needs from the whole. In Socratic terms, the light end is expressed in the purified soul of the true philosopher.

Not that the true self is off in the clouds. It's not an absentee owner. By reflecting the whole, the true self cuts through partial-order ignorance, giving us an alternative to the hungry ego. In psychologist A. H. Almaas' terms, it empowers us to exchange the false gold of the ego for the true gold of the self. Just as real gold doesn't need false gold to increase its value, the true self doesn't need to satisfy desires in order to complete its identity.

Humanity covers the spectrum. At one end is the true self, which draws us forward. It shows us who we are in the light of the whole. This light, though, casts a shadow wherever something blocks it. The shadows formed by confused desires represent the dark end of the spectrum.

Where do economies fit in?

Because they deal with self-interest—which is then equated with selfishness—economies are usually associated with the dark end. Why should we expect anything more from economies than greed incarnate?

To make matters worse, because scarcity-premises dominate modern economies, fears surface whenever the question of money comes up. Will we have enough, or will we land among the losers? Even if we win, can we make enough money to stay on top? The thirst increases, as in

Dante's description of the inhabitants of Hell. Money and the dark pole seem like soul mates.

But appearances don't tell the whole story. Economies themselves aren't dark. There's nothing dark about managing the household. What may be dark is how it's done. Addictions to desires (dark-end stuff) put shadows over economies that economies of themselves don't have.

Neither is there anything necessarily wrong with self-interest. Prosperous economies thrive on win-win, not on martyrdom. They respect self-interests and protect them. In fact, economies that compel people to act against their own best interests don't last long. Sooner or later, their members seek a different arrangement. That's what happened when the medieval burghers and other small fries rebelled against the rich, overfed barons (a McRevolt?). That's also why unions arose to counter the robber barons.

Religions agree. Self-interest isn't the problem. Hinduism, for instance, uses self-interest to spur humanity toward ultimate liberation. Hindu teachings argue that nothing can be more in our interest than to be consciously one with the whole, with God. In the chariot metaphor, it's in our interest as drivers to get to know the owner, the true self, and to find out where this owner wants the chariot to go. Given the right context, self-interest can be a positive ally to furthering the Good.

In short, economies are neither necessarily corrupt nor necessarily wonderful. They can be either or somewhere in between. They mirror us. If we live and work at the dark end, our economies will look their worst. But if we move away from this pole, they'll come along too. We regulate their course not from our heads but from our character—where we ourselves are in spiritual growth.

Consequently, discovering what regulates economies—Adam Smith's notion of an invisible hand—starts with the spectrum of human nature. Whichever pole defines our interests also shapes our economies. Economies span the spectrum, because we do.

b) Self-betterment. But there's more. Wherever we are along the spectrum, we push to better ourselves. Staying fixed is boring, and going backward depressing. The only interesting way is forward. We seek to perfect ourselves by moving away from the dark end. Indian philosopher and statesman Sarvepalli Radhakrishnan writes:

> There is a perpetual restlessness with things as they are, an eternal seeking for a better way, a continual progress toward a better world. The greatest gift of life is the dream of a higher life. Each one aspires for a deeper, intenser, and wider self-consciousness and clearer self-understanding.[9]

Economies reflect this restlessness. They show human nature on the move. As Adam Smith observed, self-betterment is a major economic force. Rather than greed, this force—the intuitive knowledge that development is possible and that we can always use more of it—drives economies. Whereas greed begins and ends with gratifying egos, the quest for self-improvement reflects the deeper drive for self-transcendence. Self-betterment patterns outwardly the inward desire for growth.

But self-betterment also has teeth. It inspires restraint. Going forward means not falling back to old habits. We measure our desires and redirect them. Motivated by self-betterment, we think twice before reverting to dark methods: the direction is wrong if we want to progress.

In economies, the restraint side of self-betterment checks exploitation. If our lives don't improve through our labors, we rebel—as the colonists did in the American Revolution and as those in oppressive, totalitarian governments are doing today. All over the world, people expect better conditions for themselves, their children, and their fellows. If economies fail to serve this aim, the invisible hand won't remain invisible for long.

c) Cooperation, which competition serves. The spectrum of human nature and the drive for self-betterment combine to regulate economies, making economies first and foremost cooperative efforts. Competition comes later, serving mainly to elevate standards and to introduce new methods. The core of economies—the reason for them to exist in the first place—is cooperation. Why? Adam Smith begins *The Wealth of Nations* by explaining how economic exchange grows out of the need for mutual assistance:

> Man has almost constant occasion for the help of his brethren. [But given human nature,] it is in vain for man to expect help from their benevolence only *[the higher end of the spectrum]*. He will be more likely to prevail if he can interest their self-love in his favour *[the lower end of the spectrum]*, and show them that it is for their own advantage *[self-betterment]* to do for him what he requires of them *[cooperation]*.[10]

In other words, if we're not saints and we need others' help, we can get it by appealing to others' self-interest and their desire for self-improvement. If it's in their interest to help us, they'll cooperate.

The logic works on us, too. The drive to better ourselves makes us help others, because we need their help in return. The ideal of creating a self-sufficient, economic island is neither practical nor progressive. It cuts us off from all the resources—the creativity and knowledge—that the rest of the world has to offer. Life becomes easier if we both seek help and give it.

Moreover, cooperation refines us. The discipline of cooperation gradually changes self-love into enlightened self-interest. We have to see what our "brethren" need before we can help them. Otherwise they won't be there for us when we need help. In fact, the more perceptive we are about others' real needs, the more successful our help to them will be. Through this process, we become more sensitive to others and less caught up in our own wants.

We participate in economies, then, because we have something of value to offer the community and because we need the specialized help of the community in return. The relation is symbiotic, like an ecosystem in nature. The individual benefits the system, while the system benefits the individual.

By contrast, interpreting the relation as a war among selfish interests makes exchange unrecognizable. It turns reciprocal benefit into a brawl. Mutual advantage disappears, replaced by mutual bilking. Such help we can do without.

Nor does a brawl count as true competition, though it's often advertised as such. Done properly, competition serves cooperation by fine-tuning it and pushing it to new levels. In a sport, the better the opponent, the better the match. Two teams or players, competing to their utmost, reach a level of performance that neither could achieve with lesser competitors.

Similarly, economic competition functions best when it serves the goal of mutual improvement. Two or more entities compete so that something better results. Guided by the invisible hand of cooperation, competition raises standards, lowers prices, increases efficiency, fires creativity, and, all in all, improves products and services.[11]

But this competitive response has nothing in common with the battleground version. Destroying competitors by driving them out of business, far from enhancing cooperation, replaces it with domination. The invisible hand disappears, replaced by the strong arms of the avaricious, or as proper Victorians used to call them, "the greedy bloodsuckers." Competition becomes an excuse for handing businesses over to bullies, who don't care about the quality of goods and services but only about controlling profits. Cooperation *and* competition fall by the wayside.

d) Liberty. The spectrum of human nature, the drive toward self-betterment and the need to cooperate, taken together, regulate economies, making them what they are. But there's one more factor to consider. We need liberty—freedom in the marketplace. Why? We need freedom to develop our talents, to fine-tune our cooperation and to better our lot.

Adam Smith, the champion of free-market economies, argued that the invisible hand guides economies toward maximum efficiency and mutual benefit *only when there's "perfect liberty"*—"where every man [is] perfectly free both to choose what occupation he [thinks] proper, and to change it as often as he [thinks] proper."[12]

Which makes sense. We need freedom to become our best. Freedom allows us to develop our talents to the maximum. If we feel our occupation isn't right for us, we can change it—not just once but "as often as we think proper." In free economies, we don't have to put up with whatever conditions come our way. We can do something about them.

Freedom is equally important to economies as a whole. It diversifies them. Free markets give all sorts of ventures a chance to prove themselves. They encourage creativity and allow it to blossom. Free markets make industries receptive to invention and innovation. They open the possibilities for problem-solving. They also allow economies to work out the best market structure.

Without freedom, economies become rigid and fixed. Vested interests and established power-structures control knowledge and suppress creativity, leaving more and more problems unsolved. Diversity together with flexibility dwindle, causing stagnation to set in. Economies become locked in their own crises, having squelched the means for resolving them.

Without freedom, we're not too happy either. We lose our options. We're stuck doing whatever the power-structures allow us, while they're stuck with a crew of zombies. The life goes out of both us and them.

We know the problem, because we're living in it. Adam Smith's free-market capitalism is the one economic system we don't have. What we really have are family monopolies, conglomerates, and multinationals that dominate economic exchange. The most polite term used to describe the arrangement is *plutocracy,* control by a wealthy elite. But when the plutocrats flex their muscles—and the public spots them doing it—we hear other terms, such as economic fascism or just plain theft.

. In such arrangements, liberty is the first thing to go. Free-market conditions function only for the few. For the majority, educational and financial limits make it almost impossible to exercise the kind of freedom that Smith described.

Not that we haven't made progress. We're better off than many. We just don't have a free market yet. In fact, perfect economic liberty has never existed, except as an ideal. Paul Samuelson, the Nobel-prize-winning economist, observed that, "We don't know whether or not 'pure' capitalism would work, because—like 'pure' Christianity—it's never been tried."[13]

Freedom in economies remains an ideal. The question is, are we aiming toward it? Are we implementing policies that liberate people and nations to interact with economies more as they choose?

Whether we make our economies more or less free depends, of course, on what we think freedom is.

According to spiritual teachings, freedom isn't a right to pursue wants with abandon. "It is no true state of happiness in which the people are given over to idleness and wasteful extravagance," Erasmus (the 16th-century humanist and theologian) wrote, "any more than it is true liberty for everyone to be allowed to do as he pleases."[14] Quite the reverse. In Hindu, Buddhist, and Christian monastic philosophies, pursuing unlimited desires doesn't just create bondage; it *is* bondage. Wants trap us at the dark end. Defining ourselves through wants makes us prisoners to those wants.

In Socrates' words, tying freedom to want-fulfillment gives us a life of "itching and scratching." Feeling itchy, we try to increase freedom by satisfying more desires. We scratch more vigorously. But scratching has the opposite effect. We end up more itchy than before. Satisfying desires as the way to freedom backfires. "Is it possible to live life happily," Socrates asked, "constantly scratching an itch?"[15]

The sixth-century Christian philosopher Boethius, writing from prison, agreed:

> Ultimate servitude is when, given over to vice, [human souls] have lapsed from the reason proper to them. . . . [They have] lowered their eyes to inferior, darkling things, . . . [and] are disturbed by destructive affections. Giving in to [these], they strengthen the servitude which they have brought upon themselves.[16]

Nonetheless, the power to get what we want is more or less how we define freedom, at least economically. It's purchasing power. Freedom is a commodity, namely, the power to fulfill wants. To get it, we have to buy it. Since only a fixed number of material wants can be fulfilled, only a few can be "free" to fulfill them. One person's gain in freedom entails loss to another. Freedom is parcelled according to money. Those with more money get more freedom. Right?

Well, it's not what the Founders had in mind when they wrote the U.S. Constitution. They had a revolution precisely to get rid of money-based definitions of freedom. Building economies on want-notions of freedom, they believed, doesn't give us free markets, much less free societies. Those most driven by wants end up dominating—the Monopoly syndrome—lessening everyone else's freedom. Freedom as a commodity of want-fulfillment doesn't work *as* freedom. More people end up without it than with it.

Instead, as religious reformers have insisted, the kind of freedom that frees everyone operates on a level beyond wants. It's not tied to money but to the soul. Freedom increases as we move toward the light end. It follows our spiritual growth.

"Perfect liberty" goes to the owner of the chariot, to Atman, the true self. True freedom characterizes a consciousness that's one with the whole and derives its being from it. Because nothing is greater than the whole, nothing lesser can dominate it. Working from the whole, the true self doesn't have to satisfy wants to achieve freedom. It's free as it is. Jesus, Lao Tzu, Krishna, and the Buddha were truly free. No horses ran them around. Scratching wasn't their idea of either freedom or the good life.

But how does a spiritual definition of freedom help on a practical level? Simple. It tells us which way to move. If the spectrum of human nature also marks the spectrum of freedom, then we know which direction to go if we want our freedom to increase. Responses that move us toward the true self and its oneness with the whole expand our freedom. Responses that tie freedom to want-fulfillment contract it. We have a choice. The direction we move along the spectrum determines how free we are.

The freedom available to economies, then, comes from us. We supply the liberty that our economies need, since liberty increases with our own spiritual growth. As a result, the invisible hand regulating economies doesn't depend just on where we are but much more on where we tend—on our own spiritual evolution. How truly free can we be?

In short, we've met the invisible hand, and it's us. We regulate economies with our responses. These responses can be shaped by two very different maps:

Rethinking economies	*Billiard-ball maps*	*Whole-seeking maps*
3. Responses	*What regulates economies?* *We do through our responses, which are shaped by*	
	a) the dark end: "Homo itchy"	a) the spectrum of human nature
	b) selfishness and ego-gratification	b) self-betterment
	c) competition, bully style	c) cooperation, which competition serves
	d) domination of the many by the few.	d) liberty as an ideal to approximate through spiritual growth.

4. Matter—energy—information—consciousness

With (1) scarcity replaced by creativity, (2) hoarding replaced by the mutually beneficial exchange of know-how, and (3) domination replaced by the invisible hand of our own evolution, we return to the mobster's question: what is economic reality? How we answer this question sets our *goals*.

Historically, the answer has developed through four stages, each accentuating a different level of economic exchange.

a) Matter. First, material goods (such as land and raw materials) dominate economic life. According to this view, the economic goal is to acquire and possess things, which is what has happened. For centuries, whoever owned the land or the physical resources controlled the economy. Since material goods are limited, it's no surprise that the scarcity-view of economics arose with this first level.

b) Energy. Land and natural resources are of little use to us, though, if we lack the power to do things with them. It's the second factor, energy (the ability to do work) that expands the uses of matter. Energy is squeezed from material resources (wood, coal, oil, gas, and now plutonium) or drawn from natural conditions (water, wind, sun). We also get energy from animal and human labor. Energy fueled the Industrial Revolution as well as the technological age. During these periods, economies shifted from matter to energy, so that whoever controlled the energy controlled the economy.

c) Information. But gradually a third, less material factor supplanted both matter and energy: know-how, skill, and expertise. Mind-power replaced muscle-power. The information age dawned, making us knowledge-transmitters rather than matter-transporters.

Information is wonderful. With it, we can tap energy sources virtually out of the air. Through radios, televisions, and satellite dishes, information systems put us in touch with invisible energy fields. When it comes to using this energy, information shows us how to create things with less matter and less energy. We do more with less.

That's not all. In contrast to matter and energy, information multiplies its resources. As Gregorian said, information already doubles every five years and may soon double every year. Scarcity of information isn't our problem. Quite the reverse. Relative to our capacity to digest all the information, its growth is unlimited. Fields such as law, medicine, science, education, and government are experiencing knowledge explosions, which reverberate through all other fields.

If anything, economies can't keep up with translating the wealth of knowledge into products and services. In the measure that they do, assets appear less as things and more as relationships within information structures. The power to produce assets lies less with what we own and more with what we know. Those businesses with the best information succeed, as do those persons with the best information skills.

As before, whoever controls the basic resource controls the economy. But with information, control is less clear-cut, less secure. Leaks and spies, independent and simultaneous discoveries, research networks, not to mention satellites and laser transmissions, make information harder to contain. The goal to possess and control information proves more elusive.

And for good reason. The earth and all life on it may turn out to be one dynamic information-structure, which each aspect reflects and on which all may draw. If that's so, then the world is less a mass of things and more a flow of information. In this flow, each part serves as a kind of receiver of the information of the whole.

Such was Leibniz's concept, for example. In his theory of monads, each monad reflects the whole. What happens in the whole, each monad feels, and what each monad does, the whole feels. More recently, James Lovelock's "Gaia Hypothesis" suggests a similar view of the earth as one interlocking, self-communicating information system.

Because information moves by its own dynamics, it's more democratic than matter or energy. Einstein's theories are public property. Because more of us have more access to more information, more of us have the opportunity to be creative with it. Equipped with know-how and a compelling image of how to use it, we can build a business, letting the economic information system supply the capital to make it go.

But the information age isn't altogether wonderful. It also brings new problems. Information opens heretofore unimagined possibilities, not all of which are wise to pursue. With the same chemical information, we can prevent or cause death. With the same stock information, we can increase or decrease market stability. With the same satellite information, we can unite or divide the world. With the same scientific knowledge, we can make the earth a living paradise or a lifeless dump.

The information stage isn't the end of economic development. What should we do with information? How can we best use it? These aren't questions of efficiency, which information can easily handle. They're questions of judgment and decision-making, which go beyond information's expertise.

d) Consciousness, ideas, and values. What we do and how we do it depends on consciousness. Consciousness is much more than an information storehouse. It's the power to arrange information into coherent forms—to see connections and structures. Whereas computers register information, consciousness turns it into knowledge. Consciousness sees the significance of information. It puts information into contexts that give it meaning, so that the information makes a difference in how we live.

How does consciousness digest information? Mainly through *ideas*. Ideas provide the link between us and reality by giving us an image of reality's order. They depict real and objective patterns—what Plato called "Forms" or "Essences." (Actually, he called them something much worse in ancient Greek.) Ideas put us in touch with reality's workings. Thanks to their grids and filters, we see reality as something more than a jumble.

Because reality's order is more than what we think it is, ideas are more than just concepts in our heads. Not any notion depicts a real order. In Heisenberg's words, our subjective realm can be in a state of confusion. What we call an idea may not tell us about the real nature of things at all. It may not put us in touch with reality but put us at odds with it. Spencer's "survival of the fittest" or Boesky's "greed is good," for instance, are often viewed as ideas, but at least according to Plato, aren't ideas at all. They're shadows of ideas—crude graspings at the real order.

But even though our grasp of ideas may be imperfect, ideas still point us toward levels of reality that lie beyond the observable. We can't see relations, patterns, or orders, only their effects. We can't see love, integrity, or truth, for example, but we see how they're understood from how people behave. Even though ideas aren't measurable, they nonetheless shape our lives. Ideas guide how we interact with the realities around us.

So much for abstractions. The practical, garden-variety expressions of ideas are *values*. Values cash in ideas and show what it means to live by them. The idea of love, for instance, includes many values—respect, caring, commitment, sensitivity, and self-transcendence. The idea of truth includes values of honesty, openness, and devotion to discovering what's true, whether we like what we find or not.

Human actions are never value-free, since even the claim of value-free behavior reflects a value in itself, namely, that values are good not to have. Scientists, for example, once claimed that science operated without values: "Just the facts." Now, however, they argue that science developed precisely because of the values held by scientists, values such as precision in observation, skepticism about accepted beliefs, honesty in reporting findings, self-criticism in the quest for objectivity, and openness in sharing results.[17]

In fact, values permeate human life. They give us practical guidance. Diligence, thoroughness, determination, and self-discipline are necessary for excellence in any endeavor. Faced with a challenge, we use these values to meet it.

Or, a value taught by virtually every world religion—reciprocity—demonstrates the power of values. Reciprocity is simply the Golden Rule: we're good to others because that's how we'd like to be treated. Or the Silver Rule: we don't beat up others because we're not keen on the same treatment for ourselves.

Reciprocity is good because it helps us see beyond the lone billiard-ball outlook. It shows that we live in a web of relationships, in which whatever we do comes back to us. If we shake the web, we bounce too. If we tear it, our strand becomes weaker. Reciprocity takes a holistic approach to relationships. Societies work better, economies prosper, and relationships improve when we adhere to reciprocity.

Moreover, values don't work alone. One of Socrates' favorite exercises was to pound out the relations among ideas and values. The wise, to *be* wise, must also be just. The just, to *be* just, must also be devoted to Truth and the Good. To seek Truth and the Good, we must study Beauty and proportion. Ideas, he reasoned, work together in a consistent and mutually affirming system. They form an integral network—a coat "without seam, woven from the top throughout." (John 19:23)

We usually talk about this network in terms of *value systems*. Value systems strengthen the guidance that ideas and values give us, especially since they work in the negative as well. If something isn't just, and if it isn't in accord with Truth and order, it most likely isn't good. If it isn't good, it isn't wise to do. The unity of ideas, which we apply through our value system, keeps us on the straight and narrow, or at least away from complete depravity.

For example, if we recognize only the values of diligence and discipline, we could use them destructively. We could apply them to bank robbing, for instance, or to extortion. Hitler had diligence and discipline. He wore only one cuff of the coat.

But if we wed diligence and discipline to reciprocity and compassion, we're much less likely to run amok. Networks of values put us in harmony with reality. Guided by the unity of ideas, we find it easier to be creative about how we work with reality's order, and we're less likely to act in ways that cause suffering.

But shaping consciousness according to ideas takes time and development. Ideas change how we live. They move us along the spectrum. According to Socrates, seeking reality's order through ideas and being transformed by them is the work of a lifetime. Just before he received the death penalty, he said, "I tell you that to let no day pass without discussing goodness and all the other subjects about which you hear me talking and examining both myself and others is really the best thing that a person can do, and that life without this sort of examination is not worth living."[18]

Which means that, two and a half millennia later, we and our economies face a new frontier. We've reached the limits of matter, energy, and even information. Not only is there more information available than we can digest, but we often use matter, energy, and information in ways that will do us in if we're not careful. The household management needs a mutation, which only a change of consciousness can bring.

Reductionism.   Not that everyone agrees with Socrates, especially when it comes to economies. There's a school of thought which claims that the consciousness-factor isn't relevant to economies. According to this view, the way to solve economic problems is to reduce them to questions of matter, energy, and information—things we can control. Values don't count among economic realities. Counting billiard balls is more exact, more masterable.

Convinced of the superiority of billiard-ball methods, economists of this persuasion drift away from Adam Smith philosophically, however much they use his name, and argue for a reductionist, value-free approach to their discipline. It sounds more "scientific." If we can reduce economies to observable facts and quantifiable forces, we can bypass the unpredictable human element, as well as the invisible, nonquantifiable stuff called ideas and values. We can control economies more efficiently.

Unhappily, this school of economic thought has dominated the Western world for well over a century. Not that all economists belonged to it. So-called value-free economics, the dissenters said, is simply a disguise for materialist economics. Values are still involved, but they're materialist values: that only material, quantifiable factors count.

In *The Unity of Law*, for example, Henry Carey challenged the reductionist, value-free approach to economies:

> Looking around, we see that throughout the largest portion of the earth there exists little but poverty and wretchedness among the millions, selfishness, extravagance, and waste among those by whom their movements are directed; the rich becoming richer, and the poor poorer from year to year. As a consequence of this, the world presents for observation little beyond a constant series of wars, rebellions, and revolutions, with terrific waste of mental and physical force, of property and of life.
>
> Seeking now to understand the cause of a state of things so sad and so destructive, the inquirer looks to the works of leaders of opinion in that country which claims to follow in the footsteps of Adam Smith; there to find, however, little but assertions that their science is limited to the consideration of material wealth alone, to the entire exclusion of mind and morals, skill and taste; that buying and selling constitute the chief aim of life. . . .
>
> Need we now wonder that a system so thoroughly materialistic should have given rise to a school from which we learn that "survival of the fittest" and crushing out of those less "fitted" constitute the bases of all natural arrangements for promoting the advance of civilization?
>
> Discoursing on the wealth of nations, Adam Smith clearly showed his high appreciation of the importance of the moral and mental elements. Rejecting the views thus presented, his Ricardo-Malthusian successors have assured their readers that their—so-called—science limited itself . . . to an exhibition of causes affecting the production, distribution, consumption of *material wealth alone*, the economist allowing "neither sympathy with indigence, nor disgust at profusion or avarice.". . . Narrow and contracted as was the *science* thus described . . . at

length it has come to be generally understood that it concerns itself little, if at all, with any societary operations outside of those of the mere trader—things that cannot be bought and sold being thus wholly excluded from consideration.[19]

By reducing economies to "the production, distribution, [and] consumption of material wealth alone" and excluding everything "that cannot be bought and sold," reductionist economists in Carey's day and ours define economies as closed systems of matter and energy. Knowledge and creativity, ideas and values, are out. They're either not relevant or mere commodities to be traded.

But closed systems run down. Economic reductionism forces the scarcity-model on economies, which, as Carey points out, makes the law of the jungle supreme. Business becomes a war, and the adversaries either aggressors or victims.

The result is precisely what's wrong with economies. From nine to five, we're expected to act like economic animals, out for the most. The rest of the time we're supposed to be caring, sensitive human beings. We're caught in contradictions, as Scrooge was: "There is nothing on which the world is so hard as poverty; and there is nothing it professes to condemn with such severity as the pursuit of wealth."[20]

As with scarcity, though, the contradictions don't come from reality; they come from a one-sided way of looking at reality. By excluding the dimensions of ideas and values, reductionism expects us to manage economies without the tools that make our management constructive. We're supposed to put away our religious and philosophical hats and make do in the jungle.

But, as we're finding out today, the method doesn't work. Materialist values trap us in more and more limits.

No-value values shut out the development we need to master crises and to manage economies well.

Overcoming limits. In fact, economic realities go far beyond trading a fixed number of billiard balls. They include all the dimensions that relate to us and our own development. Ideas of justice, Truth, and the Good are as intrinsic to economies as they are to us, since economies are us in action. We can't ignore the higher values without discovering down the road that something is missing from how we manage our households.

This is more than an issue of morals; it's an issue of *what works.* Taking all dimensions into account works better than considering only the narrowest, because the higher dimensions expand our options for coping with limits. Specifically, each dimension has limits that the next higher dimension overcomes.

Matter has certain limits that *energy* overcomes: energy moves and restructures matter. Energy changes matter's forms.

Energy has certain limits that *information* overcomes. Information minimizes the loss of energy by devising more efficient methods. "As the genetic know-how structure develops and becomes increasingly complex," Boulding writes, "the increase of know-how itself tends to push back the energy and materials' limitations and frontiers."[21]

Yet information has limits that *consciousness* overcomes. Ideas develop values that guide the best use of information. We can use information to clean up the earth rather than to suffocate it, or to take care of our own world rather than to wreck someone else's.

By expanding the context beyond matter and energy to information and consciousness, we open our economies, so that they're not bound by material limits. We put economic life back into reality—not the sawed-off realities of the reductionists but the total reality in which both we and our economies live.

To form economic goals, then, we can do it by either billiard-ball or whole-seeking methods:

Rethinking economies	Billiard-ball maps	Whole-seeking maps
	Our goal is	
	to maximize control of economies by:	to evolve economies by expanding them from:
4. Purposes	a) reducing them to fixed quantities of matter	a) matter,
	b) and energy,	b) to energy,
	c) controlling information, and	c) to information,
	d) ignoring ideas and values,	d) to consciousness, ideas, and values,
	which turns economies into closed systems.	which works as a method for overcoming limits.

How, then, can we participate in the development of consciousness? What tools help us along? Not surprisingly, the tools of the consciousness-age are philosophical: evolving consciousness by evolving the philosophies that shape it.

But what are these tools? What is a philosophy? And how do we go about evolving the ones we've got?

Rethinking Economies

By rethink-ing our—	Billiard-ball maps	Whole-seeking maps
	Economies are all about	
1. Assumptions	scarcity: unlimited desires competing for limited resources.	know-how and creativity: managing creative-ly what we have and using order to offset scarcity.
2. Strategies	*We interact with economies by*	
	maximizing our ownership of things:	developing systems of exchange:
	a) land, labor, and capital	what's common: knowledge and creativity
	b) what's different: who owns what or whom	b) what's different: how we develop and use knowledge
	c) hoarding	c) exchanging differences
	d) one-sided gain (win-lose).	d) mutual benefit (win-win).

By rethink-ing our—	Billiard-ball maps	Whole-seeking maps
3. Responses	*What regulates economies? We do through our responses, which are shaped by*	
	a) the dark end: "Homo itchy"	a) the spectrum of human nature
	b) selfishness and ego-gratification	b) self-betterment
	c) competition, bully style	c) cooperation, which competition serves
	d) domination of the many by the few.	d) liberty as an ideal to approximate through spiritual growth.
4. Purposes	*Our goal is*	
	to maximize control of economies by:	to evolve economies by expanding them from:
	a) reducing them to fixed quantities of matter	a) matter,
	b) and energy,	b) to energy,
	c) controlling information, and	c) to information,
	d) ignoring ideas and values, which turns economies into closed systems.	d) to consciousness and ideas, which works as a method for overcoming limits.

Chapter 3

Practical Philosophies:
What's Involved?

᠎🄪🄪🄪🄪🄪🄪🄪

How do we arrive at philosophies? For the most part, we pick them up as we go, usually without thinking about them. Unannounced and without proper interviews, philosophies move into our minds and tell us what's what.

Without noticing it, for instance, we make *assumptions.* We take some things for granted. These assumptions put our minds into some kind of order. They set up our mind's housekeeping.

The housekeeping, though, we tend to notice more, since our philosophies give us *strategies* for arranging the furniture of our thoughts and lives. We develop ways of doing things—of making plans and executing them.

Actually living in the house means having certain kinds of experiences and *responding* in certain ways.

Even more, it means pursuing certain *goals.* We adopt the aims that our philosophies give us and move in the directions they point.

What we've described in terms of the mind's housekeeping illustrates four factors—four tools that shape the philosophies that then steer our lives:

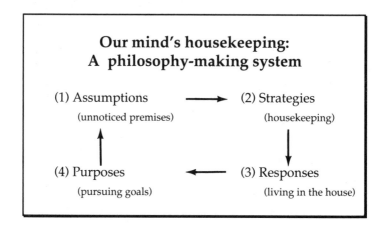

When we talk about philosophies, this housekeeping system is roughly what we mean. Not that we divide our philosophies neatly into four compartments or use the tools one at a time: we only make assumptions today; tomorrow we do our strategies; we'll respond to experiences Friday and Saturday nights, while we keep Sunday free for goals. Rather, philosophies grow with us. We develop their powers along the way.

To find out which philosophies are guiding us—and whether we're happy with them or not—we have to step back and reflect on them. Being aware of the four factors helps. It gives us a notion of what to look for. By asking questions about these factors, we entice our philosophies out of the corners and into the open where we can analyze and revise them.

I. Assumptions

Philosophical thought begins with recognizing our assumptions. Materialists make certain assumptions. Idealists make different assumptions. But we all assume something. Tart's billiard-ball credo in Chapter 1, for instance, is simply a list of billiard-ball assumptions. The assumptions outline where billiard-ball housekeeping starts. The Apostles' Creed, which the billiard-ball credo imitates, represents an opposite set of assumptions, one that points us in another direction. The Creed sets us up to investigate reality as the whole (God) and to arrange our mind's housekeeping to reflect the ideas expressed in the Creed.

But assumptions aren't always so grand. Even on a simple level, we make assumptions that are necessary to get around. Waking up in the morning, we assume that the world still exists and that our friends and family don't suddenly hate us (at least no more nor less than when we went to bed). We assume that the sun rises and that there's some reason to go on with our lives.

In fact, we get so used to our assumptions that we forget they're there. It's hard even to define them, since we pick them up from parents, friends, teachers, coworkers, and the media. The assumptions affect us nonetheless. They tell us what to expect. With them, we see order.

Not that all assumptions represent the order of things with equal accuracy. Not all have the promise of being good housekeepers. By drawing lines and defining limits, different assumptions package reality differently.

In the process, they introduce distortions. In other words, when we walk down the street, we see the world slightly skewed. Things aren't quite what they appear to be. If the distortions become too great, we go a bit nuts relative to everyone else, which means they might not let us walk down the street anymore.

Unfortunately, we can't avoid distortions by making no assumptions at all. This isn't an option, because it's not possible in practice. Rocks make no assumptions. We, however, can't avoid making them. Assumptions form the basis of our conceptual housekeeping. We can't get away from them, nor would we want to. Without assumptions about the order of things, we'd never know what to expect. Assumptions turn an otherwise overwhelming reality (like jobs, economies, or spouses) into something fathomable. They package reality into a digestible, workable form, so that we don't lose our minds.

But there's a price. What we end up digesting is often more package and less reality. That's when the fun starts. Just when we think we have our assumptions straight, we discover that what we took for granted isn't so. Some part of the world's order—how our friends behave, what methods work, or whether there's intelligent life elsewhere in the galaxy—gets turned on its head. What we assumed about reality isn't how things really are.

Yet having to rethink our assumptions isn't fatal to philosophy; it's where philosophy starts. The rethinking spurs us to bring our assumptions out into the open, so that we can examine them: what are we assuming about ourselves, others, our lives, and the world?

If our assumptions are misleading us—if they're telling us only half the story or distorting what we perceive—we can change them. But we'll never know how helpful or troublemaking our assumptions are until we put them to work, which the second philosophical tool does.

II. Strategies

Equipped with a set of assumptions, we develop strategies for filtering reality and making sense of it. Strategies give us ways both to comprehend our worlds and to function successfully within them.

In other words, our assumptions (tool 1) set up our mind's housekeeping (tool 2). Depending on what we assume, some views go in the drawer, while others go in the trash. The rest we arrange in different rooms in ways that make sense. Order emerges out of chaos.

Buddhist teachings, for instance, explain that thoughts and perceptions are like strangers passing through our house. We don't have to invite all of them to stay. Just because some notion wanders into our head doesn't mean it's our thought or that it fits with our housekeeping system. It may simply be passing through. According to our philosophical strategies, we choose which mental furniture stays and where it fits.

Without strategies for sorting out thoughts and perceptions, we'd be swamped. Information would flood us. We'd lack good methods for interacting with our friends and family or solving our problems at work. To manage our lives well—not only to arrange the house but also to do something worthwhile in it—we need strategies for acting on the input that comes our way.

The result? Our strategies give us the housekeeping systems we have. Infinite reality includes infinite possibilities. Any of these possibilities can come into being. Which of them gets actualized reflects us, the housekeeper. Depending on the strategies we bring to reality, we experience reality's order as we do.

Modern physics has been harping on this point for almost a century. Einstein's theory of relativity as well as Heisenberg's principle of indeterminacy underscore our role in what we perceive. How and when we look at a subatomic particle affects what we see. The strategies we bring to reality shape reality; that is, they shape how we experience it. We see reality differently according to the filters or maps we use.

Which means that we're not passive observers in life. There's nothing passive about keeping house. Things don't just happen to us. Stock market crashes don't just happen, neither do wars or holiday dinners. Depending on our assumptions, our strategies can be a force for good, or they can conjure the stuff of nightmares. Some strategies free us to be creative, while others lock us on courses of self-destruction. In Heisenberg's terms, our strategies either open us to the central order or lock us in partial orders.

That's what the prophecies of global upheaval around the turn of the millennium are all about. What happens or doesn't happen, they say, depends on the strategies we use. With our strategies, we choose among the infinite possibilities that infinite reality presents to us. If we persist in destructive strategies, the worlds we get won't be pretty. But we're not stuck with one set of strategies. The future isn't fixed. At any moment, we can choose differently and find ourselves in different worlds.

Which is why practical philosophies don't end with the second tool. Philosophies aren't head-games. They're maps for dealing with what goes on outside of our heads. Map-making can't be the end of the process. After we've made a few maps, we need to see how they work. Do they fit the territory? What kinds of worlds do they give us?

III. Responses

We can't package reality any way we like and still get along with it. Not any map presents the territory accurately, neither do we keep house in a void. The totality—God, Brahma, Allah, the Tao, the whole, the central order, whatever we call it—sets up an order that's bigger than we are, an order which our housekeeping methods (our maps) can't ignore.

In the third stage, then, our assumptions and strategies lock horns with reality and wrestle with it. We see our housekeeping strategies in action. As we observe their performance, we decide which strategies work and which need adjusting. We assess our philosophies: do our maps tell us what we need to know for us to work constructively with whatever is out there?

This interaction between us and reality—between our world views and the world—empowers us to take hold of our development. Though we can't change either gravity or God, we can change how we respond to them.

We can respond to gravity, for instance, by either building bridges or jumping off them. How we respond to God spans roughly the same range. In other words, we can respond to reality either by striving to understand it or by ignoring it—acting as if it isn't there.

If we choose the second option, we run into reality's order head-on. We find ourselves living in worlds that can't succeed and following maps that get us lost.

If we don't realize the role of our philosophies in creating the mess we're in, we might conclude that we're stuck with things as they are or that God doesn't like us. A less depressing response, though, would be to trace the crises to our maps—both the individual and the collective maps affecting us—and to redraw them.

How do we know when to revise our maps? If bells don't go off in our heads naturally, then lurches and jolts do the job. Our chariots hit bumps. Thanks to the knocks, we don't have to speculate about the success of different strategies. We find out in life. Experience gives us signals that are hard to miss.

By listening to the signals and responding by redrawing our maps, we exercise our power to shape experience. We respond by evolving our philosophies, which makes us and our worlds evolve, too. Waking up, we discover that there are different roads to take and other maps to follow.

To what end? Where are we going?

IV. Goals

The fourth and last tool deals with purposes and goals. It focuses the other three tools by giving them direction. Purposes define where we want to go; assumptions, strategies, and responses take us there. The goal to be a lawyer, for instance, requires different assumptions, strategies, and responses from the goal to be a physicist. The aim to lead a street gang in L.A. requires different assumptions, strategies, and responses from the aim to follow in the footsteps of Mother Teresa.

Where, though, do we get our purposes? Mostly from our relation to different contexts. The narrower the context, the more specific the goal. The context of having a body, for example, gives us the purpose to feed it and to look after its health.

As the context widens, we develop goals that link us with reality on broader levels. The context of having a family or friends, for example, expands our purposes beyond body-care to goals that build healthy relations.

The context of economies inspires a range of purposes even broader than those that link us to friends and family. Here, too, our goals reflect the way we define the economic context. For instance, defining economies as struggles to maximize personal wealth gives us one set of goals. Defining economies as mutual responsibilities for managing our human and earthly households gets us going in other directions.

Spiritual inquiry confronts purpose on the broadest level, namely, in the context of the whole, "the Great Ultimate," as Chinese philosophy calls it. Why are we here? What purpose guides human life and gives it meaning? If the Great Ultimate gives us a purpose, we'd like to know it.

V. The four as a learning system

The four tools form a system of learning. They work as a team, in which a change in one factor triggers changes throughout. Each gives feedback to the others, so that all stay out of ruts. Together, the tools keep our philosophies evolving.

Expanding our *purpose*, for instance, challenges us to rethink our *assumptions*. If a gang leader decides to follow Mother Teresa, he'll have to change his assumptions as well. Self-only or gang-only premises won't work.

New assumptions give rise to new *strategies*. The housekeeping methods change. Mother Teresa thinks and acts differently from the streetwise. Her strategies don't need guns or threats to be effective.

Different housekeeping strategies create different worlds. The gang-controlled streets of L.A. are a different world from a shelter in India or food center in St. Louis. With Mother Teresa's strategies, the former gang leader learns to *respond to life* differently. The universe changes— his universe—to reflect his changed response.

In his new universe, he discovers all kinds of *goals* that refocus his energies: helping others, ending hunger, as well as cultivating his mind and working on his inward, spiritual growth. The evolution of philosophies comes full circle, but on a higher level. The goal that sparked new assumptions, strategies, and responses sparks new goals as well.

By playing off each other, the four factors spiral growth. They create a pattern of learning, whereby we try out different philosophies and get feedback on them. We examine each of our philosophical tools to find out how we might change our use of them. For instance, we put questions to our philosophies:

1) What are we *assuming* about ourselves and about reality? What do we assume the real order is? Is it dog eat dog, for instance, or is there an order more fitted to human beings?

2) What kinds of *strategies* are our assumptions giving us? What kind of housekeeping system do they set up? Are we going forward, for instance, or do events just sweep us along? Are we driving the chariot or just being dragged around by it?

3) How satisfied are we about our housekeeping systems in action? Do they give us good ways of *responding* to experience, or are they making a mess of things? What is experience telling us about our philosophies? In other words, how big are the bumps?

4) Then, of course, there are the big questions: What is our *purpose* in life? Are our goals taking us where we want to go?

One way to bring questions of purpose close to home is to confront the death issue: If we knew that we had a year to live, how might we change our goals? How about 200 years? What if death weren't an issue at all? If life goes on, what goals enrich us in ways we can take with us when we go? Socrates suggested that we shouldn't fear death or mourn those who have died until we're sure that what happens after death is worse than what happens here. We may be in for a nice surprise.

According to the feedback we get on each question, we revise our answers. Our philosophies develop. To what end? That our maps become better guides. We develop philosophies that help us understand reality more as it is.

Granted, no map is perfect. Nonetheless, we can revise our maps. We can shape philosophies to reflect the whole more clearly and to bring us into greater harmony with it. That's what the philosophical tools are for.

VI. How the four work in economies

In fact, we've already used the tools to focus the philosophies we bring to economies. Chapter 2 discussed the assumptions, strategies, responses, and goals that make our economies what they are. Building on the first chapter, the second chapter contrasted the way billiard-ball methods on one hand and whole-seeking methods on the other use the tools to form philosophies which, in turn, shape economic life.

1) We start with *assumptions:* what do we assume economies are all about? If, as billiard-ball philosophies assume, they're about unlimited desires competing for limited resources, we start from the assumption of *scarcity.* Economies are about divvying up some fixed quantity of resources. Since we always want more (an assumption), and since there are always more of us to want (another assumption), we and our economies are in trouble. It's impossible to divvy up the scarcity in a way that will make everyone happy (yet another assumption).

2) These assumptions limit the *strategies* that are open to us. If economies are all about who gets how much of which resource, then *ownership* is the name of the game, and *hoarding* is the way to secure our interests. Moreover, what we own, others can't. A *win-lose* strategy becomes inevitable—inevitable, that is, on the premise of scarcity. Assuming scarce resources, and assuming that we all want them, we can't all win. Someone has to lose.

3) All these assumptions and strategies shape our *responses.* Driven by the fear of scarcity, we get the itch for more and scratch it by extending our assets at others' expense. Guided by win-lose strategies, we respond with *domination* and *control.* The more resources we control, the better our standing in the economy.

4) This, our philosophy tells us, is the way to get what we want, which is what billiard-ball *goals* say we're in economies to do. But the goal to maximize our control over limited resources doesn't need a very broad context, philosophically speaking. In fact, the narrower the context, the better. Ideas such as truth and justice, or values such as reciprocity and compassion, just get in the way. It's better to ignore them and to *limit the context* of economies to things we can buy, sell, and stockpile.

The economy that results from these assumptions, strategies, responses, and goals isn't the way economies have to be; it's the way billiard-ball philosophies cause them to be.

Whole-seeking philosophies, on the other hand, create economies that look completely different:

1) They *assume* that economies aren't about scarcity but about how we offset scarcity. They're about *knowledge* and *creativity*—managing creatively what we have. Instead of fighting over scarcity, we outsmart it. We use our wits to get around limits by restructuring them.

2) The *strategies* that follow from this premise free us to be creative in a way that benefits both ourselves and the systems around us. Sharing in the common resource of knowledge, we explore individual ways to develop this resource and put it to work.

The result is a *system of exchange for mutual benefit*. We need others' individualized expression, and they need ours. Win-win is the strategy that works. It's the strategy that builds prosperity, because it gives everyone a chance to prosper by sharing his or her abilities with everyone else. The synergy of exchange multiplies resources, so that there are more options for everyone.

3) Equipped with these strategies, we *respond* to economies with a commitment to *mutual self-betterment*. We

cooperate with each other so that we're all better off, and we use competition to fine-tune our cooperation. In particular, we work to *increase our liberty*, not by diminishing the liberty of others, but by evolving ourselves. As we do, our responses make both us and our economies more free.

4) All of which reflects the whole-seeking *goal*, namely, *to expand the context* in which we think, work, and live. We seek broader dimensions, which turns out to be both a spiritual and a practical method. Wider dimensions aren't vague or abstract. They constantly feed us with new perspectives for restructuring the more limited dimensions (physical, economic, social) that we deal with every day.

In economies, expanding the context in which we form our goals gives us a method for overcoming limits. Expanding the context to energy overcomes material limits. Expanding it to information overcomes energy limits, while expanding our household management to include consciousness, ideas, and values overcomes information limits, namely, that we're inundated with information, and we're not sure what to do with it all.

What makes economies what they are, then, isn't the stuff we have—the quantifiable resources—but the philosophies we bring to them. Which *assumptions* we make, which *strategies* we use, which *responses* we select, and which *goals* we seek point our chariot down one road or another. They shape economies to be what they are. As a result, the broader dimension of our philosophies overcomes the limited view that we're stuck with just one type of economy—the billiard-ball type.

To explore the wider dimensions, spiritual teachings say, we have to expand our development to include them. As the world's religions discuss development, though, it means more than building a new highway or office complex, and evolution means more than studying fossils and cockroaches. The kind of evolution they explore is *spiritual:* the ability to evolve our philosophies and to keep them evolving.

But evolving our philosophies isn't always that easy, especially if we're unaware of what's involved. How does spiritual evolution work, and how can we work with it? What does it mean to go forward in spiritual growth?

Chapter 4

What's Forward
and What's Not?

🔲🔲🔲🔲🔲🔲🔲

B ack to the chariot metaphor. The chariot is a vehicle that takes us somewhere. But where? Along the spectrum, which way are our chariots going? Backward and nowhere are our least favorite directions. Forward sounds best. But what does going forward mean?

I. What spiritual evolution isn't

One way to sharpen the picture of forward is to consider what it's not. Not everything that passes for spiritual evolution really is.

Time. Spiritual evolution isn't, for example, a linear function of time. If some philosophy is more recent, it's not for that reason alone more advanced. The latest philosophy isn't necessarily the best, just as a person living today isn't necessarily more spiritually evolved than Moses, Socrates, Jesus, Muhammad, Confucius, Lao Tzu, or the Buddha.

True, with time we get better. We learn more. But learning goes through alternating phases of forward and reverse. According to Hindu philosophy, human evolution has cycles of ups and downs that span massive lengths of time. The overall trend is upward, but in the middle of a down phase, it may not seem that way.

In the diagram, for instance, relative to 4a, 4b looks like the pits. Yet compared with cycle 1, cycle 4's low is higher than cycle 1's high. We're getting somewhere.

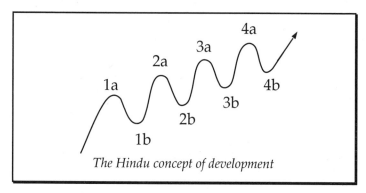

The Hindu concept of development

Variation. Neither is forward mere variation. New isn't always improved. If something is different, it's not for that reason better. Differences may or may not contribute to evolution. In biology, most mutations are unsuccessful. Their variations don't equip species to interact more successfully with the environment.

In human evolution, many developments resemble changes in costume more than in consciousness. They alter things on the surface without bringing real restructuring. Over the millennia, for instance, we've changed our methods of warfare from rocks and spears to laser beams and stealth bombers. Real development, though, would be to find ways to resolve differences without resorting to zapping and whacking. A hi-tech variation on a club isn't a sign that we're evolving.

Quantity isn't a sign of evolution, either. Neither bigness nor numerousness demonstrates evolutionary superiority. If either did, elephants or insects would be the most evolved species, while the successors of dinosaurs wouldn't have been a few tiny mammals.

So, too, in spiritual evolution. Quantitative factors don't signify the forward course. Certain philosophies may bring wealth and power to their adherents. But quantitative advantages don't make the philosophies progressive. The robber barons had lots of money, and Hitler had big armies. But that didn't make them spearheads of spiritual growth. Nor did their methods contribute to civilization. Civilization does just fine without them.

Strength in numbers is also no sure sign of evolution. That a philosophy is common doesn't mean it's progressive. Quite the reverse. Evolutionary leaps begin not with what's common but with what's different. Mutations start with individuals: the odd duck, the out-of-step thinker, or the single citizen fed up with officialdom's nonsense.

If anything, evolution favors the opposite of "might makes evolution." Those methods succeed that do more with less. Massive size and power aren't necessary for survival. More often than not, they get in the way. Just as knowledge and creativity overcome scarcity, qualitative changes out-evolve quantitative advantages.

Gandhi learned this lesson well. Britain's might didn't stop him from evolving higher models of government. In spite of the British Empire's economic, political, social, and military advantages, Gandhi's method of evolving self-rule through nonviolent, nondominating means won out.

Accretion. Because quantitative factors don't mark evolution, the evolutionary process isn't one of accretion, simply adding and adding. A mammal isn't a dinosaur with a few extra features but an entirely new design. So, too, consciousness evolution involves mutation—fundamental restructuring—so that new forms appear.

Knowledge, for example, doesn't develop by simple fact-gathering. Facts are important. But the framework into which we put facts may be wrong, that is, narrow and misleading. Within a fixed framework, we can gather facts by the millions but miss the few big concepts that help us understand things better.

Ancient and medieval stargazers, as an example, collected tons of facts about the heavens, but most of them between Ptolemy and Copernicus missed the concept of a solar system. Not that the earlier astronomers were stupid; most were very bright. They merely got stuck gathering Ptolemaic facts: they kept arranging the facts according to an earth-centered model.

Knowledge-evolution works differently. We evolve knowledge not by piling up facts but by restructuring our frame of reference—a method that historian Thomas Kuhn pointed out thirty years ago from his study of the history of science.[1] Forward means developing the categories—the *paradigms*—we use to collect and manage facts. Then the facts we gather have more meaning.

Spiritual evolution works the same way. Only marginally can we develop our philosophies by fortifying a given philosophy with more and more corroborating experiences. The art of going forward lies in restructuring our models. Propping up one model with more and more justifications doesn't establish its truth or evolutionary superiority. More likely, it makes it harder for us to let go of the philosophy—to evolve beyond it.

Technological prosperity. Nor are technological advances proofs of spiritual evolution. Air conditioning and microwave ovens are marvelous, no question. But a technologically advanced and materially prosperous culture may still be spiritually bankrupt. The best technologies don't guarantee inner growth.

Anti-tradition. Evolution isn't opposed to tradition, either. Going forward doesn't mean denying where we've been. Rather, evolution adapts the good that traditions embody, relating that good to the needs of growth. In fact, evolution builds on tradition. Without it, each new stage would have to start from scratch.

In many cases, religious, social, and political traditions came into existence precisely to help humanity grow beyond its weaknesses. They arose to protect development, not to squelch it. The evolutionary approach honors these traditions by using them to evolve further. It values traditions in their original spirit, drawing on them to keep evolution going.

Value-free. Last, evolution isn't value-free. Forward isn't any random direction. Its course is set by values.

Even in biological evolution, values play a selective role. As biologist Pierre Lecomte du Nouy argued in his classic text, *Human Destiny*, the order, intelligence, and freedom from environmental restraints that a new species expresses determines its success more than body weight, mass, or strength. Higher values enhance a creature's flexibility in problem-solving. With greater order, intelligence, and freedom, life-forms become more adaptable, therefore more able to survive.

Spiritual evolution intensifies the role of values. Intellect and cunning, without the "select mechanism" of higher values, become weapons of destruction. Reason gets caught up in dark-end impulses. By contrast, when spiritual values guide the will and intellect, we move away from the dark end. Values steer us toward constructive aims—aims more in line with the character of the chariot's owner.

In fact, ideas and values spark evolution in the first place. They get the real process going.

II. How spiritual evolution works

1) Ideas bring mutation

Evolution begins with mutation: something new appears. But the new form doesn't come out of the blue. In spiritual evolution, mutation signifies a deeper breakthrough on the level of ideas. Ideas alter the structure into which we put information. They change our filters for looking at the world when the old ones get clogged. By altering our philosophical structures, ideas reshape how we use information, energy, and matter.

But the ideas that bring mutations aren't just things beetling around our brains. For Plato and two millennia of philosophy and religion, ideas meant spiritual realities, manifestations of the whole. When one of these ideas hits us, we get a new insight into what's ultimately real. We see things differently and are changed as a result.

Biologist Rupert Sheldrake's unconventional theory of evolution—"the hypothesis of formative causation"— offers a useful parallel. In his view, universal, pre-physical forms, which he calls "morphogenetic fields," spark the appearance of new organisms.[2] These form-generating fields—not unlike Plato's Forms or Ideas—bring changes in the genotype, that is, in the hereditary code or information structure. The new genetic code then produces the new organism. For Sheldrake, evolution proceeds from the formative field (idea level) to new information to new living beings (what-we-see level).

Spiritual evolution follows the pattern. Ideas such as freedom, truth, and justice have revolutionized the world more than once and continue to revolutionize it. They made slavery obsolete. Now they're hammering away at oppression and injustice not just in governments but in families, communities, and work places. Ideas are the stuff of development. They jolt us out of ruts, so that we see things in a new light. By changing the model into which we put information, ideas change how we think and live.

To start the process, an idea breaks through. But no sooner does the idea appear than it links with other ideas. A flash of insight begins to form a web of new assumptions, new strategies, new responses, and new goals. It gets our philosophies going. Ideas feed each other, until the total form of consciousness changes.

Not that ideas affect only those areas that we usually think of as spiritual. Ideas operate as a practical force for development on all sorts of levels. They get the wheels turning in technology, business, and child-rearing.

Ideas of intelligibility and order, for example, spark the growth of science. If we assume that the universe is unintelligible and chaotic, we won't put much effort into making sense of it. But if we have a vision of order and intelligibility, we try to find out what it is. Einstein, for instance, imagined a level of order and intelligibility that physicists before him hadn't. Ideas stretched his theoretical constructs. The result was a revolution in physics.

So, too, in economies. The basic ideas that we should all be free to interact with economies as we choose and that economies should be run fairly and justly brought economies out of feudalism. In fact, these ideas still keep the economic pot boiling. The more we wrestle with what economic freedom and justice mean, the more we change our models for managing the household. The ideas alter the structures we use to organize economic life.

Exploding possibilities. When ideas change our philosophical structures, many new forms appear. One mutation becomes the seed for a forest. All sorts of possibilities emerge. The ideas of freedom and justice open possibilities for managing economies that we haven't begun to explore.

We're still working on what we can do with a simple computer chip.

As mutations expand the options for growth, what seemed impossible becomes possible. Flight, for instance, is out of the question for reptiles but the norm for their descendants, birds.

Similarly, the mutation from apes to humans didn't limit us to solving ape-problems better (getting food, shelter, and baby apes). It opened new dimensions for growth. We now can design our own jungle and do things in it that apes never dreamed of doing. And that's just the beginning. As evolution continues, what seems the norm today may seem barbaric in a few centuries (drilling teeth and cutting bodies), while future realities remain inconceivable to us now (recalcifying teeth and staying healthy).

The possibilities for change don't stop with our teeth and bones. The power of ideas to spark mutations means we're not stuck with one nature. We're not fixed as we are. If, for instance, we're inherently aggressive and insecure— if that's "just the way we are"—then war and exploitation are inevitable. We have no alternative but the evening-news version of ourselves: Homo screwed-upicus.

Yet nothing in the universe is immune to evolution of some sort, least of all humans. Through mutation, what seems impossible now—a universally nonaggressive, nondominating, nonexploiting consciousness—may become possible. By definition, mutation breaks limits, making present "realities" obsolete. In evolution, ideas "make all things new." (Revelation 21:5)

Not that mutations are easy. Each one challenges the bearer to use the new powers to advantage. As writer Arthur Koestler pointed out, evolution gave humans a big brain but no instruction manual, which is what civilization, philosophies, and religions intend to discover.

1. What gets spiritual evolution going?

The dyna-mics: what happens:	The im-pact on evolution:	What the dynamics offset:	Evolving views of ourselves:	The challenge we face:
Ideas bring mutations.	Many new possibil-ities appear.	That our nature is fixed	We're in flux, always changing.	To use the new powers to advantage

2) Open systems vs. closed systems

Since we don't reproduce at the rate of mosquitos or cockroaches, we can't leave it to new, mutant generations to figure out how to use the equipment we've got. New generations seem too mutant anyway. Even if we could clone a new breed, greater brain capacity—which new DNA could give us—isn't our problem. As Koestler pointed out, we need better manuals for the brains we have. In other words, we need more order in how we manage the mind's household here and now.

At each step of evolution, increasing order expands life; decreasing it brings death. The greater order that having wings gave to birds expanded their possibilities for life. Their powers of adaptability increased. Similarly, the order that makes a human baby gives it greater possi-bilities for life than that of an amoeba, even if the kid grows up to imitate the amoeba as a couch potato.

So, too, consciousness evolution increases order. We grow wings of the mind and soul. As we evolve, reality's order orders the philosophies we live by. Our maps' versions of order come more into line with the central order. Our manuals become more true to what's real. With better wings and better manuals for using them, we fly better.

But how do we develop greater order? Order increases only in open systems. In closed worlds, order dissipates. If we want to evolve manuals that clue us to the real order of things, openness is the way to go.

We know that now. To develop, we have to be open. Closed-minded is what no one wants to be. It shuts down learning. Yet being open is harder than it sounds. It doesn't mean being so open that every breeze blows through.

The way physics and biology discuss open and closed systems explains the problem nicely. Closed systems, though they start from order, run down. They tend toward maximum entropy—when everything levels out in total equilibrium, the cosmic blahs. Fixed limits keep closed systems from either generating or regenerating order.

To put it another way, no matter how happy ants are to create an anthill, if we put them in an ant farm and forget to feed them, we don't get catacombs of ant creativity. We get a pile of sand and dead ants: entropy in the ant farm.

Entropy is a factor in philosophies as well. Whenever a philosophy becomes the one true, final philosophy, it becomes closed. Its limits get rigid and don't allow for development. "Beware," Renaissance philosopher Marsilio Ficino wrote, "lest you get boxed into some narrow space where there is no more sky for you and nothing more that is vital."[3]

The trouble with closed philosophies is that we can't see beyond them. We can't imagine that reality could be other than the way our philosophies map it. The fourth-century B.C. Taoist sage, Chuang Tzu, wrote:

> You can't discuss the ocean with a well-frog—he's limited by the space he lives in. You can't discuss ice with

a summer insect—he's bound to a single season. You can't discuss the Way with a cramped scholar—he's shackled by his doctrines.[4]

Open systems, by contrast, don't shut themselves inside fixed limits. They grow by confronting frames of reference outside themselves. Through the exchange, new orders appear. Evolution continues.

All life-forms function as open systems. If they shut themselves off, they die. The earth, for instance, works as an open system, or life wouldn't have evolved on it. Specifically, the earth interacts with the solar system, which means it's affected by the sun's rays, electromagnetic and gravitational fields, as well as fields of consciousness.

We humans are profoundly open systems. To grow, even to be healthy, we need to interact with contexts wider than ourselves. When the utilitarian philosopher Jeremy Bentham experimented on prisoners by putting them in extreme isolation, many of them went mad.

Distinguishing between closed and open systems is the easy job. The hard part comes with seeing how open systems work. Contrary to the open-as-a-barn-door view, open systems still use limits. They maintain some internal cohesiveness, or they wouldn't be definable systems. Human beings and forests are open systems, but neither of them is without limits or we couldn't recognize them.

The difference between the limits of open systems and those of closed systems lies in how the limits function. Open systems don't use limits as absolute boundaries. Rather, they use them as tools—springboards for evolving new orders. Limits spur open systems to generate new orders to get around the limits.

The human body, for instance, is finite. Yet if we use its limits in an open way, we can create all kinds of orders that alter or extend its limits. The body's limits provide a springboard for creating new orders in food, clothing, athletics, homes, and medicine. With yoga, ballet, gymnastics, or music training, we can extend the body's limits to doing things we otherwise thought impossible.

The limits of economies work similarly. Resources are limited. But we have a choice in how we treat these limits. If we regard economies as closed systems of fixed material goods, we use limits in ways that create scarcity. In closed systems, resources run down until they run out.

If, however, we treat the limits of economies as defining open systems, we use the limits to be more creative with what we have. Economies exist precisely to help us get around limits.

On the simplest level, we create economies to get around the limit of each person having to do everything for himself or herself. A teacher doesn't have to excuse the class to grow a field of corn for lunch, while a farmer doesn't have to leave the field to show the neighborhood kids how to read and write. From such simple levels, economies evolve past one limit after another.

For evolving philosophies, openness means using the tools—assumptions, world views, responses, and goals—to evolve clearer views of ourselves and reality's order. Here, too, the tools' limits serve as springboards to new levels of understanding. When we hit a limit in how we understand things, we start bouncing around to find a way past it. Ultimately, a new, expanded view emerges.

Evolving, then, means neither becoming dogmatic about the limits we find useful (too closed) nor discarding the tools because they're limited (too open). We work out a balance. By treating limits as tools in open, evolving systems, we stay in the business of drafting new manuals— evolving new orders.

2. How do we evolve new orders?

The dyna-mics: what happens:	*The im-pact on evolution:*	*What the dynamics offset:*	*Evolving views of ourselves:*	*The challenge we face:*
By being open to the reality beyond us	Openness increases order; order ex-pands life.	Closed systems that run down	We can draft new manuals for how we live.	To use limits to create new orders

3) Niche creation

All the mutations and new models of order don't do a thing for evolution, though, if they don't find a niche in which to express themselves. Finding a niche is common parlance. But there's nothing common about doing it. For a new step of evolution, finding a niche is a life-or-death challenge.

In ecology, a niche represents the special relationship an individual or species has with its environment. It's how an animal or person works together with what's going on around it. To be successful, the relation has to be sym-biotic—two-way. The individual needs the environment to survive but also must give something to the environment in return. By forging a new relationship of give-and-take, the organism fills a niche that it created. Without this, the new form would die.

A bird, for example, can't fill a reptile's niche but must create something new, adapted to its new bird-abilities. Moreover, birds have evolved an incredible variety of niches. Before birds, the potential for these diverse niches existed, even though the reductionists among the reptiles may have thought all the available niches had been filled.

But they'd have been wrong—and for an important reason. Only secondarily does evolution fill existing niches through species expansion; primarily, evolution creates new forms. It gives the world not merely more reptiles (just what we wanted) but entirely new forms—birds.

Moreover, the significance of a new step doesn't lie in the changed form alone. In the development from ape to humans, for example, the new form (less hair and more head) was only the beginning. The great leap came in the new niches that humans created. Human evolution didn't merely increase the populations of hunter-gatherers or farmers. We evolved by inventing civilizations, which generated all kinds of new niches.

As every entrepreneur knows, creating niches forms the backbone of a growing business. For each new product or service, the entrepreneur must find a niche for it, or it will fail. It's called marketing.

Individuals develop by creating niches as well. Finding a job and building a family are niche-concerns that we all face. Where do we fit? Or more to the point, do we fit? For evolution, even not fitting has its advantages, since it compels us to create niches tailored to our growth.

So, too, in the development of consciousness. Each new idea and each new philosophy must find niches, or they'll disappear. For the many achievements that our history records, many more remain unknown. If there's no niche for the new, even great works may fail to have an impact.

In music, for example, in spite of Johann Sebastian Bach's many students, his works didn't find a place in the Western repertoire until Felix Mendelssohn performed them a century after Bach wrote them.

For that matter, Jesus' life and teaching could have passed into obscurity as another Messianic sect of Judaism, if Peter, John, and Paul hadn't universalized the message and taken it to the Gentiles. Jesus introduced the mutation as a new understanding of reality, but the apostles carved niches for it.

Misery, the grim reaper. In the philosophy of economies, though, the concept of niches worries people. The very limits that make niches cozy—that make them work as niches—become confining. If we keep growing, while the niches stay the same, the niches don't fit anymore. We run out of growing space.

An industry, for example, has room for only so many companies before the market gluts. A society can use only so many lawyers, doctors, or morticians. When the niches get stuffed to their limits, they put out the dreaded sign: "No vacancies."

The limits of existing niches depressed Parson Thomas Malthus in the late 1700s. Assuming that niches are limited by resources and that resources are limited, Malthus concluded that humanity's niche-potential is also limited.

As he reasoned, only a fixed number of niches, each of a fixed size, is available to our species. As populations increase, these niches become saturated. After the saturation point, wars, famines, and plagues step in to reduce our numbers to fit within the fixed niche limit. Kenneth Boulding summarizes:

> With a given technology the human race has a strong tendency to expand into the niche appropriate to that technology. We then, however, run into the famous Malthusian principle, that if the only thing that can check the growth of human population is misery in some form, whether this is actual food shortage or whether it is the intensification of conflict or some kind of psychological disorder (and there can be many sources of misery), then the population will expand until it is sufficiently miserable for the expansion to cease.[5]

From experience, the reasoning is hard to refute. Human life is filled with misery, separating winners from losers, those who find a niche from those who wander nicheless. The argument inspires such fear that it's used to justify any injustice, if it secures a place for us among the winners. Because no wealth or power ever ensures the position, though, the struggle goes on.

But Malthus lived before evolutionary theories were debated widely. He didn't know much about the actual dynamics of evolution. Consequently, he overlooked a few things.

First, his reasoning underestimates the role of mutations. There are limits to resources, of course, but there are no limits to how we use them, except those we ourselves impose. Ideas introduce alternatives. They open ways to get around limits. The only constant about technology, for example, is its change, from fire to steam engines to hydroelectric generators to toaster ovens. Malthus' first problem, then, is that he left out creativity. He overlooked the power of ideas to bring mutations.

Second, the "Malthusian principle" reduces evolution to accretion—quantitative expansion within closed systems. Whoever controls the most resources within the closed system survives. But dominating resources isn't an evolutionary method. It simply tries to control as much as possible of the evolution that's already occurred (the robber-baron strategy). Real evolution restructures limits, opening systems to new orders. It pushes systems beyond closed limits. With a little restructuring, the entire system mutates. New levels of order enhance the possibilities for growth throughout.

Third, accepting a restricted, closed-system view of niches, Malthusian reasoning sees evolution only as occupying the niches that already exist. But that's reptile thinking. Evolution proceeds by creating new niches, not just by filling the ranks. New forms carve new niches: birds appear, with new ways for changing the fields, forests, and windshields of the world.

Misery, the spur to evolve. What Malthus and his followers describe are closed systems, in which there's no chance of evolution. Of course closed systems reach a limit and then decay. Without food from the outside, the ant farm becomes an ant necropolis. But evolution has to do with open systems. Why should we assume that humans, the earth, or reality itself are closed, when the presence of evolution suggests the contrary?

If we reason from the premise of open systems, the situation looks quite different. We conclude that misery intensifies not because of too much evolution but because of too little. We keep trying to fill old niches, while evolution pushes us to create new ones.

We keep burning things, for example, when we need to come up with new principles of energy. We keep bringing to our economic relations the same old win-lose strategies, when it's time to focus on win-win. Or we keep trying to solve problems through analysis and specialization, when problems require that we explore more comprehensive, whole-seeking methods.

In short, we suffer precisely when we stop evolving— when we start treating our niche-creating potential as closed. Niche-creation isn't a job that stops. Since reality is unlimited, there are always new niches to explore.

In any case, that's how the philosopher Leibniz argued. He conceived of the universe as a realm of infinite possibilities. Evolution is the process of discovering these—of transcending "no vacancies" by carving new niches. The more order and complexity we gain through evolution, the more potential niches there are.

3. What do we do with new orders?

The dyna-mics: what happens:	The im-pact on evolution:	What the dynamics offset:	Evolving views of ourselves:	The challenge we face:
Create new niches: new relations of give-and-take: symbiosis	The entire niche-pattern changes, expanding the niches available to us.	That our niche-potential is closed (Malthus)	We live in a universe of infinite possibil-ities (Leibniz).	To tran-scend "no-vacancies" by carving new niches

But niche creation, like marketing new products, is risky. How can we cope with the testing time of evolution?

4) *Certainty vs. uncertainty*

Evolution is full of uncertainties. It explores the un-known—possibilities that haven't proven themselves and for which there's no precedent. Open systems regularly face things that are unexpected and untried.

In biological evolution, organisms have no choice but to plunge ahead. Evolution takes the risk for them, and they either prove themselves or die.

We're lucky. We can either go with the new or choose the less risky route. But the choice also poses a dilemma. To minimize risk, we make decisions on knowledge that's certain and that promises certain results. If knowledge is power, certain knowledge is certain power. Not surpris-ingly, the quest of modern philosophy since Descartes has been for certainty, only to find that it's certainly "damned elusive."

And for good reason. Certainty is possible only in closed systems, where the variables can be limited and their values fixed. But life isn't parcelled so neatly. In open systems, new ideas continually restructure what we know. The unknown constantly breaks through, usually at the most inconvenient moments.

By taking the unknown into account, open systems evolve knowledge without the expectation of certainty. The only thing we're certain of is that our philosophies aren't certain. They don't and can't cover everything. Reality is more. Socrates' famous maxim, "The beginning of wisdom is to know that you do not know," resembles Chuang Tzu's comment, "Calculate what man knows and it cannot compare to what he does not know,"[6] and Lao Tzu's advice, "To know that you do not know is the best."[7]

These thinkers teach the wisdom not of ignorance but of "learned ignorance," a phrase coined by Nicholas of Cusa, the 15th-century theologian and mathematician. If we qualify what we know with a realization of what we don't know, we stay open. We don't start thinking like a well-frog, summer insect, or cramped scholar.

So that's our choice. Either we can be certain, or we can evolve. If we choose the certain way, we create closed systems that narrow reality to something isolable—a method that shuts out growth. We become the proverbial big fish in a little pond. If we choose evolution, though, we face perpetual uncertainty.

Though the certainty-route is certainly more attractive, it's also more dangerous. By requiring that we squeeze reality into artificially closed systems, the certainty-route blinds us to wider contexts. Closed worlds provide an illusion of certainty—and with it, illusions of power.

The certainty is illusory, because we've excluded more of reality than we've included. If the certainty we claim isn't complete, it's also not certain. The unknown poses a constant threat to our islands of certainty—a threat that gets worse when we don't realize that it's there. The only danger greater than walking blindfolded on the edge of a cliff is not recognizing our position.

Neither is the power certain. In practice, the feeling of certain power leads to bad decision-making. Businesses become so positive that their products work under ideal conditions that they don't test them under real conditions. For instance, some firms make toys without taking into account the children who play with them.

Or they assume that their certain knowledge about a few, tested conditions gives them certain power over all conditions. It seems that's what caused the Challenger disaster. A Florida frost wasn't among the conditions for which the O-rings had been tested.

Closed-world certainty crumbles the moment it bumps into another closed world or worse, into reality. The bubble pops. There goes both the certainty and the power. Boulding writes:

> An important source of bad decisions . . . is an illusion of certainty. If our image of the future is certain, there is nothing wrong with making exact plans without flexibility. Under illusions of certainty, however, we make exact plans that can lead to disaster. With realistic images of uncertainty, we stay liquid, flexible, and adaptable.[8]

Not that we're never certain about anything. Rather, the certainty we gain—the kind sought in scientific experiments, for example—is qualified and limited. It applies to narrowly defined conditions. If we change the conditions, the certainty changes.

To assess the value of what we know, then, the old masters ("Lao Tzu" means "Old Master") were right: what we don't know is more interesting than what we know. It indicates what realities we might bump into, what we should watch out for, as well as where our future development lies.

Living with uncertainty. If evolution and its uncertainties are here to stay, how can we deal with them?

One way is to embrace uncertainty unreservedly—the skeptic's route. In philosophy, skeptics claim uncertainty about everything: God, reason, progress, ideals, the values of civilization, the use of philosophical tools, even the meaning of human existence.

But skepticism is hard to put into practice. On what do we build our lives or make decisions? On what do social, economic, and political orders rest? What do we tell the kids? Though no tool is perfect, tools are necessary. Too much uncertainty puts us at sea without a raft. We drift with the tides, not all of them good.

In business, uncertainty-advocates "say yes to risk" every time they make a deal. The greater the risk, they say, the more someone stands to gain. The question is, who?

Futures markets, for instance, capitalize on risk whole-hog. They use the uncertainties of farm production to gamble on what prices will do in the future. Speculators assume the risk, so that farmers and producing nations can sleep easily. But gambling is a strange way to manage risk—as effective as foxes guarding chickens. Starting a game of craps is one way to offset the uncertainties of the weather, but is it the best?

Whomever the commodity speculation benefits, the world's commodity producers remain buried at the bottom of the list. In practice, farmers grow poorer and world hunger increases, while food reserves are withheld or even destroyed to drive up the stakes. Farmers and agricultural countries have achieved neither economic independence nor even minimal financial security.

Clearly, living with uncertainty is easier said than done. On one hand, we can't overcome it by choosing certainty as an aim. The risks of evolution, as great as they are, are less than the dangers of standing still.

On the other hand, we can't abandon all constants and enter the surreal world of "life is a gamble." In financial matters, we'd end up with a house of cards, which, many fear, is more or less what we've got.

The middle way lies with understanding evolution and dealing with its uncertainties through a consistent discipline, one that uses the very dynamics of evolution to cope with its uncertainties.

First, uncertainties mirror our models. They're philosophy-related. If, for example, we adopt philosophies that are based on screwball assumptions, we heighten uncertainty. We're more likely to be wrong. Or if we adopt aggressive, we-they, win-lose strategies, we intensify stress and insecurity. Structuring our relations on conflict, we have more reasons to be afraid. Even if we win, others want to knock us down. The same philosophies that put us on top make us targets.

The best way to reduce these uncertainties is to mutate beyond the philosophies that create them. Instead of waiting for philosophies to produce their worst-case scenario— for greed to drive us into a depression, for instance—we can restructure them. How?

Insofar as mutation begins with ideas, we can explore ideas and let them restructure our philosophies. Education, for example, both acquaints us with existing knowledge and prepares us to develop further. It introduces us to the world of ideas. By investigating ideas, we prime ourselves for change. To paraphrase Louis Pasteur, mutation favors the prepared mind. As our philosophies evolve, many uncertainties simply fall away.

Second, order reduces uncertainty. The risk of driving a car, for instance, becomes manageable the more everyone follows the rules of the road. In information systems, the order given by the context reduces the ambiguity of messages. In ecology, the more complex a system, the greater its options for adjusting to stresses. In politics, the more ordered a society, the more swiftly it can respond to disasters. In economies, the more exchange is ordered according to values of trust, integrity, and reciprocity, the less we fear fraud or theft.

In other words, the more diverse our knowledge, the more we're able to cope with things we don't expect. Order equips us to reduce uncertainties where we can and to adapt creatively where we can't.

Since order emerges only in open systems, we invite evolution by avoiding closed concepts. As paradoxical as it seems, uncertainty is lessened not with certainty but with openness to evolution. The second way to reduce risk, then, is to keep evolving—to stay open to the evolution of new orders.

Third, if evolution requires niche-creation and uncertainty comes from the fear of no vacancies, we can tackle uncertainty by creating niches of our own.

Doing this, though, means following the inward, which is generative, rather than the outward, which is fixed. Creative people, from artists to entrepreneurs, follow inner leadings as the way to develop something new. They don't settle for what's already established. Paul's advice was, "Adapt yourselves no longer to the pattern of this present world, but let your minds be remade and your whole nature thus transformed." (Romans 12:2, NEB)

In other words, instead of waiting for existing niches to push us out, we can follow the logic of evolution and get on with creating new niches. True, creating niches involves leaps into the unknown, but the alternative is to have no alternative.

Fourth, we can tackle uncertainty by understanding what is constant. In the worlds we see, everything changes: matter, energy, information, and consciousness. Expecting any of these to be fixed is a delusion. According to the Buddha, it's ignorance. In fact, he taught that expecting the impermanent to become permanent leads to suffering. When things shift, we go bananas.

Not that nothing is constant. What's constant is the ultimately real—the Absolute, Unconditioned Reality, the whole that governs both order and changes. In ancient Greek terms, through the flux of the many flows the One. The more we understand the One, the more we base ourselves on the true constant in life. "We should let ourselves be guided by what is common to all," the philosopher Heraclitus said, "yet, although the Logos is common to all, most men live as if each of them had a private intelligence of his own."[9] In a similar vein, the third-century Chinese thinker Wang Pi wrote:

> If we investigate things by approaching them as a united system, although they are many, we know we can handle them by adhering to the one. . . . Differences vary in a thousand ways, but the [one] leading, ruling principle remains.[10]

Seeking what's constant by evolving how we understand reality, we master uncertainty. Instead of trying to make islands of impermanence constant, we strive to comprehend what's truly permanent, namely, the central order. Not that we become certain about this either. The whole, for all our seeking and contemplation, lies beyond our grasp. Rather, realizing what's certain, we strive to understand it. Correlatively, we know our limits—our position on the cliff.

4. How can we handle evolution's uncertainty?

The dyna-mics: what happens:	*The im-pact on evolution:*	*What the dynamics offset:*	*Evolving views of ourselves:*	*The challenge we face:*
By facing uncertain-ty, coping with the unknown	We gain a realistic under-standing of evolution and of our role in it.	Lust for certain knowledge and certain power	We assess what we know in the light of what we don't know.	To make uncertain-ty serve evolution

5) *When niches become ruts*

Uncertainty isn't the only challenge in evolution. Paradoxically, creating a successful niche brings dangers of its own. The success itself makes further change unwelcome. We hate to leave it. Just when we're getting good at grade school, for instance, junior high comes along. Just when parents get the knack of parenting, the kids grow up. Just when we master a project, we finish it. In these cases, the niches outgrow us, and we have to move on.

But moving on isn't always so clear-cut. Instead of niches outgrowing us, we can outgrow them, whether they're jobs, relationships, or simply habits of thinking and acting. Outwardly, we could go on as before. After all, when we've put so much into building a niche, how can we give it up? Inwardly, though, the give-and-take is becoming less mutually beneficial. The boundaries of the niche begin to pinch.

The longer we postpone change, the more the niche becomes a rut. We can't leave it, yet we find it harder to make it work. What's going on? What makes a change of niche so resistible?

The drive to maintain equilibrium. It's not that we're born stick-in-the-muds or misoneists—haters of innovation and change. The problem comes from how niches work. They're systems. Like all systems, they constitute a self-complete network, needing no further change to succeed. In fact, through feedback mechanisms, systems operate to neutralize changes, so that the order they embody doesn't revert to chaos.

In other words, niches are self-perpetuating. For every change, the systems compensate, bringing things back to equilibrium. As a thermostat maintains a constant temperature in a house, niches maintain a set balance with their environment. All things being equal, niches could continue their relation with the world indefinitely.

In fact, that's the great value of niches. They provide a stable environment for evolution. If everything were in flux, nothing new could be established. Chaos isn't a friend to growth. Rather, order is needed for greater order to emerge. Since we're basically creatures of habit, this suits us just fine. We like nothing better than to settle into a niche that fits us and to pass the days in its reassuring environment—our own nest.

But there's a limit. When we've developed a niche to its fullest, stability ceases to be an asset to growth and instead becomes an obstacle. Even though the established niche is strained and approaching a crisis, the system continues to resist restructuring. That's what it's supposed to do.

Whether the niche represents a marriage, a family, a business, a personal relationship, or a philosophy, it resists change. Collective niches are even more tenacious. Industrialists and academicians have definite niches, as do scientists, engineers, bankers, administrators, doctors, and politicians. When niches harden into institutions, their inertia seems insurmountable.

To keep niches loose, we have to find ways to use niches to advantage without becoming locked in them. One way to do this is to recall what niches are for in the first place.

They're not for advancing development once and then fixing us in concrete forever after. Creating great niches isn't the goal of spiritual evolution; evolution itself is. Niches serve as tools of the process, not as ends of it. They provide the nurturing environment that evolution requires. Though we use niches to evolve, evolution pushes us beyond adaptation to any one niche.

As a result, successful niche management lies not in building the niche to beat all niches but in evolving: keeping the process going. Many different niches can play a role in spiritual growth.

How, though, can we cope with a stream of niches flowing through our lives? By letting the process happen. Evaluating where we've been, for instance, we can sort out which aspects of our niche-development build a bridge to the new and which aspects are better off left behind us as history.

Looking forward, we can stay open to possibilities. We don't have to cross off those impossible hopes and secret aspirations. True, some dreams may not fit within our present niche-structure, but they may yet find their place as we evolve.

Using niches to evolve, instead of stopping with a few because they've been successful, gives us a chance to do things we never thought we could. It keeps us evolving. Together, valuing the best of what's established and continuing to create new niches becomes a rhythm. We have our niches and evolve too.

5. How can we beat success?

The dyna-mics: what happens:	The im-pact on evolution:	What the dynamics offset:	Evolving views of ourselves:	The challenge we face:
By over-coming a niche's resistance to change	Evolution continues: we don't get stuck in any one niche.	Successful niches that turn into ruts	We're not here to build great niches but to evolve.	To have our niches and to evolve too

6) Standards for transformation

What's the effect of all this evolving? Ultimately, total transformation. Changing just one niche sparks changes throughout the entire niche structure. To borrow Jesus' parable, a little yeast leavens the whole lump. The new sets off a chain of restructuring, so that even familiar relations, placed in a new context, take on new meanings. The effect is what we've come to expect of interrelated systems: parts don't change without affecting the totality.

In life, each person's development has an impact on everyone else's. We don't have to be presidents or saints for this to be true, either. In Frank Capra's movie classic, *It's A Wonderful Life*, George Bailey's apparently unexceptional life affected the character of the whole town and the lives of everyone in it. His quiet development transformed his entire world without his realizing it.

The totality of change, however, makes us ambivalent. We seek evolution, because it gives us reasons for hope. We can be other than we are, and life can be restructured for the better. At the same time, the scope of change is scary. What if it goes in the wrong direction? What if

George Bailey hadn't existed, and an army of Mr. Potters—Mr. Billiard-Balls—took over?

To answer this concern, spiritual evolution includes the development of *standards*, so that we can evaluate change. Standards help us gauge where we're going. How?

Standards combine values, so that we can apply them consistently. The standard of free speech, for instance, combines the values of freedom of thought and freedom of expression with the values of exchanging different views and of respecting individual philosophies. Though the standard admits a wide range of interpretations, it gives us a general yardstick for assessing change in society.

So, too, with free competition. Many values converge to define this standard. Some relate more specifically to economic concerns: economic self-determination, diversity, nondomination, the right to better our lot. Others cover the basic values that keep freedom from turning into license: integrity, trustworthiness, responsibility, mutual respect, and honesty. Freedom comes to the marketplace, if not as current practice, at least as a standard to help guide the development of economies. The standard tells us whether we're moving toward it or not.

Ultimately, we use standards to guide our evolution along the spectrum. Standards steer us away from the confused end. They keep our philosophies evolving, so that they become better maps of what's real. And they keep us evolving, so that we're more like who we are at the spectrum's light end.

But even standards aren't fixed. They change with us. Our understanding of freedom and justice develops, and our sense of values changes. The question of where we're headed, then, sparks a continual re-examination of the standards that guide us. To evolve means not only to follow standards but to evolve them as well.

6. Which way are we evolving?

The dyna-mics: what happens:	The im-pact on evolution:	What the dynamics offset:	Evolving views of ourselves:	The challenge we face:
Develop-ing stan-dards that evaluate the direc-tion of change	Standards keep us moving in healthy, construc-tive direc-tions.	Change in the wrong direction: toward the confused end	Our lives are shaped by values that steer us for-ward.	To con-tinue to evolve the standards we live by

7) Evolving practical philosophies

All these methods of evolving—investigating ideas, developing new orders, creating new niches, facing uncertainty, overcoming resistance to change and clarifying standards—get us going on the main job of spiritual growth, namely, evolving practical philosophies. We use the methods to experiment with the philosophical tools. As we find assumptions, strategies, responses and goals that work, we extend knowledge. Our experiments turn the philosophical tools into different ways of knowing.[11]

1) Knowledge begins with *know-what.* If we assume, for example, that the sun rises each day and will continue to do so for our lifetime at least, and the assumption is backed by all the assumptions physics gives us about the cosmos, we call that assumption knowledge. Know-what defines our assumptions about what's going on around us. It expresses what we take to be the real nature of things.

By analyzing our assumptions, we extend the founda-tions of our knowledge. The result isn't a set of dogmas or a catalogue of facts but a well-thought-out and rigorously tested set of assumptions. We know what we're assuming, and we know these assumptions work.

Few physicists, for example, test every law they accept. Thanks to the discipline of physics, they have good reasons to assume that all the laws are valid. So too, few citizens check every media story or government report they hear. Because we can't investigate everything for ourselves, we have to trust the research and accounts of others.

We accept know-what assumptions, then, because it seems reasonable to do so and because we have little practical alternative. Most of the time, acting on our know-what assumptions brings predictable, reliable results.

2) On the basis of know-what, we devise *know-how*. We become economic in the broadest sense of acting on what we know, of putting our know-what to work. Based on what we know about human nature and child development, for instance, we develop different strategies for raising children. If the kids come out more or less okay, we say we know how to bring them up.

To put it another way, whereas know-what gives us a vision for doing something, know-how gives us the means for doing it. Whereas know-what opens countless possibilities (if the universe is this or that way, we can do such and such), know-how shows how to cash them in.

3) But should we pursue all the worlds that know-what and know-how bring within our reach? Philosophies include a third stage: *know-whether*. We develop criteria for judging what works and what fails, which strategies produce which consequences, and which possibilities are best to pursue. With know-whether, we select responses that shape our worlds in ways we deem best.

Know-whether is usually discussed in the language of ethics and morals. What should we do? What is the Good, and what leads to it? To get rid of the intruders in our homes—pollution, war, drugs, crime, poverty—we have plenty of know-what and know-how. We need more know-whether: the knowledge to make wise decisions.

4) But decision-making doesn't occur in a vacuum. It depends on our purposes: **know-why**. What are our goals? The goals we pursue affect (1) *what* we seek to know, (2) *how* we make knowledge practical, and (3) *whether* we create one world or another. Purposes shape our philosophies, which then shape our worlds. We understand both ourselves and reality relative to our goals.

United we evolve. Traditionally, *know-what* means science and academia, *know-how* business and technology, *know-whether* law and politics, and *know-why* religion and philosophy. The question is, do these fields have anything to do with each other?

These days, not much. At least, that's how it seems. Specialization requires that we don't stick our noses into more than one field.

1) Scientists just discover facts (know-what); values (know-whether) aren't their concern. They "describe" instead of "prescribe."

2) Technology and industry turn the economic wheels (know-how); whether something is ethically right (know-whether) isn't their business. Business is their business.

3) Law and politics steer the ship of state (know-whether) but dodge issues of goals and purposes (know-why). If we ask whose interests lawyers and politicians serve, we get everything from doublespeak to anxiety attacks.

4) Religion and philosophy discuss ends (know-why), but usually off in some ivory or ivy-covered tower, remote from the -what, -how, and -whether issues that occupy us everyday. Besides, who listens to these disciplines in the "real worlds" of money and power?

But the splitting-up method doesn't work. Questions arise in the practice of know-how, for example, that only the other three can answer. Pollution, for instance, says we're doing too much know-how with not enough -what and -whether. Scandals say our -whether and -why are completely out of whack. For philosophies to be practical, they need all four ways of knowing combined. Knowledge grows in healthy and balanced ways only when all four aspects pull together.

The splitting doesn't work for another reason: it's not what actually happens. We never completely exclude any aspect, since -what, -how, -whether, and -why issues permeate all facets of life. We can't get away from them. It's just that our spotlight in one area gets so bright that the others lie in shadows. We don't realize how much all four play roles in what we do.

For that reason, the spotlighting method is dangerous. For instance, we think that if we *can* do something (know-how), we *should* do it (know-whether) without considering the whether-issue carefully. Know-how takes over know-whether decisions, even though it's not qualified to do this. That's what bothered many of the physicists working on the Manhattan Project to build the atomic bomb. They mastered know-what and know-how, but they weren't sure about know-whether and know-why.

If we focus on one way of knowing and don't think about what we're doing in regard to the rest, we're at a disadvantage. We operate on only one-fourth of our total reflective power. For three fourths of our philosophical life, we accept second-rate standards: junk philosophy.

If we keep using the spotlighting method, even our own forte suffers. As Renaissance philosopher Tommaso Campanella noted in *The City of the Sun*, "Anyone who knows only one science [way of knowing] knows neither that one nor any other well."[12] When what we do in one area doesn't make sense within the whole picture, our expertise isn't successful. It's not a help.

Practicality, though, isn't the only reason to unify our philosophical awareness. It's good for evolution. Isolated, the ways of knowing fall into ruts. To evolve, each needs the new blood that its philosophical soul-mates offer.

7. How can we develop our philosophical powers?

The dynamics: what happens:	The impact on evolution:	What the dynamics offset:	Evolving views of ourselves:	The challenge we face:
By testing assumptions, strategies, responses, and goals and turning them into knowledge	Expands our know-what, know-how, know-whether and know-why	Specializing in one area and excluding all others	We're philosophers on all fronts, and these philosophies shape how we live.	To develop four-fourths of our philosophical powers

But what mandates evolution? What keeps us evolving even when we haven't the slightest inclination to change? To paraphrase the most basic philosophical question, why is there evolution rather than no evolution?

What's Forward?

The dyna-mics: what happens:	*The im-pact on evolution:*	*What the dynamics offset:*	*Evolving views of ourselves:*	*The challenge we face:*
1. Ideas bring mutations.	Many new possibil-ities appear.	That our nature is fixed	We're in flux, always changing.	To use the new powers to advantage
2. Being open to the reality beyond us	Openness increases order; order expands life.	Closed systems that run down	We can draft new manuals for how we live.	To use limits to create new orders
3. Creating new niches: new rela-tions of give-and-take: symbiosis	The entire niche-pattern changes, expanding the niches available to us.	That our niche-potential is closed (Malthus)	We live in a universe of infinite possibil-ities (Leibniz).	To tran-scend "no-vacancies" by carving new niches
4. Facing uncertain-ty, coping with the unknown	We gain a realistic under-standing of evolution and of our role in it.	Lust for certain knowledge and certain power	We assess what we know in the light of what we don't know.	To make uncertain-ty serve evolution

The dynamics: what happens:	*The impact on evolution:*	*What the dynamics offset:*	*Evolving views of ourselves:*	*The challenge we face:*
5. Overcoming a niche's resistance to change	Evolution continues: we don't get stuck in any one niche.	Successful niches that turn into ruts	We're not here to build great niches but to evolve.	To have our niches and to evolve too
6. Developing standards that evaluate the direction of change	Standards keep us moving in healthy, constructive directions.	Change in the wrong direction: toward the confused end	Our lives are shaped by values that steer us forward.	To continue to evolve the standards we live by
7. Testing our assumptions, strategies, responses, and goals and turning them into knowledge	Expands our know-what, know-how, know-whether, and know-why	Specializing in one area by excluding all others	We're philosophers on all fronts, and these philosophies shape how we live.	To develop four-fourths of our philosophical powers

Chapter 5

The Ups and Downs of Evolution

I. Descending and ascending

As inventive as we humans are, we didn't invent evolution; it invented us. Darwin sketched a process that myth-tellers and sages pondered millennia before him. But neither he nor they created evolution. Instead, something about reality made evolution happen, which made us happen.

Inquiring about evolution's source takes us to the heart of spiritual teachings—to questions of ultimate reality. According to spiritual teachings, reality operates as a totality: the One or central order. This totality impels evolution. It's the ultimate source of order and life.

Western theology refers to evolution's source when it talks about the Spirit of God, the power of Christ, or the influx of the Good. Because of what's ultimately real, we evolve. We're brought forward by virtue of the whole context in which we exist and have life.

As it turns out, the notion cuts across religions and cultures. There's Tirawa Atius of the Pawnee Indians, the Supreme Being beyond forms that gives rise to forms, as well as Awonawilona, the Zuni name for the universal Principle that is the source of life. And of course we can't leave out the Hindu's Brahman, the One from which all comes, the Muslim's Allah, the Maker of all that exists, and China's Tao, the Mother of all things.

One way or another, spiritual teachings suggest, the reality that transcends us also includes us and spurs us to evolve. The Bible's rendition, for example, "And the Spirit of God moved upon the face of the waters," (Genesis 1:2) parallels the *Katha Upanishad* (one of a collection of Hindu sacred texts written between 700 and 300 B.C.):

> Beyond the senses is the mind, and beyond mind is reason, its essence. Beyond reason is the Spirit in man, and beyond this is the Spirit of the universe, the evolver of all.[1]

Dionysius, an anonymous fifth-century Christian theologian whose writings were famous through the Renaissance (he or she is called Dionysius only because of some historical mix-up), reasoned similarly:

> All being derives from, exists in, and is returned toward the Beautiful and the Good. Whatever there is, whatever comes to be, is there and has being on account of the Beautiful and the Good. All things look to it. All things are moved by it. . . . Here is the source of all which transcends every source. . . ."For from Him and through Him and in Him and to Him are all things" says holy scripture.[2]

Under the impact of the whole, chaos gives way to order not once or twice but with a rapidity that defies statistical probability. Within the limits of physical explanations, scientists describe conditions necessary for the order we see to have appeared, but they don't identify the cause. According to spiritual teachings, the source lies beyond physical conditions.

What do they mean by this?

The higher orders the lower

As the spiritual teachings reason, evolution can't be one-dimensional. It has to involve more than atoms knocking around, because the chance of atoms coming together into the order needed for an intelligent organism, much less a human brain, is virtually nil.

Moreover, systems bound by fixed dimensions (the dimension of billiard-ball things, for example) shut out evolution. In closed worlds, order runs down. It doesn't increase by any physical law we know. To account for order, we have to broaden the scope not just horizontally but also vertically. We have to expand the dimensions to include less limited realms.

To use an analogy, iron filings scattered on a sheet of paper don't show any order. If we put a magnet under them, though, a pattern appears. The filings move in ordered ways which we can't account for within the two-dimensional plane of the sheet of paper. The order comes from the three-dimensional world of the magnet, which in turn is governed by the fourth dimensional time-mass-energy continuum that shapes magnetic fields.

The order that evolution brings, spiritual teachings say, emerges in much the same way. Evolution occurs when higher levels of energy, information-fields, and consciousness intersect lower levels and restructure them. Under the impact of higher levels, physical and mental limits change and recede, allowing greater order to appear.

This movement—higher dimensions spurring development in lower—is just what spiritual teachings suggest when they trace evolution to God. The One has an impact on the universe, causing it to evolve beyond fixed or fragmented forms. Because nothing can get outside the One, all things feel its influence. All things are touched by the impulse to evolve.

In Judeo-Christian terms, the whole operates as divine Providence: "an intelligent, superintending principle, who is the governor and will be the final judge of the universe."[3] Providence represents the vertical, higher-to-lower impact of the central order on humanity. It's the influx of grace, which effects our spiritual growth.

Descending and ascending

To define the process more clearly, religion, philosophy and, recently, some sciences discuss evolution as the result of complementary movements of descent and ascent: downs and ups.

In the first movement, the whole descends. The totality unfolds its wholeness, touching all levels of existence. In Judeo-Christian and Muslim theology, God shapes creation. The infinite isn't bound by the limits that make systems closed. Quite the reverse, it breaks through limits. Its descent introduces greater order and complexity.

In the second movement, there's an effect. New forms of order and wholeness appear, as creation patterns its origin. We ascend to reflect the whole more fully.

This descent-ascent rhythm makes most religions, Christianity in particular, incorrigibly upbeat. In spite of dark-end stuff, they say, the trend for humanity is upward and civilizing.

This upbeat outlook doesn't come from watching the news or reading political or military history. It comes from a philosophical stand: reality impels evolution, and, however confused we might be, reality is bigger than we are. It's the greater power. Its descent drives our ascent.

Not that we've ascended. We are, though, developing. We still tolerate violence in movies, but at least we don't flock to the Colosseum to get human blood splashed on us.

What's important isn't where we are but where we're tending—the spiritual process that's at work.

Ancient, Medieval, and Renaissance thinkers referred to evolution's two-way process as "originating and returning." The fifth-century philosopher Proclus, for example, wrote: "Every effect remains in its cause, proceeds from it, and returns to it."[4]

Similarly, Dionysius reasoned that God "generates everything out of himself as from some omnipotent root, and he returns all things back to himself as though to some omnipotent storehouse."[5] Dionysius quoted another unknown writer, "Hierotheus," who described the process as "an everlasting circle":

> Let us say that there is a simple self-moving power directing all things to mingle as one, that it starts out from the Good, reaches down to the lowliest creation, returns them in due order through all the stages back to the Good, and thus turns from itself and through itself and upon itself and toward itself in an everlasting circle.[6]

Fourteenth-century Christian mystic John Ruusbroec spoke of "God coming to us" and "our turning to God":

> God is always giving new gifts, and our spirit is always turning back to God in accordance with the ways in which it has been called and gifted by God, and in this encounter it constantly receives new and higher gifts. In this way a person is constantly advancing to a higher form of life.[7]

Though the teachings differentiate the movements into down and up, originating and returning, they regard them as occurring simultaneously—as one flow. Both movements go on at once and continue together.

Jesus' life, for instance, illustrates evolution's two-way movement as one, spiritually impelled process. He 'came from the Father' to exemplify the way of spiritual growth.

Then he 'returned to the Father.' But throughout, he remained one with the Father: "No man hath ascended up to heaven, but he that came down from heaven, even the Son of man which is in heaven." (John 3:13) Jesus' life patterned the universal process that he exemplified and taught. He "originated" and "returned" as a natural, ongoing way of life.

Yet evolution's two-way movement isn't a uniquely Western concept. Chu Hsi, the influential twelfth-century Confucian scholar, analyzed the movement similarly in his commentary on the *Doctrine of the Mean*:

> The Book first speaks of one principle; it next spreads this out, and embraces all things; finally, it returns and gathers them all up under the one principle. Unroll it, and it fills the universe; roll it up, and it retires and lies hid in mysteriousness.[8]

Hindus describe history as reflecting these cosmic downs and ups. Brahma and Vishnu, the creative and sustaining aspects of God, evolve the universe through enormously long time periods, called "yugas." Then Shiva, the reintegrating aspect, draws all existence back to the One. This divine rhythm is symbolized in yogic teachings as breathing out and breathing in, mirroring God's exhaling and inhaling of the universe.

Neither does the concept belong exclusively to thinkers of the past. The rhythm of descent-ascent or originating-returning has resurfaced in the theories of contemporary physicist David Bohm. Bohm was a protégé of Einstein's as well as a friend of the late Indian religious philosopher Jiddu Krishnamurti. In Bohm's view, reality operates as a *holomovement*. The whole has its own order, enfolded within itself. This *implicate order*—what's implicit in the whole—makes itself explicit by unfolding its whole-order through space and time. The result is the *explicate order* of the human and physical universe—the time-space order we live in. Bohm writes:

> I can give an idea of enfoldment by thinking of taking a sheet of paper, folding it many times and, say, sticking pins in it, cutting it, and unfolding it, and you've made a whole pattern. So the pattern is enfolded [in the implicate order], then it unfolds [in the explicate order].[9]
>
> We are suggesting that it is the implicate order that is autonomously active while . . . the explicate order flows out of a law of the implicate order. . . .
>
> The implicate order has its ground in the holomovement, which is vast, rich, and in a state of unending flux of enfoldment and unfoldment, with laws most of which are only vaguely known, and which may even be ultimately unknowable in their totality.[10]

Unlike many physicists, Bohm includes consciousness in his theories. He takes the holomovement as the common ground between matter and mind. These two represent different projections of one, higher-dimensional reality:

> The more comprehensive, deeper, and more inward actuality is neither mind nor body but rather a higher-dimensional actuality, which is their common ground and which is of a nature beyond both. . . . In this higher-dimensional ground the implicate order prevails.[11]

As reality's implicate order unfolds, Bohm explains, evolution occurs. Simultaneously, evolution enfolds everything back into the central order. Through the holomovement—the constant flow of unfolding and enfolding—evolution spirals upward, introducing higher forms of matter, energy, information, and consciousness.

The whole, of course, remains what it is. Nothing can be added to the totality of being. What changes are the limits of the explicate order: material and mental limits fall away. Because of the descent of the whole, the universe changes, and we change. The effect of all this holomoving is our ascent: we evolve.

In light of these downs and ups, what we experience as evolution is really our way of taking part in reality's total process. The impulse to evolve comes from a source beyond us. We evolve, because we exist within the whole and are included in its dynamics. Evolution is how we participate in reality's workings.

II. Revelation

If being open to the descent is the way to evolve, how do we do it? Are there maps showing how we can respond to the descent with our ascent—with spiritual growth?

Revelations exist for this purpose. They serve as guides for spiritual growth, scouts in a territory that's relatively new. After all, several millennia of wrestling with spiritual evolution is fairly recent for a creature several million years old.

What are revelations? According to spiritual teachings, they appear as a result of reality's descent, the influx of grace. Coming from the whole, revelations introduce clearer expressions of reality's ultimate nature and of how we fit into it. By giving us a better understanding of the central order, they make it easier for us not to be fooled by partial orders.

Revelations are, in fact, one of the most obvious ways that the whole has an elevating impact on humanity. The whole touches prophets or messengers and gives them a vision. "Every nation has its Messenger," the *Qur'an* says. (Sura 10:47) The messengers then express their revelations in language adapted to their worlds. They communicate the new understanding to their cultures, which usually means they reinterpret existing symbols. People begin to rethink their philosophies and their corresponding ways of life.

Which leads to the second side of revelation's total process. Whereas revelations happen as a result of the descent, understanding them involves an ascent. To understand revelation is to evolve in the direction that it points. We wrestle with revelation's meaning. As we do, our philosophies gradually reflect the central order more and partial orders less. We enfold consciousness and life back into the structure of the whole. Naturally, this changes how we manage our worlds. We work out problems in more whole-seeking ways—ways that pattern outwardly our inward ascent.

By coming from the whole and leading back to the whole, revelations combine descent and ascent—both sides of the holomovement. Their unfolding projects a new vision of the central order onto human consciousness. Their enfolding occurs as we understand the new vision and are transformed by it; we draw nearer to evolution's source.

Maps for evolving maps

Exemplifying evolution's two-way process, revelations are well-qualified to speak on it. The descent that is their origin builds into their message the ascent that is their reason for being. They come from the whole precisely to show the way of evolving toward the whole.

As a result, revelations do more than tell us what to think—which maps we're to believe. They distinguish themselves as revelations by mapping spiritual evolution—the process. Their maps aren't about spiritual stuff up in the clouds; they are maps for where we are, namely, on the move. They show us how to engage in the spiritual process that makes up our lives.

If we're talking like philosophers, we'll call these *meta-maps*. Revelation's maps go beyond any one map. They're on a level above, because they map the process through which we develop our maps. In other words, they're maps for evolving our maps in a spiritual direction.

This means that revelations don't necessarily designate a specific world view or philosophy as the one which alone is right. They're not answer machines. They can't afford to be, since, if revelations gave all the answers, they'd work against growth. If we could just go to revelations for all the right answers, we wouldn't have to develop. We could become robots of righteousness. Would we ever learn to add or subtract if we were always given the right answers?

True, we can interpret revelations this way (it's been done). We can read into them a set of beliefs that we're supposed to accept. We can also look to them for answers about whether we should apply for a new job, expand a business, or get married.

But this use of revelation raises thorny questions: How do we know that the beliefs and answers we're getting from revelation are what the revelation itself reveals? How do we know we're not using revelation to justify thoughts we already had or actions we wanted to take all along? Is our interpretation right?

Revelation's meaning is notoriously hard to interpret, because it moves with us. Students of the Bible, as of any inspired text, often feel as if they're reading a passage for the first time, even though they've read it many times before. What happens is that they've touched the ascending side of revelation. The revelation changes them, until they find themselves reading the text with new eyes. Suddenly, new dimensions of meaning stand out.

That means we're getting more from revelations than just what to believe or what to do when and with whom.

Only secondarily do revelations sketch out beliefs and answers. Primarily, they give us methods for evolving ourselves. Beyond the specifics, revelations provide methods for evolving the maps we live by, so that we develop and can work out our answers on our own.

Approaching revelations this way brings out their timeless quality. Answers change with growth, as do beliefs, but the *method of growing* persists. If revelations gave only beliefs or answers, they'd soon be outdated. We'd outgrow them. But revelations don't work this way. The more we evolve, the more we value their message, because we know from our own experiences how successful their methods are in effecting spiritual growth.

For example, we no longer depend on the answer to what to do if our ox gores our neighbor's goat. But we still find compelling Moses' revelation of a higher law that's binding on human action. To evolve is to align ourselves with divine law. In Heisenberg's words, it's to come more into harmony with the central order. Moses' revelation isn't about oxen, sheep, and goats; it's about the method of spiritual growth.

Another example is the Buddha's Eightfold Path, which lies at the heart of Buddhism. The path is simple enough: "Right knowledge, right aspiration, right speech, right conduct, right livelihood, right effort, right mindfulness, and right concentration."[12] Yet this much venerated teaching can be perfectly annoying as an answer. If we knew what was right, we wouldn't need to consult the Buddha or his Path. Being told to do all those things rightly doesn't necessarily help us.

If, however, the Buddha's Eightfold Path isn't only about morals—if, as well, it charts our development—then what is right changes as we change. The spiritual values remain constant, but how we understand them evolves.

A six-year-old's "right knowledge" of building blocks isn't "right knowledge" for an adult, especially one building skyscrapers. The more we evolve by understanding the values and by letting them transform us, the more we master their rightness.

In short, accepting the Buddha's or anyone else's revelation as a doctrine to be believed isn't nearly as effective as using it as a map of spiritual growth. We can outgrow beliefs about the spiritual, but we can't outgrow methods of spiritual growth. What revelations give of enduring value, then, aren't maps but meta-maps: maps for evolving maps.

Four meta-maps from the Bible

Using revelations this way—as maps for evolving maps—we can appeal to them to help steer the evolution of our philosophies. Insofar as philosophies are shaped by (1) assumptions, (2) strategies, (3) responses, and (4) goals, each of these must develop in order for our philosophies as a whole to evolve. As it happens, four of the most famous teachings in Western religion—all from the Bible—can be used as maps for evolving these four factors.

1) Since philosophies begin with *assumptions*, we want to know from revelation what kinds of assumptions invite spiritual growth and which lock us in closed worlds. The *seven days of creation* give us an idea. They map assumptions that open us to reality's nature. By opening us to evolution's source, these assumptions expand our philosophies beyond closed premises. In the process, they show which assumptions make us more creative.

But the practical value of the seven days' assumptions doesn't sink in until we see what's at stake. Hence, Genesis contrasts the seven days with the story of Adam and Eve, which depicts opposite assumptions—those that lead to "the Fall." Together, the two creation accounts map the *spectrum of assumptions* about what's real and what's not— what works and what fails.

2) Assumptions give rise to *strategies*. As we've seen in Chapter 3, strategies give us tools for understanding reality and interacting with it. They cash in our assumptions and make them practical.

But not all strategies free us to evolve. Many enslave us. To sort them out, the *Commandments* map *strategies that liberate.* Describing both offensive and defensive methods, the Commandments identify strategies that diminish our freedom and show how we can change them. Positively, they map strategies for winning both inner and outer, spiritual and economic, liberty.

3) Strategies, in turn, shape how we *respond to experience*—experience being the holomovement appearing in our own life's clothing. Because we can't control the holomovement, we can't control all that happens to us. We can, however, choose how we respond. The *Beatitudes* map responses that *align us with spiritual growth* and thereby *empower us to evolve.*

4) What's the point of all this? What *purpose* drives our philosophies? Instead of giving a fixed answer, the *Lord's Prayer* offers a method for revising our answers. To keep our philosophies evolving, it says, we need to *evolve our purpose in life* as well.[13]

The "Holomovement," The "Everlasting Circle"

The whole, the totality
The Spirit of God
Tirawa Atius, Awonawilona
Brahman, Allah, Tao
Divine Providence
"The Son of man in heaven"
The implicate order of the whole

Higher dimensions   expand the limits of   lower dimensions

The descent of the   brings about   the ascent of
whole   creation.

"Originating"   "Returning"

Jesus came forth   Jesus returned to
from the Father.   the Father.

The unfolding of   effects   the enfolding of the
the implicate order   explicate order
                             back into the
                             whole.

Revelation brings a   Understanding
new vision of the   revelation leads to
central order.   the central order.

The explicate order:
humanity—history—economies—the world
We're in the middle of a process that unites us with the whole.

Chapter 6

The Days of Creation: Assumptions that Make Us Creative

🔲🔲🔲🔲🔲🔲🔲

I. What gets creativity going?

S carcity spooks us. If we think there's not enough to go around, we panic. We start buying up what's still available, which only makes scarcity worse. Sooner or later we run out of things to buy, which is what we're afraid of in the first place.

Creativity breaks the cycle. By generating new orders, creativity overcomes scarcity in ways that actually multiply our resources. We beam messages around the world electronically, instead of sending piles of paper. We develop new strains of wheat that are more productive per acre. Or we discover new methods of harnessing energy, so that we do more with less. The new forms restructure how we manage resources, which in turn pushes back the limits that spook us. Creativity outsmarts scarcity. It makes scarcity obsolete.

Where does creativity start? With our assumptions—the first tool of practical philosophies.

Assumptions define the world in which we work. By setting limits, they mark off a territory in which we can be creative. Within the limits, our assumptions tell us what's possible and what's impossible. They tell us how creative we can be.

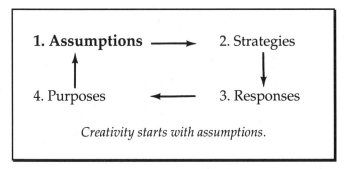

1. **Assumptions** ⟶ 2. Strategies

4. Purposes ⟵ 3. Responses

Creativity starts with assumptions.

The Taoist images of the well-frog and summer insect (Chapter 4, II.2) make the point. A frog living in a well doesn't have a chance to be creative about designing a home in the ocean or bay. His assumptions keep him in the well. The same with the summer insect: her creativity ends with the first frost.

Charioteers live inside their assumptions too. If we assume that horses just run wild, we won't be very creative about making bridles and tack. Even if we've got the tools for driving, we won't be creative about using them. We'll just let the horses run, while the reins flop about in our hands. Our assumptions put the possibility of steering the chariot out of reach. It doesn't occur to us.

Then, of course, there's the contrast between billiard-ball and whole-seeking assumptions. *Billiard-ball assumptions* (such as those Charles Tart summarized in the billiard-ball credo: Chapter 1, III) tell us that the world is made up of sharks eating big fish, who eat smaller fish, who eat minnows, who eat larvae. No matter how big we are, there's always someone bigger who's ready to eat us.

The "struggle for survival" makes conflict inevitable. We focus all our creativity on either stirring up conflict or escaping it.

But is this so? Is conflict the way things are, or is it the way our assumptions cause things to be? In the award-winning film, *The Mission*, writer Robert Bolt argues the latter. When the wealthy slaver justifies the massacre of native Indians and Jesuit priests with the claim, "Thus is the world," the Cardinal replies, "No, thus have we made the world."

Why is the slaver's assumption wrong? Not because slaving and massacring don't happen. And not because billiard-ball assumptions don't create pain-in-the-neck dominators. What's wrong with the assumption is that things don't have to happen that way. As it turns out, slaving and massacring aren't laws of nature. They occur when our assumptions tell us that's how to succeed. To have the biggest horse and chariot, we have to trample all the other horses and chariots around.

But trampling isn't creative. Quite the reverse. It decreases the total creativity available to the system. That's why the slaver's assumption doesn't work. Assuming that conflict is the way of things, he ends up destroying the very systems on which he himself depends. He reduces the diversity of the systems around him, which cuts off their sources of regeneration. Worse, his assumption makes him think he has no other option. Why?

If the slaver accepts the limits that his assumption gives him as the way things must be, then he locks himself in an artificially closed system—a world that's closed conceptually. In this world, he calls the shots. He controls the variables. He dominates.

But there's a problem. In closed systems, options are limited, and resources fixed. The slaver has to dominate others in order to control the scarce supplies. Instead of solving scarcity, his assumptions intensify it. When he runs out of natives to capture, he has to expand his territory. More, he has to destroy anyone who stands in his way. The world created by his assumptions requires it: enslave or be enslaved, control or be controlled. Through the grid of his assumptions, scarcity and conflict seem inevitable—laws of economic survival.

According to *whole-seeking assumptions,* scarcity and conflict are inevitable only if we don't question the limits that billiard-ball assumptions impose. Creativity starts the moment we do: maybe the limits reflect not reality but our way of looking at reality. Maybe they aren't as fixed as we thought. Maybe we're outgrowing the limits. Maybe we'd be better off assuming something quite different.

In short, creativity gets going the more we question our assumptions. By examining limits and rearranging them, we open the doors to new possibilities. By inventing a new starting-point, we give creativity a chance. In turn, creativity gives us a chance not to be spooked by scarcity. By changing our assumptions, creativity changes the game.

II. The spectrum of assumptions

The two accounts of creation

Creativity is the first issue the Bible takes up. It's where Genesis begins: "In the beginning God created the heaven and the earth." (1:1)

The Bible opens by giving its own view of where creativity starts: with the whole. The whole, being unlimited, restructures limits and creates ordered variations of its own wholeness. In David Bohm's terms, the holo-movement is creative. It's the ultimate source of creativity. Because of it, things take shape and hang together.

This assumption—that creative power stems from the whole—echoes throughout the seven days of creation: "God said," "God saw," "God called," "God divided," "God created," "God made," "God blessed."

Assuming simply *that* creativity comes from the whole, however, doesn't say *what* creativity actually involves. In fact, such a general statement leaves us almost as much in the dark as before: "The earth was without form, and void; and darkness was upon the face of the deep." (1:2)

So the text elaborates its assumptions. Through symbols taken from nature, the seven days of creation depict assumptions that open us to the whole—God—and enable us to tap the creative process that the whole generates (creation, genesis): (1) The whole brings light. (2) It orders values according to the firmament. (3) It causes the dry land to appear and plants to grow. (4) It unifies everything under the stellar system. (5) It sparks life in abundance. (6) It shapes generic man in the likeness of the whole and (7) integrates creation back into its own self-completeness.

But the seven days go by us quickly. They present reality's infinitely self-creative activity in fewer than a thousand words. To make matters worse, their assumptions sound abstract, remote from what we experience day to day. So what if God *is* self-creative and creates a perfect universe? How does that relate to the everyday worlds we experience?

To bring the issue closer to home, a second version of creation, the Adam-and-Eve story (2:6–5:24), describes something more familiar: worlds built on partial-order assumptions. What creativity do we have if we disregard the whole and instead try to work out our lives from premises of fragmentation?

The second account of creation answers with a story. In it, God isn't the only actor, and man, though already created, is made again, only this time from dust and breath. The vision of God's unfolding creativity disappears, replaced by a script that swings between farce and tragedy—a mixture typical of the ancient storytelling traditions that the second creation account resembles.

It doesn't have a happy ending, either. The entire family gets bumped from the Garden. One son even murders his brother and then spawns a line of murderers. It's the prototype for all the novels that get made into mini-series.

But why the two accounts? Not because the first isn't convincing or didn't take. Rather, the two accounts tell us different things we need to know if we want to be creative.

The first view of creation shows where real creativity lies. Creativity is a universal process, because it's a function of the whole. To exist at all is to be included in reality's creative power. This, the seven-days account implies, is a fact of our lives.

What cuts us off from this process? Or rather, what makes us think we're cut off? What turns a naturally creative universe into a self-destructive world of slavers and dominators? The second version of creation answers by presenting an inverse image of the first. It shows the order of the seven days seen "through a glass, darkly." (I Corinthians 13:12) It depicts the kinds of assumptions that trap us in conflict-torn, noncreative worlds.

The two creation accounts thus present a *spectrum for evolving our assumptions*. The first describes real creativity as God's self-creative power. To be creative, we need to develop assumptions that open us to this source. The second analyzes why we fall for billiard-ball assumptions and stop being creative as a result. We look at the world, we see trampling, slaving, and massacring, and, like a rabbit frozen by a snake's eyes, we forget that our own assumptions make things this way.

How can we move toward the spectrum's creative end? To answer this, we need to know the poles. Which assumptions make us creative, and which don't?

1) Light vs. mist

The first day characterizes creativity's source: "And God said, Let there be light: and there was light." (1:3)

Light symbolizes intelligence and enlightenment. It illuminates. When the light breaks, we don't see shadows of reality but reality as it is. Light symbolizes creativity in action, namely, the power of intelligence to generate ideas and to forge new insights.

Light appearing by God's word presents the basic assumption that real intelligence reflects the whole. It's not the private possession of gray matter upstairs but a reflection of reality's own nature. In Bohm's terms, intelligence is a function of the holomovement, which unfolds light through the influx of ideas. This intelligence, enfolded within the whole and unfolding constantly, provides the creative force of the universe.

Assuming that we aren't the origin of creativity—that true creativity comes from the whole and pervades the universe—makes us truly creative, because it opens us to a source that's unlimited. We relax the boundaries that we carry around in our heads and feel freer to let go of them. The assumption allows us to become a channel for a far greater creative power.

The second story, by contrast, opens with the opposite of light: "But there went up a mist from the earth, and watered the whole face of the ground." (2:6) (The term for "mist" is also rendered "flood" or "gush of waters.")

In contrast to light, mist symbolizes ignorance and confusion—an impersonal, cosmic muddle. Mist obscures. In it we glimpse only shadows and traces, not a complete picture. We see parts without their contexts and then try to make sense of what we see. But it doesn't work. The parts appear fuzzy and distorted, while we can't see the big picture at all.

As a result, assuming that we can be creative in a mist brings a flood of disjointed perceptions. We create something here that fouls things up there. Without a clear image of the whole context around us, we can't be creative in a whole way. In worlds of mist, "Things fall apart; the center cannot hold."[1]

It's not hard to guess which of these assumptions makes economies more creative.

Assuming that reality is the source of intelligence and creativity, we evolve assumptions that structure economies on this basis. On the simplest level, we base our economies on knowledge and the creative use of it. We assume that prosperity stems not from possessing things but from exchanging ideas. Knowledge increases knowledge. The more intelligence flows in an economy, the more knowledge multiplies to make the economy prosper.

Moreover, if knowledge and creativity ultimately stem from the whole, then we don't own them for ourselves to the exclusion of others. Rather, we create systems in which knowledge and creativity flow freely, with the effect of generating universal prosperity. In a fluid, information economy, we all have wealth, because we all have access to the prime resource—the knowledge and information—that makes the economy prosper.

According to mist-assumptions, however, economic success isn't about knowledge and creativity. It's about making money on other people's ignorance—on their lack of information or their uncertainty about the future. The greater the confusion, mist-operators reason, the more those in the know can profit.

It's not hard to find examples. From several years of stock-market scandals, we know how insider trading capitalizes on mist, inflating it with leaks and rumors. Then, of course, there's selling the Brooklyn Bridge or phony real estate in Florida. Dishonest car mechanics play the same game. If auto entrails aren't our forte, we'd better make plenty of money doing something else if we want our car back from the shop.

But economies aren't about tricking everyone out of money. Legitimate profits are tools to help us do what economies are really about, namely, managing the household. Mist-assumptions, however, don't make us more creative about household management. Deceiving people with mist—using their lack of knowledge against them—doesn't contribute to an economy. It doesn't produce, nor does it offer a service. It doesn't exchange anything.

The emptiness of mist shows itself most when economies are in crises, as they are now. In the face of debts, inflation, lagging production, and mounting pollution, tricks are useless. They don't push back limits; they make us think there are more limits than there really are.

Neither do mist-premises work on their own terms. When economies resemble a mutual con game, all information becomes suspect. When we hear something, we wonder if it's genuine information or a well-laid trap. Which is deceit, and which is real? What information can we trust? When misinformation (mist) dominates, the very notion of an information economy faces a crisis.

Mist-premises aren't good, then, not because moralists say so, but because mist-premises don't work. They shift economies to bases that are empty and lead nowhere. They cut us off from true creativity and distract us with tricks.

The creation accounts open, then, by contrasting two starting-points: Do we begin with light or mist, intelligence or ignorance? Which premise makes us more creative? The questions call for a sorting out, which is what follows.

1. Light vs. mist assumptions

First-account assumptions vs. Second-account assumptions	Whole-seeking assumptions vs. Billiard-ball assumptions	Assumptions that make us creative vs. Assumptions that hinder creativity	True-economy assumptions vs. False-economy assumptions
Light vs. Mist	Intelligence comes from the whole. vs. Ignorance, confusions	Using knowledge to be creative vs. Manipulating ignorance	Building on the flow of knowledge vs. Making money on others' ignorance

2) Firmament vs. dust and breath, the two trees

Sorting things out is the second day's specialty:

> And God said, Let there be a firmament in the midst of the waters, and let it divide the waters from the waters. And God made the firmament, and divided the waters which were under the firmament from the waters which were above the firmament: and it was so. And God called the firmament Heaven. (1:6–8)

Ancient myths often described the sky (firmament) as a sheet of hammered metal that mirrors light and separates the waters. The image is a good one for symbolizing a universal ordering power. The light of the first day reflects off the firmament, while the waters of the void (a symbol of thoughts) are arranged into a cosmic order.

As in the first day, the ordering power is of the whole. The firmament sorts everything out according to what's ultimately real. The whole becomes the reference point. It separates what's higher (the waters above the firmament) from what's lower (the waters under the firmament).

Sorting things out is essential for creating new orders. We can't create when everything is thrown together in a jumble. We have to assume that some things work and others don't, and that creativity has to do with distinguishing between them in a new or better way.

Moreover, if we assume that creativity sorts things out according to what's ultimately real (the firmament of heaven), then we can also assume that creativity involves learning. Even when the mist of the second account confuses us, we're still included in reality's ordering activity. As a result, we'll learn. We'll experience the ordering of "the waters" as a clarifying, purifying process that goes on continually.

The Adam-and-Eve story, by contrast, doesn't focus on processes but on states—worse, states that oppose each other. To put it philosophically, the story assumes primal duality—two forces, two powers, two coequal realities set in opposition: spirit vs. matter, good vs. evil, gain vs. loss, us vs. them.

The trouble is, duality makes conflict inevitable: Which state comes out on top? Which dominates? The premise turns the world into a battleground.

Adam, for instance, isn't made by God's word but from "dust of the ground" and must have life breathed into him. He's a mixture of matter and spirit, lower and higher. This doesn't make life easy. Adam faces the opposite pulls of a centaur—a human head and torso joined to the body of a horse. It's a battle for the human half to persuade the horse half to behave.

As if Adam's double nature weren't enough to illustrate the dualistic assumption, the story describes two trees growing in Eden: the tree of life in the middle of the garden and the tree of the knowledge of good and evil—a duality double feature. The *knowledge* of the second tree isn't the issue, but the fact that the knowledge is *premised* on ultimate dualism.

Dualistic premises make it hard for creativity to get going, because we can't decide which way to go. The polarized states pull us in opposite directions. Our efforts to go forward are cancelled by fears that hold us back. The human half can't be creative in one area, when the horse half carries it somewhere else. Thanks to our philosophical schizophrenia, we end up not going anywhere.

When it comes to being creative in economies, we face the same issue. How can we sort out the conflicting values that vie for attention? Are things as either-or as they seem?

According to the second day, no. In fact, we're more creative when we look to whole systems as the "firmament," the creative context for sorting things out. We order values so that the whole and our evolving relationship to it lead. We seek the whole view of things, which means we include each aspect and value and weigh them all in the balance.

The sorting-out approach makes conflict unnecessary. Conflict happens when two values compete for superior importance. One value dominates. Yet this isn't a creative ordering of values; it's a way of forcing a war among them.

Ordering values means seeing how each has its place within the totality. Assuming a multidimensional order—a spectrum of contexts and values nested within the whole—we're much more likely to explore how each value serves a vital function within the whole process. Different values don't then fight; they work together in a larger development. Their very differences fuel the creative process.

In the centaur image, for instance, the human head and horse body fight only if they're on the same level, locked in opposition. One wins by excluding the other.

If, however, we include both, we explore ways to work out a mutually supportive relation. The human-end, being more intelligent than the horse-end, can steer the horse's raw, physical power without tyrannizing it. In fact, the human can be creative in doing what's best for itself and the horse as well. To paraphrase Socrates, when the soul guides the body, the natural order is established, and both are healthy.[2]

The firmament's method of ordering values inspires us to manage economies more creatively. Important factors— quality, safety, education and research, social and environmental consequences, working conditions, as well as the well-being and equitable compensation of workers themselves—aren't sacrificed for short-term gains or obscene profits. Not that profits have to be sacrificed, either. Good management makes businesses beneficial to workers and consumers, the earth and societies—and profitable as well.

But when values aren't ordered according to what's important within the totality, they all fight it out on the same level. The battle stymies creativity with false alternatives. Either we make profits, or we clean up the environment. Either we cut money for health care, education, and the arts, or we sacrifice national defense. Or, according to Neo-Malthusians, either we die from war, famine, and plagues, or we multiply until there's standing room only.

In creativity, what there's really no room for is the narrow, either-or logic. Either-or premises blind us to alternatives. If we value the environment, there are profits to be made in cleaning it up. And, as we're discovering with Eastern Europe's restructuring, there's more to a nation's security than rusty missiles and doomsday bombs. Economic exchange for mutual benefit can preserve a nation's freedoms much more effectively. The same with Malthus' breed-like-rabbits-till-we-die view. Other options emerge with better education, improved methods of distribution, and more responsible governments.

According to the second day, then, the way to break through false alternatives is to sort out our values within a whole context. Having values isn't enough. To be creative, we need to order them in ways that make sense within the whole. Assuming such a "firmament," we can explore ways to affirm each value's place within the totality. From there, we can generate options that dualistic premises and their false alternatives leave out.

2. Firmament vs. dust-and-breath, two-trees assumptions

First-account assumptions vs. Second-account assumptions	*Whole-seeking assumptions vs. Billiard-ball assumptions*	*Assumptions that make us creative vs. Assumptions that hinder creativity*	*True-economy assumptions vs. False-economy assumptions*
Firmament dividing the waters vs. Adam made of dust and breath, two trees in Eden	The whole is the source of order. vs. Primal duality, polarized states	Ordering values within the whole vs. Conflict from false alternatives	Profits serve wise management. vs. Profits dominate at cost to everything else.

But how we order values reflects us: who we are and what we're here for. If our assumptions tell us that we're here only to make money—Homo money-grubber—then this value comes out on top every time. To do what the second day proposes, we need to consider the assumptions raised by the third: how do we define ourselves?

3) *Earth and herbs vs. Eden and Adam's naming*

If meaning is determined by context, as we know it is from language and life, then our meaning—our identity—depends on the context we use to define ourselves. The third day defines us in the biggest context: it identifies us with the whole, symbolized by "Earth."

> And God said, Let the waters under the heaven be gathered together unto one place, and let the dry land appear: and it was so. And God called the dry land Earth; and the gathering together of the waters called he Seas. (1:9–10)

In contrast to waters, dry land is definite and constant. Though things change on the surface, the earth remains the earth. That God calls the earth into being symbolizes the whole as the constant in life. The whole is, so to speak, our earth. It's what we stand on, so much so that theologian Paul Tillich called God the ground of our being. Of course, he may not have had the third day in mind when he said this.

In turn, the whole defines who we are. Though everything in human life and the physical universe changes, the whole remains what it is. It's the ultimate context of our being. Instead of identifying us with what's temporary or superficial (e.g., sex, age, salary, social group, moles, warts, and scars), the third day assumes that our ultimate identity is rooted in the spiritual. "Earth" defines us according to what's ultimately real.

This basic assumption that our true and most basic identity is spiritual—that we're defined by our relation to the whole—makes us creative, because it puts us in touch with primal forces of creativity. There's nothing limited or rigid about the whole. It's where creativity starts. Identifying with the whole gets our creativity going.

To show this, the third day introduces along with the earth all the plants, trees, and herbs growing on it.

> And God said, Let the earth bring forth grass, the herb yielding seed, and the fruit tree yielding fruit after his kind, whose seed is in itself, upon the earth: and it was so. And the earth brought forth grass, and herb yielding seed after his kind, and the tree yielding fruit, whose seed was in itself, after his kind. (1:11–12)

In ancient cultures, herbs were seen as gifts from God, catalysts for the soul in regaining our innate wholeness. Plants were used for both food and healing—to put people in touch with their own creative self-regeneration.

Which makes sense symbolically. Even when a forest fire burns everything black, new shoots appear almost overnight. Looking at a seed, who would think it had the power to bring back entire trees? No one has to hold a gun to a seed to make it do this, either. When a seed finds its home in the earth, it just starts growing.

The symbols of the third day suggest that that's how creativity works for us as well. The identity we gain from our relation to the earth "bears fruit." It makes us creative and generative, starting with ourselves. As we find our home in the whole, we become more creative about who we are and why we're here. Identifying with the earth engages us in self-transformation.

The result is profoundly creative. Changing ourselves changes the course of things more powerfully than changing only technologies or governments, because it touches the actors behind these forms—us. It restructures problems at their root. As we're transformed, we manage things differently, which means our families, schools, governments, businesses, and environments end up transformed as well.

The second version of creation, however, paints the opposite picture of identity, which yields opposite results. It shows how we get caught up in living static, superficial, self-absorbed lives, when we really didn't mean to.

It all starts with Eden. Adam is put in Eden, a place reminiscent of ancient, royal pleasure gardens, probably from Assyria or Babylon—not the Bible writers' favorite holiday spots. Pleasure gardens, as the name suggests, exist to satisfy the self and its desires.

That Adam is put in Eden shows what he's assuming about himself. He identifies not with the whole (earth) but with a psychophysical ego that's only interested in satisfying its own wants and desires (Eden). Eden becomes Adam's context for defining who he is.

Putting his feet up in Eden seems great, until Adam finds out what's involved. Before too long, he discovers that Eden is no paradise.

First, he has "to dress it and to keep" it. (2:15) Dressing and keeping private pleasure gardens sounds wonderful. The trouble is, what begins as fun ends up a burden. With all his energies devoted to maintaining Eden, Adam doesn't have much time for anything else.

Second, there's trouble in the garden. Adam isn't allowed to eat of the tree of the knowledge of good and evil, "for in the day that thou eatest thereof thou shalt surely die." (2:17) The Bible drops a clue about which tree is ultimate and which isn't.

Third, Adam lacks a "help meet." (2:20) Eden alone doesn't bring satisfaction. After running all day on the treadmill to dress and keep Eden, Adam isn't sure the garden's pleasures are worth it. Anyway, it's no fun satisfying our own pleasures. It's more fun to have someone to share them with. But Adam doesn't have anyone. He's lonely, and not just because Eve hasn't been made yet. As psychologists explain, a self that exists only to satisfy its own wants doesn't have room for anyone else.

Fourth, beasts are formed "out of the ground." In Aesop's fables, like most stories of the ancient world, animals symbolize qualities of character. The qualities in Adam's world, though, are "of the ground." They symbolize lower instincts—the opposite of what Adam needs to overcome loneliness.

Last, Adam names the animals. In the seven days' account, God names everything; the whole defines the character of what is. But here, Adam names the beasts: he labels everything according to his Eden-identity and so projects his own insecurities onto the world. In his view, whatever he names something (good, bad, friend, enemy) is what it is. "And whatsoever Adam called every living creature, that was the name thereof." (2:19)

Some things haven't changed since the Bronze Age. Adam stuck in Eden tells the story of economic life today.

First, we have to dress and keep our corner of economies, so that they give us some pleasure for all the work they require.

Second, dressing and keeping private Edens has two sides: moving ahead and falling behind, buying pleasure and getting bored with it, acquiring something and becoming burdened by it. Worse, dualistic assumptions pit us against each other to get what we want. Even though we suspect that something is wrong with this premise (eating of the tree of good and evil brings death), we don't challenge it. Our assumptions convince us that's just the way economies are.

Third, in a struggle for economic survival, we feel inadequate and insecure (lacking a help meet). Assuming that we're all out for ourselves puts walls between us. It creates the "lonely crowd." We don't trust anyone.

Fourth, thanks to insecurity and loneliness, we feel driven to use lower qualities (the beasts made from the ground) to secure our own interests. If it's us or them, anything goes. Survival legitimizes predatory behavior.

Last, to cover our tracks, we name everything according to our economic assumptions (Adam names the animals). Robber barons become "captains of industry," fraud becomes "clever advertising," usury becomes "interest," and theft passes under a host of names: "inflation," "rising rents," "extra fees," "higher taxes," or "bailing out an industry" (we all suspect why). We don't have to conquer the world to exploit it; we can simply rename it.

The question is, is Eden a good map of reality? From the start, Eden-assumptions have philosophical problems. They treat the self like a fixed quantity, one that doesn't change. The self becomes locked in its own closed world. If something doesn't benefit the self, it's not worth our while. There's no room in Eden for anything more than self-gratification. According to Hindu and Buddhist teachings, there's no worse taskmaster than the grasping ego.

The third day's assumptions give just the opposite picture of who we are. In relation to the whole (earth), the self isn't fixed. It's not even a separate thing. Beyond our social, physical, and psychological forms, we're defined by our deep connection to what's ultimately real. This relation is both definite (it's the ultimate context that defines who we are) and unlimited (it contains infinite possibilities for expression).

As a result, the third day gives us an open-ended identity, which creativity challenges us to explore. As our self-definitions shift from a pleasure-pain to a whole-seeking context, we find ourselves engaged in one of the most creative processes we can imagine, namely, evolving ourselves—moving with the whole by allowing ourselves to be transformed by it.

Our economies get better as we do. If we bring to economies a narrow sense of selfhood, our economies become narrow as well. They function in small-minded, pleasure-seeking ways. They grow full of problems, since no one has time for anything but keeping up private Edens. But if we allow ourselves to be more creative about who we are, we bring more to economies, because there's more of ourselves to bring. They're enriched, because we are.

3. Earth vs. Eden assumptions

First-account assumptions *vs.* *Second-account assumptions*	*Whole-seeking assumptions* *vs.* *Billiard-ball assumptions*	*Assumptions that make us creative* *vs.* *Assumptions that hinder creativity*	*True-economy assumptions* *vs.* *False-economy assumptions*
Earth and plants growing on it vs. Adam is put in Eden to dress and to keep it.	Identity comes from the whole context. vs. Identity comes from the context of wants and pleasures.	Creative self-transformation vs. Getting trapped inside egos and their desires	Changing economies by changing our self-concepts vs. Reducing economies to private Edens: a fight to survive

We're back to the issues we encountered in Chapter 1. Economies reflect us and our philosophies. To send the nuisance visitors packing, we need to rethink our assumptions. According to Genesis, we need more earth-selfhood assumptions and fewer Eden-selfhood assumptions—and for a very practical reason: economies need from us more creativity than what the Eden-self can give.

But what does it mean to identify with the whole? How do we do this?

4) *Stellar system vs. Adam's rib and Eve's confusion*

Identifying with the whole identifies us with reality's central order—its "axis mundi." In the study of the history of religions, the "axis mundi" refers to what's central, the hub (axis) of the world (mundi). It's that around which everything turns and by which everything is governed. The most common symbol for it is a tree, which acts like a cosmic pillar that reaches up to the sky (heaven) and connects it with us on earth.

The fourth day uses the stellar system as a kind of axis mundi. The One governs the universe through its system and then extends this system down to us, so that we're governed by it too:

> And God said, Let there be lights in the firmament of the heaven to divide the day from the night; and let them be for signs, and for seasons, and for days, and years. . . . And God made two great lights; the greater light to rule the day, and the lesser light to rule the night. . . . And God set them in the firmament of the heaven to give light upon the earth. (1:14–17)

In a sense, there's nothing new in the fourth day—no new elements. The fourth day simply arranges the light, firmament, and earth of the first three days into a system: the sun, moon, and stars giving light to the earth. But this doesn't mean there's nothing creative going on. A system has been set up, which becomes the hub of creativity.

Specifically, the system brings everything together to form a creative matrix for growth. Within a unifying system, everything works in a creative relation with everything else, because the system provides the link by which each part draws on all the others and is touched by them.

The assumption of the fourth day, then, is that the whole brings creation together to form a working system. It establishes the higher unity behind all the diversity we see. From this unity comes the creative ordering of things. Thus, the unifying system of the whole "give[s] light upon the earth," "divide[s] the day from the night" and marks signs, seasons, days, and years. It establishes the ultimate order that brings a creative, evolving order to earth.

What does this assumption mean for us? Identifying with the whole puts us in touch with the center of creative power—the place where everything comes together. Taking the central order as our axis mundi makes us creative with its system. It brings our enlightenment (light upon the earth) and orders our growth (signs, seasons, days, and years). In George Lucas' *Star Wars'* terms, as we unite with "the Force," it empowers our development.

But how do we unite with "the Force"? According to the first four days, by evolving our assumptions. The more we assume that what's at the core of our being is a spiritually creative process—(1) the light breaking, (2) the firmament ordering values, (3) the dry land showing what's both constant and self-regenerative, and (4) the stellar system drawing everything together in a dynamic unity—the more we experience this process as the power moving us.

In Hindu terms, the first four days' assumptions open us to the true self, to Atman, which works like our own personal axis mundi. On one hand, Atman is one with the whole, Brahman. On the other hand, it focuses the whole in a specific way. It brings the whole home to where we are and shows what it means to be one with it. Like the stellar system, Atman "give[s] light upon the earth." It infuses what we do every day with higher dimensions, which then take us in new directions.

The cross is a universal symbol for how this works. The horizontal line of our ordinary life is cut through by the vertical axis mundi—the descent of the whole, expressed as our true self. The meeting point is profoundly creative. It generates thoughts, actions, and worlds unimaginable from the world of the line alone.

As we putter along the horizontal line, we have a better chance of being creative if we're open to the vertical and listen to it. Socrates listened to a voice that guided him, mostly by stopping him from doing something stupid. Elijah listened to the "still small voice" (I Kings 19:12) that saved his life and led him to Elisha, who became his successor. In Hindu terms, these thinkers listened to Atman, the true self, which guided them beyond the limits of Eden-defined egos.

The second account of creation, by contrast, shows where Eden-premises lead. They don't link us to the whole by any axis mundi. Rather, their assumptions cut us off from the central order and bury us in partial orders. We assume that we're separated and detached. That's what Adam assumes.

Adam doesn't listen to anything. He falls asleep. His mind turns off to the whole. He shuts himself off from his connection to wider contexts.

Jehovah then takes a rib from Adam to make Eve. Creativity here doesn't mean bringing everything together into a unity. Instead, it means breaking up systems into partial orders.

As a result, Adam and Eve don't unite with "the Force." They leave their father and mother (their origin in the whole), so they can put their pieces together in order to "be one flesh." They shut themselves off from creativity's source, so they can match up body parts and do a little creating of their own.

Last, they don't take the central order as their axis mundi. Eve is confused about what's in the "midst of the garden." (But then, she was just a rib when the Lord gave Adam the rules.) The confusion is philosophical. The tree of life, the fruit of which they may eat, is in the middle of the garden; it's the real axis mundi. But when the serpent questions her, Eve assumes that the tree of the knowledge of good and evil, of which they may not eat, is central. She takes duality to be her cosmic premise. In other words, the nightly news finally got to her.

With these assumptions, creativity comes to a halt. There's no vision of the central order, just a confusing collection of partial orders. The assumptions given by the first four days get turned upside down.

First, instead of awakening us to our relatedness to the whole (light), fragmenting assumptions make us asleep to it. We drift into a mist. We don't realize our fundamental relation to the universe via the central order. We assume that we're on our own and that what we do doesn't affect anyone else.

Second, instead of aligning us with one ultimate order (firmament), narrow assumptions swamp us with irreconcilable dualities: completeness vs. incompleteness, man vs. woman, the serpent vs. God, the tree of life vs. the tree of the knowledge of good and evil. We're torn between false alternatives.

Third, instead of identifying us with the whole (earth), narrow assumptions identify us with private Edens and center our lives around dressing and keeping them. We marry ourselves to wants and ambitions.

Fourth, the upshot of all these assumptions is fragmentation. We assume that we and the universe are made up of so many disjointed, partial orders. Creativity doesn't involve any unifying system (sun, moon, and stars governing earth). Instead, the tree of duality is central (the confusion). Creativity means breaking things into odd bits—bodies and ribs. The only order we have is what we piece together; in which case, how strong is our glue?

Economies grapple with the same spectrum of assumptions. On one hand, we suspect that there's a fundamental, spiritual order that we need to understand in order to manage economies well. On the other hand, it seems as if fragmentation is the way things are, and the only way to deal with it is to impose an order of our own.

If we choose the second route—Adam's—we assume fragmentation and increase it. We treat economies as if they were Monopoly boards. The way to succeed is to break things up, so that we can piece them together again to our own advantage. Using robber-baron methods, we fragment the competition, industries, resources, or communities, so that we can put them back together again in ways we can control.

But there's a snag: we end up the ones fragmented.

For one thing, Adam's assumptions separate our aspirations—the things we dreamed of as children and tell our own children about—from the task of making money. Assuming that we have to compartmentalize ourselves, we fill our waking hours with jobs we hate or merely endure. We give up the hope that we can both make ends meet and live lives of meaning.

With our personalities so divided, Homo economicus crowds out Homo sapiens ("sapiens" meaning "wise" and "full of knowledge"). We take out a rib, the one concerned with getting money, and wed ourselves to it. For its sake, we put the dreams on the shelf.

Busy with the partial order, we don't see our relation to the worlds around us, much less to the central, spiritual order. We just do business. We forget the whole and bury ourselves in fragmented worlds, thinking they'll give us a sense of completeness.

But they don't. By reducing humans to money-making machines, fragmenting assumptions make us feel even less worthy. The mind and soul dimensions drop out. Before too long, Homo economicus gets confused—as Adam and Eve did—about what's the hub of the universe. If it's the tree of the knowledge of good and evil, and getting money or not defines what's good or evil, then anything is good if it makes money.

The fourth day's assumptions point us in the opposite direction—a direction economies are more than happy to follow.

First, we assume that economies work as whole and integral systems and that we can't separate ourselves from them. If we're related to economies at all, we're related to the whole ball of wax. What we do affects them, and what happens to them affects us. Instead of ignoring this relatedness, we're awake to it.

Second, to find out where we fit in, we assume that listening to Atman, the vertical line of the cross, makes us more creative than dividing ourselves into Homo greedy at work and Homo caring at home. If creativity comes from the whole, we're more creative when we let its creative power flow through us (give light upon the earth and mark signs, seasons, days, and years).

Third, drawing on our relatedness to the whole, we assume that each of us has a unique contribution to make to economies. These contributions don't put us at odds with economies: they don't make us leave our origins (our "father and mother"). They reinforce the bond. Economies need us, and we need them. They need our creative talents, which we pour into jobs and businesses, while we need their system to be creative. After all, we can't be creative in a void.

Last, we assume that economies have as their axis mundi the same unifying system that governs the rest of life. Working in economies can be as much a meditation on the central order as working in churches, perhaps even more so, in that economies hit us where we live. They speak a language we know to concerns we share.

4. Stellar-system vs. Adam's-sleep assumptions

First-account assumptions vs. Second-account assumptions	*Whole-seeking assumptions vs. Billiard-ball assumptions*	*Assumptions that make us creative vs. Assumptions that hinder creativity*	*True-economy assumptions vs. False-economy assumptions*
Sun, moon, and stars give light upon the earth. vs. Adam sleeps, and Eve is made from Adam's rib.	The central order works as a unifying system. vs. Fragmentation, partial orders	Uniting with the system unites us with its creative power. vs. Patching pieces	Working from our relatedness to economic systems vs. Fragmenting ourselves with a Monopoly-approach

So where have we been? The first four movements of each creation account lay the groundwork. They show which assumptions make us creative and which don't. The last three movements show why this matters. Creativity either takes off or it nose dives.

5) *Teeming fish and fowl vs. the Fall*

On the basis of the unifying system, the fifth day explodes with life:

> And God said, Let the waters bring forth abundantly the moving creature that hath life, and fowl that may fly above the earth in the open firmament of heaven. And God created whales, and every living creature that moveth. . . . And God blessed them, saying, Be fruitful, and multiply, and fill the waters in the seas, and let fowl multiply in the earth. (1:20–22)

Abundance—"multiplying" and "filling the waters"— gives us an idea of what the creative power of the whole can do. It doesn't make just one fish; it fills the oceans. It doesn't stop with minnows; it makes whales. It doesn't limit creation to bugs and snakes; it makes birds that fly in the open firmament of heaven.

We don't need much skill at symbol interpretation to get the point here. The creative power of the whole super-abounds. It's not meager and miserly. The whole creates with fullness and abundance. Spiritual creativity generates a plenitude.

Moreover, it does this by taking off limits. The creativity of the whole makes the impossible possible. After all, the size of whales and the flight of birds seem, at least for us humans, fairly impossible. Real creativity jumps barriers. The story of life appearing on earth is a great symbol for this. The more creativity supersedes limits, the more possibilities for life there are.

With all this teeming and multiplying, the fifth day tells us what we can assume about the creativity that comes from the whole. Infinite reality is infinite in expression. The unifying system (the fourth day) opens countless possibilities for mutation and discovery (the fifth day). From the standpoint of the whole, there aren't hard and fast limits to creativity, not at least in the way we usually think of them.

In fact, the assumption that limits have the last word isn't a premise of revelation. The only limits to spiritual creativity are those that limiting assumptions impose. Partial-order premises put lids on what's possible—lids we don't need and that the whole doesn't give us.

The second account shows what comes of lids. Limit-bound assumptions give us lack instead of abundance, demoralization instead of inspiration, disillusionment instead of development, and separation from the whole instead of oneness with it.

In the story, we get the Fall. Thanks to narrow assumptions—(1) ignorance, (2) duality, (3) Eden-bound identity, and (4) fragmentation—we fall away from the source that makes us creative. When billiard-ball assumptions drive us out on our own, we discover that we haven't got what it takes. We can't do in isolation what we can do when we're connected with the whole, backed by it, and drawing on it.

In other words, the Fall typifies the assumption that we're not good enough, that we lack something. Eve obviously feels lacking, or she wouldn't have jumped at the serpent's offer. Not that Eve is alone in assuming this. Adam's quick to munch, too. For that matter, fears about not having enough haunt everyone. We don't have the money, authority, or influence to do what we want. We lack the knowledge or cleverness to pull things off. We lack the love and good friends to be happy. We lack the character we need for the life we face. Or maybe we just lack luck. Whatever, our assumed lack lets the serpent in the door. We're listening.

The way to compensate, the serpent claims, is to raise ourselves to number one, and here's how: to eat of the tree of the knowledge of good and evil. This opens our eyes and makes us "as gods."

That is, we overcome lack by coming out on top in closed, billiard-ball worlds, zero-sum games. Within limits, we compete to be the best, the wealthiest, the most powerful, the most famous, successful, loved, intelligent, knowledgeable, even the most spiritually advanced. If we're separated from God, the next best thing is to become as gods, which is the serpent's bait to Adam and Eve.

It doesn't matter whether we have to use dirty tricks to achieve god-status, either. In fact, dirty tricks are the ticket in. According to dualistic premises, the way to succeed is to know good and evil and then to use evil to get the good we want.

So Eve eats the fruit that seems "good for food," "pleasant to the eyes," and "desired to make one wise," and gives it to Adam as well. She accepts the premise that "knowing good and evil" (3:5) opens people's eyes and makes them godlike.

But the fruit is misadvertised. Granted, it opens Adam and Eve's eyes, but not to enlightenment. They awake disillusioned. They know that they're naked (3:7). Unfortunately for the hot-blooded, nakedness is used as a negative symbol throughout Genesis. Rather than exalting them, the eye-opening exposes their separateness and makes them ashamed. They feel their lack—in this case, their lack of clothes—more intensely.

What does the Fall on one hand and whales and birds on the other have to do with economies?

In the marketplace, the Fall assumes all sorts of guises. There's the J. R. Ewing fall: the assumption that good guys finish last, so being the worst bad guy is the way to win. For J. R. types, being creative means cleverly destroying someone else's business. We're creatively pursuing our individuality when we're doing a good job of chiseling people out of what's theirs.

Sociologist Robert Bellah[3] complains that this perverse notion of individualism is wrecking America and the world. It's demoralizing. Worse, it's not creative. Like the slaver in the film, *The Mission*, it either feeds on others or tramples them. But it doesn't create. Into the middle of a prospering economy, it thrusts a bottomless pit which, like some ancient idol, must be continually fed innocent victims to keep it from devouring everyone.

Then there's the fall that early 20th-century economist Thorstein Veblen described. In his view, economies fall when people stop making money from producing and start making money from shortages.

If there's plenty, Veblen explained, we can't drive up prices. In addition, we have to work harder to manage all that stuff. But if there's lack, a shortage of things, we can concentrate wealth easily.

First, we can put prices wherever we want, especially if the shortage is in a product everyone needs.

Second, we don't have to work as hard, since we're making money on what's not available rather than on what is. We can take it easy, which is what Veblen found "the leisure class" doing all over high society.

And third, we can stockpile what's withheld from the system to increase the value of what we own and to guarantee future profits. In Veblen's words:

> The owner or manager of any given concern or section of this industrial system may be in a position to

gain something for himself at the cost of the rest by obstructing, retarding, or dislocating this working system at some critical point in such a way as will enable him to get the best of the bargain in his dealings with the rest.[4]

Owners and managers do this because of what they assume about their role in economies: it's not to be creative, it's to make money. As Veblen put it:

> The businessman's place in the economy of nature is to "make money," not to produce goods.... The highest achievement in business is the nearest approach to getting something for nothing.[5]

To those who assume that economies are about production and distribution, contriving shortages makes no sense. Yet to the owners and managers who fit Veblen's description, the very real possibility that economies could produce the necessities of life cheaply, efficiently, and in abundance seems crazy, if they can make fortunes by holding things up.

What these falls have in common is their assumption that eating of the tree of the knowledge of good and evil makes us wise and prosperous—that it makes us creative: "as gods."

J. R. types assume win-lose versions of the tree. If others lose, they're winners by default. Veblen's owners and managers assume have/have-not dualities. The more others haven't, the more the owners can charge for what they have, so that the have-nots have even less and the haves even more.

The problem is that the assumptions don't work. They don't make people gods, otherwise J. R. types and captains of industry wouldn't land in jail or have to hire public relations people to mend their images. Laws wouldn't be passed to outlaw their methods, and economies wouldn't disintegrate after a good dose of them.

More importantly, the assumptions don't make people creative. Restricting or limiting production—inventing lack—isn't creative. Nor is contriving someone's demise. The assumption that knowing good and evil elevates us to the winner's circle actually robs us of our power to contribute to economies. We just take and always at the expense of the system on which we ourselves depend.

According to fifth-day assumptions, we're far more creative without dualistic premises. Given a good system that includes everyone (the fourth day), creativity works by taking off limits and breaking restrictions (the fifth day). Then resources and prosperity abound.

This happens regularly with inventions. As physicists learned more about atoms and electrons, they broke barriers of knowledge. When they applied this knowledge to technology, they sparked not one industry but dozens, from power companies to electronics, from light bulbs to radios to televisions to personal computers. The lid was off. Economies experienced their own version of teeming and multiplying.

Moreover, we've all benefited from the revolution. We don't have to squint over candles, retype manuscripts, or hear news of our friends and family by pony express. We don't have to cut down trees for fuel. And the revolution isn't over. We're only beginning to see what's possible with computer, communication and information systems.

The serpent, then, is just plain wrong. There's more prosperity in win-win (the tree of life) than in win-lose (the tree of the knowledge of good and evil). And there's more prosperity in letting creativity take off limits than in imposing more.

Which set of assumptions works better is ultimately shown by the results of each, which is what follows in the Bible texts.

5. Teeming-life vs. Fall assumptions

First-account assumptions vs. Second-account assumptions	Whole-seeking assumptions vs. Billiard-ball assumptions	Assumptions that make us creative vs. Assumptions that hinder creativity	True-economy assumptions vs. False-economy assumptions
Teeming fish and fowl, great whales	The whole brings life in abundance.	Taking off limits expands our options for growth.	Letting knowledge renew economies
vs.	vs.	vs.	vs.
The Fall: Adam and Eve eat of the wrong tree.	Lids: limits are fixed and absolute.	Winning in closed systems is the way to success.	Contriving loss and shortages

6) Animals and man vs. curse and murder

The greatest measure of an assumption is what it does to us, beyond the effect it has outwardly. Assumptions change us. We're remade in their likeness. In the sixth movements, the two creation stories look at what the two sets of assumptions do to us. Some assumptions give us a blessed life, others a cursed existence. Our assumptions permeate our life and shape the character of our existence.

In the sixth day, we find out where whole-seeking assumptions take us: we're made in the likeness of the whole. The sixth day opens with the appearance of animals:

> And God said, Let the earth bring forth the living
> creature after his kind, cattle, and creeping thing, and
> beast of the earth after his kind: and it was so. (1:24)

Here, the animals come into being by God's word.
They're not made out of the ground, as in the third part of
Adam and Eve's story. Instead, the animals of the sixth
day typify spiritual qualities; they're creations or manifestations of the whole.

They're also our first clue to who we are in the light of
the whole. As we cultivate higher qualities, these qualities
form our nature. We have the opportunity to learn from
the animals and to incorporate the spiritual qualities they
express. Consciousness empowers us to draw upon the
entire universe of spiritual ideas and values, which we
then can weave together in different and individual ways.
Through this development, we become individualized
expressions of the whole.

According to the sixth day, this individualized expression of the whole constitutes who we really are. It reveals
our true nature:

> And God said, Let us make man in our image, after
> our likeness: and let them have dominion over the fish of
> the sea, and over the fowl of the air, and over the cattle,
> and over all the earth, and over every creeping thing that
> creepeth upon the earth. So God created man in his own
> image . . . male and female created he them. And God
> blessed them, and God said unto them, Be fruitful, and
> multiply, and replenish the earth, and subdue it: and have
> dominion over the fish of the sea and over the fowl of the
> air, and over every living thing that moveth upon the
> earth. (1:26–27)

The sixth day depicts the true genus to which we
belong, namely, the image and likeness of God: Homo
divinus. The sixth day's assumption is that our ultimate

nature is the whole reflected. We belong to the category of the God-man, God-being. Spiritually seen, we're whole and free, entirely equal before God. There are no grounds for subjugating anyone here.

Moreover, our spiritual nature is creative. Through oneness with the whole, we participate in its creativity. Our whole-reflecting nature gives us "dominion over the earth." It gives us power to be creative with the universe of God's expression—to be creative with God and like God.

In short, our true nature (Homo divinus, male and female) unites all higher qualities (the creatures of the earth) in a form that reflects the whole (is made in God's image and likeness) and acts creatively from at-one-ment with God (has dominion).

Unfortunately, the phrases "have dominion over the earth" and "subdue it" have been used to justify the exploitation of nature. "Subdue the earth" appeals to Veblen's owners and managers in a way "replenish it" doesn't. To own is to take from, not to care for.

Even more to the point, such convenient interpretations overlook what kind of man has dominion. It's not Adam. As we'll see, Adam's lot is to till the ground. The being that has dominion is the God-being, Atman. We have spiritual dominion—the only kind given here—only in the measure that we align our assumptions with the whole. The more we're working in harmony with the whole and reflecting it, the more we share in its power to work creatively. From it and through our oneness with it, we have dominion.

As a result, spiritual dominion carries a great responsibility, namely, to act in God's image and after God's likeness and not to act from partial-order interests. It brings the responsibility to be creative from the whole, through it, with it, as well as for it. That's how Dionysius described the holomovement;[6] that's how we work when we work at one with it. Spiritual dominion is oneness with the whole in action.

The American Indians, for instance, knew spiritual dominion and also knew its responsibilities. An unknown speaker expressed this understanding in a speech later titled, "How can one sell the air?":

> All things are bound together.
> All things connect.
> What happens to the Earth
> happens to the children of the Earth.
> Man has not woven the web of life.
> He is but one thread.
> Whatever he does to the web,
> he does to himself.[7]

Spiritual dominion has nothing in common, therefore, with beating up the earth or each other. It's as remote from aggression, exploitation, and domination as it can be, because it emerges with a specific form of consciousness. Only a consciousness molded in the image and likeness of the whole has dominion. A consciousness patterned on partial orders has the opposite experience, as the second account shows.

In Adam's story, no one has dominion—not even God. In the first account of creation, God is represented as "Elohim," a noun with a plural form but a singular meaning. It gives a sense of the One that's also manifold in expression. Grammatically, it also suggests a concept of God that unites masculine and feminine qualities: it's a feminine noun, "Eloah," with a masculine plural ending, "im." It gives a pure and spiritual sense of God, as we can tell from how Elohim creates. Creation appears spiritually—by God's word. There's no mucking around with dust and ribs.

In the second account, by contrast, we find the Lord God, "Jehovah," a name that suggests an ancient, tribal concept, roughly equivalent to "King God." Jehovah appears less than whole. For instance, King God doesn't know where Adam and Eve are hiding and has to be told who ate what on whose advice. To add to the confusion, King God joins Adam and Eve in believing the serpent's lie, namely, that knowing good and evil is godlike. (See Genesis 3:22.)

In view of the assumptions that lead up to this point, it's no surprise that the concept of God is muddled. Trying to make sense of the whole from these second-account assumptions doesn't work. Through their grid, everything seems disjointed.

Especially humans. The story paints human nature in dismal tones. When King God confronts Adam with what he's done, Adam passes the buck to Eve and even to God: "The woman whom thou gavest to be with me, she gave me of the tree, and I did eat." (3:12)

But Eve responds correctly. She traces the Fall to the serpent, here symbolizing primal delusion—much like the mist from which the whole story starts.

Thanks to the serpent, instead of gaining dominion, Adam and Eve are cursed to live in pain and toil. Eve bears children "in sorrow" and has to answer to Adam as well: no small curse. At least, though, male domination is identified as a curse and not as women's original lot. As readers of myths soon discover, seeing something as a curse and not as a natural state is the first step on the journey toward breaking the curse.

Adam, though, has his own problems. His is the curse of economic slavery, the opposite of spiritual dominion. He has to till the ground for a living, until he ends up in it. For his sake, even the ground is cursed:

> In sorrow shalt thou eat of it all the days of thy life; thorns also and thistles shall it bring forth to thee. . . . In the sweat of thy face shalt thou eat bread, till thou return unto the ground; for out of it wast thou taken: for dust thou art, and unto dust shalt thou return. (3:17–19)

In other words, dualistic, partial-order assumptions curse both Adam and Eve to live fragmented, struggle-for-survival lives. Adam's life isn't one of freedom and dominion but of economic slavery.

Even the obvious solution is forbidden: Adam and Eve aren't allowed to eat of the tree of life. From the story's beginning, the two trees represent not only opposite assumptions but also different ways of learning: either by understanding (the tree of life) or by suffering (the tree of the knowledge of good and evil).

Having chosen the second way, Adam and Eve have to learn from their own experiences that duality brings death. Simply telling them didn't work. It didn't click.

The lessons aren't long in coming. Adam and Eve have two boys. Cain, the older, tills the ground, while Abel keeps sheep. But Cain gets jealous when Abel's offering is favored over his.

As symbols go, the preference is logical: tilling the ground is the curse on Adam, whereas keeping sheep—nurturing higher qualities—is a step toward the nature we have from the whole.

Instead of learning from Abel, though, Cain murders him. It's the old saw: when in doubt, kill the competition—Cainsian economics.[8]

To make matters worse, Cain absolves himself of responsibility by affirming his premise of fragmentation: "Am I my brother's keeper?" (4:9) Cain exercises neither dominion nor responsibility, because of what he assumes to be his lot. If he's living an isolated and ultimately cursed life, he's stuck, so why not behave accordingly? The urge to get ahead by fighting may be in his blood, but it got there by way of his philosophy.

As it turns out, Cain's philosophy doesn't work. His actions don't advance his interests. Killing Abel doesn't gain him the blessing. Instead, he's cursed to be an outcast and a fugitive—the most severe punishment in the ancient world. He can't even be killed to end his misery.

The Bible isn't exactly subtle about which nature is more creative. On one hand, Atman—the nature that bears the image and likeness of God—is free to be creative with the whole. Our spiritual nature has dominion.

On the other hand, the creature of dust and breath (the one shaped by billiard-ball assumptions) is cursed to suffer and to cause suffering. A fragmented consciousness isn't free, nor is it creative. It's a slave to its own fragmenting assumptions.

But is the true nature more creative in economies as well? In the famous "real world," don't we have to behave like Cain to survive?

Not according to the first record. The nature made in the image and likeness of God takes a comprehensive approach. We assume that the whole is there (in this case, the whole system that makes up economies), that we're part of it, and that we act constructively the more we understand it and work with it. To this end, we consider our actions in larger contexts. We look at the relation of what we're doing to what's going on around us.

In his *Theory of Moral Sentiments*, Adam Smith sought support for this approach from the Stoic philosophers, whom he admired:

> Man, according to the Stoics, ought to regard himself, not as something separate and detached, but as a citizen of the world, a member of the vast commonwealth of nature.

To the interest of this great community, he ought at all times to be willing that his own little interest should be sacrificed. Whatever concerns himself, ought to affect him no more than whatever concerns any other equally important part of this immense system. We should view ourselves, not in the light in which our own selfish passions are apt to place us, but in the light in which any other citizen of the world would view us.[9]

Again, Smith took this view of human nature because it seemed the only practical view to take. The comprehensive, citizen-of-the-world approach inspires each member of economies to be more creative and to contribute to the system as a whole.

6. Animals-and-man vs. Cainsian assumptions

First-account assumptions *vs.* *Second-account assumptions*	*Whole-seeking assumptions* *vs.* *Billiard-ball assumptions*	*Assumptions that make us creative* *vs.* *Assumptions that hinder creativity*	*True-economy assumptions* *vs.* *False-economy assumptions*
Animals made; man made in God's image and likeness vs. Adam and Eve are cursed; Cain kills Abel.	We're Homo-divinus: our first nature is spiritual. vs. We're isolated and cursed to suffer.	A comprehensive approach brings true dominion. vs. Destructive means put us ahead.	Managing economies with a citizen-of-the-world approach vs. Private and public interests fight: Cainsian economics.

By being creative in wider contexts, we transcend the battles of private good vs. public good, Cain vs. Abel, Adam vs. the earth—us against the world. Instead, we see possibilities for working with whole systems. We find ways to do business that affirm both our own development and that of everyone and everything involved.

7) Completion and rest vs. Cain into Nod

The first account ends with rest and completeness:

> Thus the heavens and the earth were finished, and all the host of them. And on the seventh day God ended his work . . . and he rested. . . . And God blessed the seventh day, and sanctified it: because that in it he had rested from all his work which God created and made. (2:1–3)

That God rests doesn't mean we've got an exhausted deity ready for a vacation under some newly made palms. Completion and rest express the basic assumption that creation is integrated with the whole. Creation is complete. It's not only created from the whole but also valued as the whole's own self-expression. It's the whole expressed.

As such, each aspect of creation has its perfection from the whole. Creation is perfect in that it's perfectly valued as an integral part of the totality. The whole wouldn't be what it is without each aspect. Integrated with the whole, each aspect takes on its perfect meaning. What's been created is also "sanctified" and "blessed."

On this basis, there's rest. We come back to the creative quietude from which the days of creation started, but on a higher level. Now things aren't without form, they're not void, and there's no longer darkness. Instead, there's the stillness of everything coming from the whole and finding its place within the totality. The rhythm of "coming from" and "returning to" enfolds the universe in a process that's good and that brings peace and fulfillment.

How is this assumption creative? It says there's a time to stop and to value what's been done. Knowing when a work is complete is essential to every creative process. Artists, for example, need to know when their paintings are finished, otherwise they'll ruin them. Some artists don't rest until every hair is in place. Others stop with a few clean lines. The trick lies in seeing when everything fits in a unity—when the totality works.

According to the seventh day's assumption, whether something is finished or not depends on the whole context. Only the whole-view can rightly value what's there. In a painting, each line doesn't have to be perfect on its own. Isolated, how could it be? Instead, assuming a day of rest means seeing the perfection that the totality gives each part and letting the totality determine when the creative process is complete. The whole says when something is finished—when to rest.

In the second account, however, rest is what Cain never finds. After being cursed to be "a fugitive and a vagabond in the earth," Cain goes "out from the presence of the Lord" and dwells "in the land of Nod." (4:16) "Nod" means "wandering" with overtones of "oblivion." Cain's assumptions don't allow him peace or fulfillment. They keep him on the move. Assuming that he's separate and detached, he's driven to compensate for his isolation. But nothing compensates. Cain never stops. He wanders in oblivion.

In no-man's land, Cain and his wife have a child, whom they name "Enoch," meaning "dedicated." They even build a city and call it Enoch. But to what are their son and their city dedicated? Six generations later we find out. Lamech becomes a murderer like his ancestor, Cain: "I have slain a man to my wounding, and a young man to my hurt." (4:23)

Though Cain and his descendants suffer, they don't use the experience to learn. By not analyzing their assumptions, they perpetuate and even multiply suffering.

Adam and Eve, however, do learn. Their third son, Seth, has a son, Enos, and "then began men to call upon the name of the Lord." (4:26) Six generations after Seth comes another "Enoch," one "dedicated" to the Lord. This Enoch becomes the legendary prophet of the ancient world. "And Enoch walked with God: and he was not; for God took him." (5:24) By patterning his premises on the whole, Enoch enters a new world.

From Adam and Eve, then, come two opposite lines. Cain's descendants are cursed by assumptions that lead to oblivion. Enoch, however, evolves his assumptions and so "walk[s] with God." He leaves the worlds of curse and conflict behind. Enoch shows what's possible.

But how is rest possible in economies? Dozing in the hammock on a summer afternoon isn't the first image that comes to mind when we think of modern economic life.

As with all the other days, the seventh's assumptions speak to our economies by way of our philosophies. Rest isn't something to be won or earned. It's a premise to start from, otherwise it eludes us. If, for instance, we use economies to win rest—to establish peace of mind through financial security—we never get it. The more we have, the more we need to secure our position, as the philosopher Porphyry observed (Chapter 2, II.2). Our requirements for security go up. The only real rest from financial pressures comes when we're six feet under.

The seventh day, by contrast, doesn't dangle rest in front of us like a carrot. It gives us rest from the start. Whether we rest or not depends on what we assume about reality and our place in it. If we're woven into the whole, we don't have to run. What we need is at hand. From the whole, we have unlimited access to all the creativity, wisdom, and adaptability we need to manage human affairs wisely.

We don't have to make ourselves or every part of our lives perfect before we can rest, either. Since what's perfect depends on the whole context, and since we're not the whole, we can't know whether we or things about our lives are perfect or not. Within the totality, what we're already doing may be perfect, and we simply may not realize it.

The challenge we face, then, isn't of gaining rest but of accepting it—of valuing what the whole gives us. If we have peace, rest, and fulfillment from the whole, we don't have to kill ourselves looking for them elsewhere. Rather, we can assume that what the seventh day says is so: that perfection comes from the whole, and that it perfects us.

Guided by the seventh day's assumption, we rest in the spiritual process. Moving with the downs and ups of the holomovement, we're "sanctified" and "blessed." We take our peace and fulfillment from higher levels. Lao Tzu's *Tao Te Ching*, the central text of Chinese Taoism, captures the seventh-day tone and relates it to economies:

> Which is more valuable, one's own life or wealth?
> Which is worse, gain or loss? . . .
> He who is contented suffers no disgrace.
> He who knows when to stop is free from danger.
> Therefore he can long endure.[10]
> There is no greater guilt than discontentment.
> And there is no greater disaster than greed.
> He who is contented with contentment is always
>   contented.[11]
> He who is contented is rich. . . .
> He who does not lose his place [with the Tao] will
>   endure.[12]

7. Rest vs. wandering-in-Nod assumptions

First-account assumptions vs. Second-account assumptions	*Whole-seeking assumptions vs. Billiard-ball assumptions*	*Assumptions that make us creative vs. Assumptions that hinder creativity*	*True-economy assumptions vs. False-economy assumptions*
Creation is complete; God rests. vs. Cain goes into Nod; the line from Seth to Enoch	Being integrated with the whole vs. Being driven by incompleteness	Knowing when to stop: the totality vs. Trying to make each part perfect	Accepting fulfillment spiritually vs. Thinking that money brings peace

Assumption for assumption, then, the two creation accounts map the spectrum. By doing so, they put within our reach one of the most powerful human freedoms—the freedom to evolve our assumptions about reality and hence to restructure our relation to it.

But the potential for freedom brings a challenge: can we actually, practically, master this freedom? After all, Cainsian economies aren't figments of our imagination. The opening chapters of Genesis may well describe the poles of a spectrum, but the distance between them seems unnavigable.

Going the distance is the story of Exodus. To help us along the way, the Commandments map strategies that lead to the Promised Land.

The First Account of Creation

The first view of creation	Whole-seeking assumptions	Assumptions that make us creative	True-economy assumptions
1. Light	Intelligence comes from the whole.	Using knowledge to be creative	Building on the flow of knowledge
2. Firmament dividing the waters	The whole is the source of order.	Ordering values within the whole	Profits serve wise management.
3. Earth and plants growing on it	Identity comes from the whole context.	Creative self-transformation	Changing economies by changing our self-concepts
4. Sun, moon, and stars give light upon the earth.	The central order works as a unifying system.	Uniting with the system unites us with its creative power.	Working from our relatedness to economic systems
5. Teeming fish and fowl, great whales	The whole brings life in abundance.	Taking off limits expands our options for growth.	Letting knowledge renew economies
6. Animals made; man made in God's image	We're Homo divinus: our first nature is spiritual.	A comprehensive approach brings true dominion.	Managing economies with a citizen-of-the-world approach
7. Creation is complete; God rests.	Being integrated with the whole	Knowing when to stop: the totality	Accepting fulfillment spiritually

The Second Account of Creation

The second view of creation	Billiard-ball assumptions	Assumptions that hinder creativity	False-economy assumptions
1. Mist	Ignorance, confusions	Manipulating ignorance	Making money on others' ignorance
2. Adam made of dust and breath; two trees in Eden	Primal duality, polarized states	Conflict from false alternatives	Profits dominate at cost to everything else.
3. Adam put in Eden to dress and keep it.	Identity comes from the context of wants and pleasures.	Getting trapped inside egos and their desires	Reducing economies to private Edens: a fight to survive
4. Adam sleeps, and Eve is made from a rib.	Fragmentation, partial orders	Patching pieces	Fragmenting ourselves with a Monopoly-approach
5. The Fall: they eat from the wrong tree.	Lids: limits are fixed and absolute.	Winning in closed systems is the way to success.	Contriving loss and shortages
6. Adam and Eve are cursed; Cain kills Abel.	We're isolated and cursed to suffer.	Destructive means put us ahead.	Private and public interests fight: Cainsian economics.
7. Cain goes into Nod; from Seth to Enoch	Being driven by incompleteness	Trying to make each part perfect	Thinking that money brings peace

Chapter 7

The Commandments:
Strategies that Liberate

🔲🔲🔲🔲🔲🔲🔲

I. Freedom expands with evolution

I f we want to extend our freedom, evolution is the way to do it. At least that's how freedom has increased so far. Whether we look at the evolution from plankton to mollusks, lizards to birds, apes to humans, or foraging tribes to diversified civilizations, each step forward increases freedom. By evolving, we become more free.

The bond works the other way, too. The more freedom we master, the greater our ability to evolve. With freedom, we investigate new ideas and try out new forms. We see more possibilities, which means that we develop in more directions. Freedom allows evolution to take off.

In other words, freedom and evolution support each other. They feed back and forth, until both jump to new levels. In fact, without one the other dies.

The bond is important when it comes to formulating strategies that liberate. If we just work for freedom and leave out evolution, we don't get the freedom we wanted, because we don't evolve to the level that freedom requires. The freedom we gain isn't grounded on real growth.

For example, children can't exercise adult freedoms until they've matured to them. If we give kids freedom before they've grown to it, we hurt both them and ourselves, as every parent discovers. The children don't learn what freedom involves, while the parents become hostages to hellions.

Or, to take another case, pushing for more freedom in society without putting equal energy into intellectual, moral, and spiritual development invites anarchy. We don't base freedom on the development that's necessary for us to use freedom wisely. The strategy is dangerous. When freedom takes precedence over inward discipline, maintaining order takes precedence over freedom. Tyrants step in to tell us we've gone too far. With a little more evolution, we could have told ourselves.

Unfortunately, we hear variations of this argument when governments justify oppressive methods. The ruled, we hear, lack the maturity to manage their own freedom. Citizens should be treated like children by those who know what's best for them, which, of course, those in power always do. To the politically elect, "the masses are asses."

Granted, we're not a planet of philosopher-kings. It's just that we masses don't have a corner on the qualities symbolized. Prize donkeys—and pachyderms—lead the herd. This being so, the remedy doesn't lie with limiting freedom but with fostering evolution—everyone's.

Freedom is a big issue in economies, perhaps even *the* issue. Adam Smith predicated the invisible hand on perfect liberty. Economic freedom—or at least a system that aspires to it—is the one export from the West that the rest of the world always welcomes. For that matter, the people of the West wouldn't mind more of it, either. In contrast to feudal and colonial systems, free markets aim at replacing economic domination with economic self-determination, however much their practice falls short of this ideal.

If freedom is the most valued asset of free markets, then their success depends on the quality of freedom that we bring to them—on what we understand freedom to mean. Is it grounded on evolution or not?

The spectrum of freedom

Cain's notion of freedom, for example, won't work. For him, increasing his own freedom meant decreasing Abel's. That's the crudest definition. It quantifies freedom and then parcels it out as if it were a fixed, closed quantity. If someone has more of it, someone else must have less.

Socrates, by contrast, didn't assume that ideas such as freedom and justice could be quantified. He was interested in investigating qualities that are essential and universal. Ideas apply to us all equally, he reasoned, not because we're all the same but because ideas tell us about what's basic—the way things are no matter who we are.

Universal ideas are like concepts of physics. Gravity applies to us all equally, even though we don't all weigh the same or have the same shape. Moreover, if gravity holds one of us to the earth, it isn't at the expense of letting another drift off into space.

So with freedom. Freedom isn't a fixed quantity. We can't simply list quantities of freedom on asset sheets and then decide who's to get how much. It's not equivalent to dollars: one dollar, one unit of freedom.

Nor does the fact that one person masters greater freedom mean that there's less available for everyone else. Quite the reverse. If someone gains a new understanding of freedom, everyone else has a better chance of tapping into the same vision and benefiting from it.

That's what happened with the Magna Carta and later with America's Declaration of Independence. These new models of freedom expanded the understanding and practice of freedom all over the world. The wider vision of freedom spread. As it did, it extended the experience of freedom for generations to come.

But the universal, nonquantifiable nature of freedom makes it hard to define, as Plato discovered about ideas in general. In the end, Plato's dialogues don't define ideas once and for all—much to the frustration of students ever since. Reading the discussions with Socrates, we can break our brains thinking about freedom, justice, beauty, and the Good. Yet after all that work, the dialogues don't reward us with tidy definitions.

Defining freedom, as Plato suggests, is more like what we do in a discipline. Music, for instance, defines harmony through a system of values and concepts. Musical harmony has to do with notes, keys, rhythm, and how they all blend together. As a result, we never really finish defining harmony, since there are always more dimensions to consider. Defining harmony engages us in a development through which we understand music theory better and gain a better practical ear. We continually expand our understanding of how harmony works and explore new ways to express it.

Defining freedom involves a similar process. Freedom concerns our strategies. What can we do, and what can't we? Which way shall we act? We don't answer these questions with words but with the actual strategies we adopt. Some strategies multiply our options. They extend our freedom. Other strategies don't allow us much freedom at all. Either way, we choose our strategies, and they tell us how to proceed. As we use them, we discover whether we're more or less free.

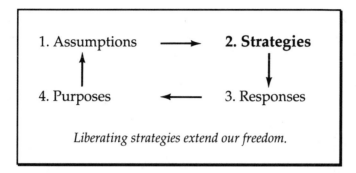

1. Assumptions ⟶ **2. Strategies**

4. Purposes ⟵ 3. Responses

Liberating strategies extend our freedom.

Choosing strategies doesn't happen in a vacuum. Strategies follow on the coattails of our assumptions. Cain's assumptions led him to choose strategies of trampling. Enoch's assumptions, by contrast, guided him differently. His whole-seeking assumptions gave him whole-seeking strategies: Enoch "walked with God." The strategy made him free. He wasn't confined to Nod as Cain was.

Mapping the spectrum of assumptions, then, the two creation accounts also map the spectrum of freedom. The seven days depict the ideal: spiritual freedom through oneness with the whole. By walking with God, Enoch exemplified perfect liberty; Cain's world didn't bind him. He was free to act in harmony with what's true and real— to exercise spiritual dominion.

By contrast, mist-premises bound Adam, Eve, Cain, and Abel, boxing them in narrow worlds. Not realizing that their assumptions deprived them of freedom, they suffered. Worse, they saw no way out. Their notions of freedom didn't ground freedom on evolution. As a result, they not only didn't evolve, they regressed. In the process, they lost what real freedom they had.

To Eve, for instance, freedom meant choosing between opposites. By eating from the tree of the knowledge of good and evil, she thought she asserted her freedom.

To Adam, freedom meant choosing irresponsibility. He blamed Eve for his troubles—and not her alone but God for making her. (3:12) To Abel, freedom meant choosing the good side of duality. To Cain, it meant choosing the bad. But to none of them did freedom mean the freedom to evolve. As a result, none of them were free. They lived self-bound. Their notions of freedom didn't bring freedom.

Only when Adam and Eve gave birth to Seth and Seth led to Enoch did the story turn around. By challenging mist-premises and patterning assumptions on what is, Enoch evolved. Consequently, he was the only one in the second story who was truly free. He was even free to change worlds: he ascended. Enoch's life says that, in spite of mist, falls, and a ton of curses, liberation is still possible.

But the Bible doesn't yet say how Enoch became free. "Calling upon the name of the Lord" and "walking with God," though relevant, are vague. What does it mean to do this? Which strategies liberate? Correlatively, how can we break the hold that mist-premises have on us?

Strategies for freedom: offensive and defensive

Though the patriarchs wander in and out of bondage, freedom doesn't become an issue until the Children of Israel become slaves in Egypt and Moses leads them out. Leaving Egypt with Pharoah's blessing isn't easy, but with higher help and a few special effects, Moses manages it. Staying out of Egypt, though, turns out to be the real challenge. In the desert, the people have to master freedom for themselves. Moses can't do it for them.

At first, they escape into the wilderness. That's the fun part: they spoil the Egyptians of their jewels and slip through parted seas. Crossing the desert is where the fun stops. The twelve tribes wander without obvious sources of food, water, or shelter, until slavery in Egypt seems like paradise:

> And the children of Israel said unto [Moses and Aaron], Would to God we had died by the hand of the Lord in the land of Egypt, when we sat by the flesh pots, and when we did eat bread to the full; for ye have brought us forth into this wilderness, to kill this whole assembly with hunger. (Exodus 16:3)

This time, Moses doesn't just step in and fix things for them. He doesn't, for instance, materialize an Eden-like oasis or an air-conditioned supermarket. Instead, he gives them strategies that enable them to master freedom for themselves. Coming out of slavery involves more than a change of address. Their strategies have to change too. They can't keep on using the strategies that worked while they were in slavery if they want to get out.

Actually, the Israelites are in luck. They're given two sets of strategies: one to advance freedom through spiritual growth and a second to prevent backsliding into some new form of oppression. They get an offense and a defense. As it turns out, the Commandments, carved on two blocks of stone, cover both.[1]

The first section (Exodus 20:2–11 or Deuteronomy 5:6–14) presents strategies for working out our relation to the ideal or, as theologians say, our relation to God. It gives guidelines for evolving our assumptions to approximate those of the first creation account. The strategies we find here give us a good offense. They take us forward in spiritual growth, which makes us free from the inside out.

The second section (Exodus 20:12–17 or Deuteronomy 5:16–21) warns us against strategies that appear to offer us more freedom but really don't. It watches our outside, so that this doesn't snare us while we're getting our inside free first. Theologians characterize this section as showing our relation to others. Since the temptations to settle for less than freedom don't arise from our relation to God but from our relations with each other, the second group of Commandments forms the rear guard, the defense.

When a lawyer asked Jesus which was "the great commandment in the law," Jesus answered by summarizing the two strategies:

> Thou shalt love the Lord thy God with all thy heart, and with all thy soul, and with all thy mind. This is the first and great commandment. And the second is like unto it, Thou shalt love thy neighbour as thyself. On these two commandments hang all the law and the prophets. (Matthew 22:36–40)

Loving God involves strategies for developing whole-seeking philosophies. It's a strategy of evolving consciousness by evolving the philosophies that shape it, so that we're more guided by the ultimately real, by God.

Loving our neighbors as ourselves involves strategies that use whole-seeking philosophies as the most practical guide for working out our relations with each other. It's a strategy of living by the ideas that whole-seeking philosophies present.

Together, the two strategies get us going on the quest for freedom. They don't treat freedom like an object to be bartered but like a discipline that binds in order to liberate. More than handing out freedom—this much to some, that much to others—the strategies mold us to be free. The result isn't that we *possess* more freedom; it's that we *are* more free.

That's the best kind. If we only *have* freedom, we can lose it. It slips through our fingers when we aren't looking, since others always want it. But if we *are* free—if we evolve a consciousness that is free—then we embody freedom. The exercise of freedom shifts to a more powerful level.

Even in prison, for example, Gandhi didn't lose his freedom. Quite the reverse: he went to prison precisely because he was free. His inward evolution gave him a free consciousness that wouldn't accept outward oppression. Being in prison couldn't affect the freedom he'd gained through spiritual growth.

In short, *the first set of Commandments* shows how to master freedom by evolving our relation to God, the whole. But because we haven't developed to the degree of Enoch, Moses, Jesus, or indeed Gandhi, *the second set of Commandments* warns us to avoid methods that would hinder spiritual growth—ours or someone else's. These two complementary strategies form the discipline that actualizes freedom.

Now for the specifics: which strategies rob us of freedom, and which help us get it back for keeps?

II. The offense:
Going forward spiritually

1) *Being guided by the whole*

We aren't free, for example, when we get stuck in some closed, rigid system. It could be a job or a relationship. It could be the way we look at ourselves or the world. It could also be the way we manage our economies. Whatever, closed systems don't evolve. Their limits are fixed. That's why living in them becomes so oppressive. We can't grow any more than the limits allow us. To break the bondage, we need a strategy that loosens the hold that limits have on us.

The Commandments open with a strategy that does just that. The first statement looks to the whole as the source of both freedom and evolution: "I am the Lord thy

God, which have brought thee out of the land of Egypt, out of the house of bondage." (20:2)

The whole isn't bound by any limits, certainly not by those that weigh on us. It transcends all closed systems—all limits as we know them. As a result, in the light of the whole, some things just aren't as necessary as they seem. Their limits could be arranged differently.

Looking to the whole, then, is our ticket out of closed worlds. The more the whole-context guides us, the less closed worlds have the final say. True, we may not know exactly what the whole is, but at least we know it's more than any finite system.

The strategy of casting our lives in the context of the whole widens our perspective. Instead of accepting limits as absolute (the limits of a relationship, job, or philosophy, for instance), we question them. If we're working out our lives ultimately in relation to God, we don't have to accept lesser limits as final. They may not be as absolute as they seem.

This strategy breaks the bonds that we find oppressive; it frees us from "houses of bondage." Once free of a limit, we're freer to evolve beyond it. Even though we may have found certain assumptions and strategies—certain limits—useful in the past doesn't mean we have to stop with them. A liberating strategy reminds us of this. It makes us wary of our assumptions and open to evolving them. We're free to question the limits and to rethink them.

The upshot is that we're more receptive to the light of the first day of creation. We're more open to letting the spiritual perspective shed light on what we do. Some ways of doing things may not prove as intelligent or creative as we thought. The light of the first day presents alternatives: it gives us a vision of what's intelligent from the whole, from God. The first statement of the Commandments suggests that we listen to the alternatives—that we follow the vision.

The first offensive strategy

Statement of Command-ments	*Strategy for evolving in-ward freedom*	*Impact on freedom and evolution*	*Strategy for evolving economies*
Coming out of houses of bondage	Being guided by the whole	The whole-context gives us a ticket out of closed worlds.	Not letting jobs turn into houses of bondage

2) Not having other gods

But how do we get caught in closed systems in the first place? Easily—demands draw us into them. One demand after another weighs on us. After a while, we're so hassled by bills, taxes, families, and jobs that we don't have time or energy left to evolve. The demands gain power over us to control what we do. They become as gods.

The Commandments' second offensive strategy, "Thou shalt have no other gods before me" (20:3), turns the situation around. Not having other gods means not letting lesser contexts supplant the whole context. We can give ourselves to the whole in a way that we can't afford to give ourselves to anything else.

The reason is practical. Only the whole keeps evolution going. It's the only context that guarantees our growth in freedom, because it's the only context that, as the first statement says, doesn't honor the limits that make systems closed. Accordingly, the whole is the only context to which we can safely entrust our freedom. As long as we attune ourselves to this context above and beyond every other, we're bound to evolve.

By contrast, a strategy of putting demands first isn't liberating. It invites demands to trap us in one house of bondage after another. The day-to-day pressures swallow us, keeping us so busy that we don't get around to development. We become slaves to the never-ending demands, as they become our gods—not very nice ones, either.

The Commandments don't address this issue because it's esoteric theology. They speak to it because it's dead common. Whether we're living in the Iron Age or the plastic, Sinai or suburbia, making gods out of the demands of life isn't a good strategy. It's not a strategy that liberates.

But does this mean that we're supposed to abandon all demands and join the street people? Tempting as this may sound to freedom-niks, there are other ways of dealing with demands. Jobs and financial pressures don't have to be treated like gods in order to be met. In fact, that's the least liberating way of handling them. Before long, they make all the decisions for us.

According to a whole-seeking order of values (the second day of creation), not all demands are equally binding. The "firmament dividing the waters above from the waters beneath" provides a framework for sorting out which demands are worth meeting and which aren't. It sets up a hierarchy of demands, in which only one occupies top place: the demand to understand God. The rest are weighted according to this ultimate priority.

In other words, the second offensive strategy sorts out the demands we face according to the criterion of spiritual evolution. If a demand serves spiritual growth, it's worth meeting. But if it interferes with development, the best strategy is to leave it alone. According to the Commandments, it's not worth risking our freedom and growth to do something that's not even that important within the big picture.

The second offensive strategy

Statement of Command- ments	Strategy for evolving in- ward freedom	Impact on freedom and evolution	Strategy for evolving economies
Having no other gods before the one God	Not letting lesser contexts supplant the whole-context	A hierarchy of demands frees us to evolve how we meet all demands.	Economic demands don't take over, which means we're free to keep evolving.

3) Not making graven images

But development has its own traps. We can lose freedom by valuing a stage of growth too much. Something can strike us as so worthwhile that we're tempted to make a god of it, too. We put it at the center of our lives. Who needs the whole, when we've got this wonderful stage to keep us occupied?

Science, rendered as scientific materialism, is one of the most popular graven images. There's gold leaf all over it. Then there are the old favorites: making money or gaining power. Even families and friendships, despite all the good they do, can become graven images. They can become the whole world.

Whatever the specific image may be, we hook into an activity, a stage of growth, and then we don't want to get unhooked. It seems so all-encompassing that we're loath to leave it.

The strategy that the Commandments give counteracts this over-appreciative tendency. No stage is so great that it warrants becoming the whole for us:

> Thou shalt not make unto thee any graven image, or any likeness of any thing that is in heaven above, or that is in the earth beneath, or that is in the water under the earth. Thou shalt not bow down thyself to them, nor serve them: for I the Lord thy God am a jealous God, visiting the iniquity of the fathers upon the children unto the third and fourth generation of them that hate me. (20:4–5)

Along the spectrum of development, stages come and go. They're good if they take us forward, evil if they hold us back. The value of a given stage relates to where we are in development. But that's not the whole story. Because evolution goes on, even stages that once were good can hinder growth after their purpose has been served. They become evil, in that they make it harder for us to evolve beyond them.

At one time, for instance, Augustine's notion of a just war was a revelation. It said we had to have a good reason for slaughtering a city. Breaking the monotony with a little raping and pillaging wasn't good enough. In the age of nuclear weapons and international terrorism, however, claiming that some wars are just simply isn't helpful. Any war—just or unjust—can wipe us out.

Moses' law of "an eye for an eye" is another case. Moses gave the law in an age of tribalism, when an attack on one person sparked escalating exchanges of revenge that wiped out entire tribes. To get all twelve tribes through the desert intact, Moses had to limit retribution: only one eye for one eye, only one life for one life. Today, the law sounds barbaric. We agree with the laws of Jesus and Muhammad, who said that, though the law of eye for an eye may be fair retribution, the law of forgiveness is much better. In Gandhi's words, an eye for an eye simply makes the whole world blind.

Business and money-making are stages of development, too. Hindu philosophy, for example, describes four stages of human life: student, householder, thinker (forest contemplative), and teacher (wandering monk). Money-making goes in the second: managing the household. But as important as it is, money-making isn't the pinnacle of human evolution. To treat it as if it were gets in the way of the larger development. We don't go beyond being householders.

Above all, the strategy of not making graven images speaks to evolving our philosophies. Good teachings are adapted to our development. But as we develop, the same teachings may not serve as well. According to legend, for instance, the Buddha told his nearest disciple, Ananda, to discard whatever lesser precepts and rules wouldn't help new generations on their way to enlightenment. Being a good disciple, of course, Ananda kept everything.[2]

To move our evolution along, then, the Commandment presents a strategy for valuing stages without getting trapped in them. Relative to what came before, each stage introduces much that's good, otherwise we wouldn't have bothered with it in the first place.

The trouble is, if we treat a stage not as a relative good but as an absolute good, we make a graven image of it. An aid to growth becomes an end point, which makes it hard for us to grow beyond it. We get locked into fixed notions about God (heaven above), about human and physical life (the earth beneath), or even about evil (the water under the earth). Bowing down and serving the images gets in the way of freedom and growth.

Not making graven images—not bowing down and serving them—means not substituting specific stages for reality itself. Only the whole is ultimate: "There is no God but God"—Islam's first pillar. By not confusing current stages with the ultimate, we reserve our total service for seeking what is ultimate ("I . . . am a jealous God"). At the same time, we preserve our freedom to change relative to any given stage.

The third strategy joins forces with the third day of creation. The third day suggests that we take our identity from the whole, from earth, as the constant in life. The Commandments say we have a better chance of doing this if we don't make a graven image, an Eden, out of any one self-image. If we do, we won't be free, because we'll have to bow down and serve this image, just as we have to dress and keep our Edens. We'll get stuck in one notion of who we are and why we're here. We won't evolve.

The third offensive strategy

Statement of Command-ments	Strategy for evolving inward freedom	Impact on freedom and evolution	Strategy for evolving economies
Not making graven images and not bowing down and serving them	Not treating one stage as if it were the ultimate	We're free to evolve beyond any one stage.	We don't regard household managing as the end of existence.

4) *Loving God and keeping the commandments*

But what if we goof and make a few graven images? Are we sunk? It depends on our strategy for handling mistakes. If goofs get the better of us, we'll lose our freedom. Either we won't let go of past blunders, or we'll be afraid to move on for fear of doing worse. Either way, we won't evolve, and we won't be free. Mistakes will hold us back.

The fourth statement of the Commandments tackles the problem with a strategy that uses mistakes for evolution: "And shewing mercy unto thousands of them that love me, and keep my commandments." (20:6)

Making mistakes is part of development. It's how we learn. We can do something right for ages and not realize why it's right. But if we do it wrong just once, we find out what happens. We discover the why.

If we're to evolve, our strategies have to let this process happen. They have to allow room for mistakes, so that we learn in ways we don't forget. Our strategies can't treat errors as one-way tickets to outer darkness.

If they do—if our strategies don't allow any bungle space—besides asking the impossible, they make us crazy. When there's no room for error, one mistake might ruin us. To save our necks when the dreaded deed happens, we ignore the slip if we can, hide it if we can't, and, if exposed, justify it any way possible. Through a trail of half-truths, anti-mistake strategies take us deeper and deeper into unreal worlds, until we can't face things as they are.

The Watergate cover-up, for instance, turned a professional mistake into a plethora of personal and national tragedies. But that's only one example. There are countless less publicized cases of industries and governments hiding their mega-boo-boos—to the good of no one.

A case we all know is the dumping of toxic chemicals. We're swimming in all sorts of mind-boggling poisons, yet no one wants to claim responsibility for them. Here, the mistake isn't the poisons, which may have been produced with good intentions for products we all buy. The mistake is not confronting the mistake—not accepting mercy. If we don't know what's been dumped and where, how can we begin to clean it up?

If we can't confront mistakes, we can't correct them, which means we're not free to evolve beyond them. We're stuck. We come to the real problem with anti-mistake strategies: they assume a static view of reality and put us in their static world. We do everything right, or we fail. There's nothing in the middle—no developing steps, no room to put things right. We're either chosen or damned, depending on how many blunders we make. We become so afraid of winding up damned that we don't take any steps at all.

By contrast, the fourth offensive strategy doesn't buy the anti-mistake approach, because it's not practical for either freedom or evolution. Instead of harping on mistakes, the Commandment talks about mercy.

Mercy wouldn't come up unless mistakes are part of the growth-process. Clearly, the Commandment expects us to make our fair share of mistakes. If we were all perfect, we wouldn't need mercy. Showing mercy for mistakes is, in fact, the most logical strategy to take on the basis of the fourth day of creation's assumptions.

On the fourth day, reality is assumed to be a dynamic, open system—one that makes the universe, including us, evolve. The stellar system gives light upon the earth and marks progress through signs, seasons, days, and years. In this context, mistakes aren't mistakes at all. They're part of learning. What's really going on is our development in understanding reality's whole system (loving God) and in learning what it means to be governed by it (keeping the commandments).

The strategy that liberates, then, uses mistakes for development. The moment we learn from a mistake, we're free to evolve beyond it.

But does the Commandment's strategy work in economies, which aren't that merciful? If we miscalculate, don't we lose?

In the short term, yes. But for successful entrepreneurs, that's not the end of it: they come out ahead every time, because they come out wiser for what's happened. There aren't many success stories that aren't peppered with great losses along the way.

We lose, the entrepreneurs tell us, only when we don't learn from our losses. If we do learn, one mistake opens countless possibilities for us to work successfully with the systems around us.

Yet learning per se isn't enough to apply the Commandment's strategy. It makes a difference *what* we learn. Learning revenge, for instance, doesn't bring out the merciful side of economies. "I lost once, so I've learned since to do whatever it takes to win" only justifies Cainsian methods. We don't evolve our grasp of economies with this profound insight.

Real learning focuses on how systems work and how to work with them. Given that economic systems build on exchange for mutual benefit, loss tells us when mutual benefit isn't happening. Some outside factor—like greed or the weather—is throwing the system out of whack. Or maybe the system itself needs to change.

Whatever, loss is a problem for us to solve. It's a problem to be solved by evolving better economic systems, much as heat loss in engines is a problem to be solved by building better engines. Loss isn't what makes economic systems work; it's what economic systems work to offset.

Loss per se, then, isn't evil. It's feedback we need. The only evil we face is our not learning from the feedback. It's double evil to build loss into the system by designing strategies that create loss and then pass it on to others.

Even in economies, then, the Commandment's strategy liberates. By applying our mistakes to evolution, we construct—to borrow the phrase that elected George Bush—"kinder, gentler" systems. The strategy shows mercy, as long as we keep using our mistakes to evolve.

The fourth offensive strategy

Statement of Command- ments	Strategy for evolving in- ward freedom	Impact on freedom and evolution	Strategy for evolving economies
Showing mercy to those who love God and keep the command- ments	Using mistakes to understand the whole and to be governed by its system	Mistakes don't shut down devel- opment; by learning from mistakes, we're free to evolve beyond them.	We learn from loss and so construct economies that offset loss more effectively.

5) Not taking God's name in vain

As we're evolving, though, it's easy to settle for facile explanations. There's so much going on during growth that it's nice to have some things made simple, so that we don't have to wrestle with everything all at once. But there's one area where this strategy doesn't apply, namely, to the question of what's ultimately real. This one we've got to think through deeply. Why?

According to the Commandments' fifth statement, if we reduce reality to a few narrow, superficial concepts, we trivialize it, which in the end trivializes us, too: "Thou shalt not take the name of the Lord thy God in vain; for the

Lord will not hold him guiltless that taketh his name in vain." (20:7)

Other translations render "not tak[ing] God's name in vain" as "not misus[ing] God's name," that is, not making false oaths with it. Granted, using God's name to swear at people isn't a good strategy, however tempting. But there's a deeper issue here. Beyond our choice of expletives, what concept of reality do we swear by? The "name of the Lord thy God" raises the issue of what we understand about reality's nature and how we arrive at that understanding.

For example, if we try to settle the subject through empirical methods, we don't have a subject to settle. God doesn't mean anything. We can't measure the central order or test the whole in a laboratory. If we assume that these methods tell us all there is to know, we'll end up thinking God doesn't exist.

Yet God isn't like an owl or a lemur that some enterprising biologist can sit up all night to observe. Methods useful for theorizing about rocks and animals don't fit the infinite. If we apply these methods to the infinite, useful as they are for studying nature, we'll end up with vain concepts about God.

But even if we grant God's existence, we're still faced with the question of what we're talking about. If we interview 100 people—and, according to surveys, 95 out of 100 claim to believe in God or a Universal Spirit—we'll get 95 different definitions.

Defining God by popular opinion, however, isn't a sure method, either. If God means whatever we think it means, then there's nothing really there beyond our thinking. God ends up as much a vain, empty concept as if we subjected it to the owl and lemur watchers.

Not impressed by such methods, many theologians in this century and the last claimed that God is dead. But they weren't actually talking about God; they were talking about the modern world's view of God. Swearing by either materialist or opinion-poll methods, we don't have much chance of making sense of what the whole is or means on its own terms.

What's wrong, they said, is that we've all become prisoners to a few, over-specialized methods. Empirical methods record what our senses pick up. They don't tell us how to interpret the debris, and they certainly don't prove that that's all there is. Opinion-poll methods tell us what people think, but they don't tell us whether or not what people think is right or true. If our concepts begin and end with these methods, we can't reason beyond them. Our understanding of reality stops when our methods reach their limits.

So what? So what if we have a lackluster notion of God because of the one-sided methods in vogue today: what difference does it make? According to the Commandment, plenty: we're not held "guiltless" for sticking to these methods.

Yet that's when the Commandment gets annoying. Why should we suffer from the world's narrow methods? We didn't invent them. The Commandment, though, isn't dishing out heavy-handed morality. It's saying something philosophical and practical: as our philosophies go, so go our worlds.

If our philosophies—individual plus collective—claim that ultimate reality isn't any more than what we can measure with the senses, then we aren't, either. We're just warm bodies struggling for survival in a universe that has no real meaning. We wind up living in the vain, one-dimensional worlds that vain, one-dimensional methods produce. Vain concepts about God don't stop with God. They pay us a visit as well.

They also visit economies. If narrow methods reduce economies to superficial concepts—making money or scrambling for possessions—they trivialize the role that economies play in life. Economies have the potential to make life pleasant instead of unpleasant, easy instead of hard, progressive instead of barbaric, fair and free instead of cruel and enslaving. Economies can't move in these directions, though, as long as reductionist methods confine them to vain, superficial concepts.

If, for instance, we reduce our economies to gain-loss struggles—unlimited desires competing for a few limited things—we don't find out what happens in economies or what makes them succeed. We discover only what makes them fail. According to the gain-loss definition, there's no direction for economies to move toward but war. Conflict is inevitable. If our philosophies give us that concept, we're not held guiltless. That's how our economies go. Our day-to-day "economic realities" look fairly grim.

How, then, is reality—whether ultimate reality, our own reality, or economic reality—sought rightly and not in vain? The fifth day of creation gives a clue with the birds flying "above the earth in the open firmament of heaven." Relative to us, reality is open above. There are structures we don't see, orders we don't understand, and forces we don't know. Reality includes more than what test tubes, computers, and atom-smashers can reveal—and they've revealed a lot this century.

The best strategy for dealing with wider dimensions isn't to ignore them just because they don't fit into test tubes. It makes better philosophical sense, the Commandment suggests, to consider what we don't know and to begin to explore it—not to be "vain" about ultimate questions. That way, our strategies stretch our methods and stretch us. We're free to evolve both.

The fifth offensive strategy

Statement of Command- ments	Strategy for evolving in- ward freedom	Impact on freedom and evolution	Strategy for evolving economies
Not taking the name of the Lord in vain	Not reducing God to empty concepts by using inap- propriate methods	We're free both to use specialized methods and to evolve others as well.	We expand our concept of economies beyond superficial definitions.

6) Laboring six days

But suppose we're faced with the worst case. Suppose narrow methods and worse philosophies have already done a job on us. Suppose we're mired in vain concepts. Suppose we've accepted them as accurate portraits of our- selves and the world. What happens? Without a strategy to break the cycle, we're stuck. The methods undermine both the development we've made so far and our ability to evolve further. It's hard to get past the vain concepts.

For instance, there's the popular notion that we're all economic animals, and the world out there is a jungle. Or, for those who feel more at home in the water, it's a shark meet, in which we're all either sharks or meat. As pro- found as these insights may be, they're most likely not the apex of our evolution in self-understanding. If, however, we accept them as true pictures, our work is cut out for us. We're stuck spending our lives either imitating sharks or warding them off.

The curse of vain concepts is Adam's problem. He's cursed to be a one-dimensional man—Homo economicus and nothing more. He's condemned to till the ground by the sweat of his face, until he's dust for the potatoes and carrots he's tilled. A bumper-sticker slogan, "We work, and then we die," sums up Adam's life. There's not much room for meaning.

The Commandments' sixth offensive strategy shows how to reverse the worst-case scenario—how to get the meaning back. There's more to us than one dimension. The strategy for uncovering the more is to "labor six days" to find out what our true nature is.

> Remember the sabbath day, to keep it holy. Six days shalt thou labour, and do all thy work. (20:9)

We usually pass over this bit in the Commandments, since it mentions what we do on all the days that aren't Sabbaths (work days), and we figure that the Bible is only interested in what we do on Sabbath days. But in fact it suggests a strategy for non-Sabbaths as well. It suggests that we look to the *first six days of creation* to find out what counts as real work.

Specifically, the six days of creation define work as a creative process—the creative unfolding of what's real. Moreover, it's a creative process that unfolds who we are. The days of creation's assumptions about reality also apply to us, since we're part of reality.

The sixth day states this outright: generic man reflects the whole and shares the nature of the whole. What's been revealed about God says something about us, since the context that is God defines our meaning.

According to the sixth statement of the Commandments, then, our real labor—the work that overshadows all the specific jobs—is to take part in reality's creative process. It's the labor to use the six days' ideas and values to evolve who we are, so that we experience more of the nature we have from the whole.

And it is labor. It's work. The six days' assumptions challenge us to rethink all sorts of attitudes that we've picked up along the way.

For instance, the notions that we're here to work till we drop, or that our character is fixed, set in stone after the first seven years, aren't liberating. Nor is the view of human evolution that goes from macho man to yuppie-on-the-move to terminal sweetness-and-light. There are dimensions to us that the images miss. Reclaiming the meaning we have from the whole means questioning the images, so that we can evolve beyond them.

In other words, the sixth statement brings the fifth home. If our philosophies characterize reality in superficial ways, we'll think about ourselves the same way: that's the fifth statement. The sixth statement says that when this happens, a life of labor and toil follows. Bad philosophies trap us in one-dimensional patterns of what it's like to be us day to day. If we don't rethink the philosophies ("labor six days"), they'll have us digging in the dirt until we're buried in it.

Of course, we can use the Sabbath for a rest. But more than that, we can use the six days to break the cycle. The six days engage us in the creative process of restructuring our concepts—of finding out what's ultimately true about reality and ourselves.

If we use the six days this way, everything changes—both we and our work. To be us means to be part of a larger spiritual process. To work means to evolve, no matter what symbols or activities we use to do it. We can use our families, our friendships, our businesses, our governments—anything—for spiritual evolution. One way or another, what we do and how we do it make a difference in people's lives—in the development of consciousness, as well as in our own inward growth.

By recasting work in a spiritual context, the Commandments' sixth offensive strategy uncovers dimensions of
work that shark-meet models hide. To say that we work
for money describes only a tiny thread of the whole fabric.
In the end, we're working to evolve our understanding of
reality and to find out what it means to be governed by it.

In fact, even if we buy shark-meet models, we do so
because we think that's the way reality is, and sharking is
the way to succeed in it. We're still wrestling with reality
questions and trying to find out what it means to participate in reality as we see it. The Commandments' sixth
offensive strategy simply points to what we're doing and
suggests turning it into a conscious strategy, so that we go
forward more aware of our philosophies and of how
they're affecting us. That's where consciousness-evolution
starts.

The sixth offensive strategy

Statement of Command-ments	Strategy for evolving in-ward freedom	Impact on freedom and evolution	Strategy for evolving economies
Remembering the Sabbath; laboring six days	Laboring to evolve who we are in light of reality's own creative process	We're free to evolve beyond super-ficial con-cepts of what it's like to be us day to day.	We expand our concept of work beyond merely making money.

7) Resting on the Sabbath

But can labor give us our true nature? According to the
sixth statement, it does, because we're laboring to see

through vain concepts in order to rediscover our original, spiritual meaning.

But there's more going on. In the seventh statement, the Commandments expand the picture of what's really happening. The seventh offensive strategy exposes a final trap in working out our relation to God. If we think that freedom and spiritual growth are gained entirely by our own efforts, we shut out grace. The strategy of working for freedom and evolution backfires. We stop being open to the descent, the influx of the whole, which means that we close ourselves off from the very source of freedom and evolution.

The story of how the Buddha became enlightened makes the same point. Once the Buddha realized that a life of luxury wasn't all that fulfilling (he was raised a rich kid in a medium-sized palace) and that the world was filled with suffering, he set out on a spiritual quest to find a solution. Raised a Hindu, he took this quest to include spiritual instruction, contemplation, and severe asceticism: heavy-duty work. But after he'd studied with all the best teachers and nearly starved and frozen himself to death, he didn't feel any more enlightened. So he stopped. He sat down under a tree and waited for enlightenment to come to him. It did.[3]

The Commandments' seventh statement recommends this strategy. After we've done our six days' labor, there's a time to stop, rest, and be open to the descent:

> The seventh day is the sabbath of the Lord thy God: in it thou shalt not do any work, thou, nor thy son, nor thy daughter, thy manservant, nor thy maidservant, nor thy cattle, nor thy stranger that is within thy gates: for in six days the Lord made heaven and earth, the sea, and all that in them is, and rested the seventh day: wherefore the Lord blessed the sabbath day, and hallowed it. (20:10–11)

To rest is to accept what is. In working out our relation to God, this strategy completes all the others, because it says we can accept the relation we already have to God. The Commandments' offensive strategies are actually ways for us to accept what's already established. Man in God's image and likeness is already created. It's not a nature we have to contrive.

Moreover, we're already part of the whole, since the whole isn't something we can get outside of. That's why we care about it in the first place. If we weren't part of the whole, we wouldn't have to bother with it. We could make up any order we liked. But if we're already living in its context, then it's in our own best interest to understand the whole and not to work in ignorance of its order.

Whereas in the six days we work to find out what this means, the seventh says it helps if we include a strategy of accepting what's already created—what's true spiritually.

On one hand, the message of the six days is right. It's necessary to "work out [our] own salvation." That's how Paul put it in his letter to the Philippians (2:12). It's also the last instruction that the Buddha gave as he died. Given the screwball concepts that come our way, both from within and without, it's a job to see through them all and to avoid being duped.

On the other hand, we can't do this without grace, that is, without accepting that reality has a say in our development, too. Even if we wanted to, we couldn't mastermind evolution, because evolution transforms us beyond where we are now. From where we are, we can't say what we will or should be. We can only say that, with spiritual growth, we'll become more like what the sixth day says our true nature is. John's first letter says:

> Now are we the sons of God, and it doth not yet appear what we shall be: but we know that, when he shall

appear, we shall be like him; for we shall see him as he is. (I John 3:2)

Nor is resting on the Sabbath a bad strategy for economies. But it's more than taking it easy on Saturdays and Sundays. It's a strategy of not getting locked into the way economies are at present and therefore of being open to what they may become as we ourselves evolve. We rest from how we currently manage our money-side, which means we put our present strategies into neutral. Doing this, we make ourselves and our economies more open to what's possible.

The seventh offensive strategy

Statement of Command-ments	Strategy for evolving in-ward freedom	Impact on freedom and evolution	Strategy for evolving economies
Not doing any work on the Sabbath	Being open to grace, which is the source of evolution	We don't confine our evolution to present models but are free to be remade by grace.	We're not dogmatized by how economies are but are open to what they may become.

III. The defense: Watching our tails

The trouble is, the nature we have from the whole hasn't appeared yet. At least, it hasn't appeared on the news. Neither have economies outgrown all their bad habits. It's a fair guess to say that we're all still developing. In that case, we and our economies need protection. Other-wise, stages that we're still outgrowing get in the way.

We stumble over immature philosophies and methods, which, given the chance, can jeopardize the freedom and evolution we've won. To secure our growth, then, we need to couple strategies for advancing freedom with strategies for guarding it—for watching our tails.

1) Respecting law and obligations

Our freedom is jeopardized, for instance, when we don't honor obligations. Without strategies based on mutual respect and a commitment to the agreements that grow out of that respect, societies slip into chaos, starting with economies. Each person lives by his or her own law: everyone does whatever he or she wants to whomever he or she wants. In such a world, we're lucky if we can hang on to the most basic liberties—liberty of life and purse.

The Commandments' first defensive strategy tackles this problem by appealing to respect for law. Laws define obligations on all sides. More than that, they express a universal commitment to meeting those obligations. By honoring laws and using them to build mutually beneficial relations, we make sure our relations with each other don't threaten the freedom and growth we've gained. Laws protect us from ourselves at our worst.

But telling people to respect law is a bit dry. If you're out in the desert with folks who need to be told not to get too cozy with the sheep, you need a more graphic image, one they'll find convincing. So Moses uses the universal relation between parents and children:

> Honour thy father and thy mother: that thy days may be long upon the land which the Lord thy God giveth thee. (20:12)

The choice of image couldn't be better. According to most theories of psychological development, the parent-child relation is the parent to all the relations we form later in life.

It's also where respect for law starts. Honoring parents opposes strategies of "I am my own law," since parents are the first to challenge this notion in children. Early on, our parents let us know that we're not alone, and we're not the center of activity. We're to obey the rules, as everyone else does—or else. Further, parents let us know about the obligations that go with relationships, which more or less boil down to the Golden Rule.

We honor parents, then, by not behaving like jerks. That is, we respect them by respecting what they've taught us about laws and obligations.

But a little family experience tells us that not all obligations are legitimate; not all serve freedom or growth. A lawful approach to human relations does more than secure obligations; it also limits them.

Family ties, for instance, don't give us a right to burden our housemates with unlimited demands. Equally, political alliances, business partnerships, religious ties, friendships, or marriages don't entitle one party to impose unlimited restrictions or expectations on another. The reason is simple. The demanders become more dependent, while the demandees feel burdened and trapped. Neither party grows, and neither is free.

What tells us whether or not obligations are legitimate? Again, spiritual evolution. Whatever responsibilities nurture spiritual growth warrant respect; whatever expectations hinder it should be re-evaluated.

Jesus gave this rule of thumb when his mother and brothers came to ask him for a favor. He replied (surely to the delight of his family), "Who is my mother, or my brethren? . . . whosoever shall do the will of God." (Mark 3:33,35) Whereas Moses used honoring parents to teach respect for law, Jesus pushed the symbol further to define what's worthy of respect: not blood ties per se but the extent to which a relationship "does the will of God." Does it serve spiritual growth or obstruct it?

Defending freedom, then, begins with honoring the legal and moral instruments that put our relations with each other on a right basis, so that we're all freer to evolve.

The first defensive strategy

Statement of Command-ments	Strategy for protecting freedom	Impact on freedom and evolution	Strategy for protecting economies
Honoring parents	Building relations on a respect for law and obligations	Making laws and obliga-tions serve growth frees us from obli-gations that hinder it.	Protecting economies from "I am my own law"

2) Not using destructive means

But aren't there times when we need to break the law and use destructive means in order to achieve good or defend it? The second statement is categorical: "Thou shalt not kill." (20:13)

Whatever the problem, the Commandments' second offensive strategy says, destructive strategies won't solve it. They won't, for example, pave the way for mutual respect. Nor will they support mutual growth. They cer-tainly won't make the one killed or injured freer. That being so, the killer isn't freer, either. The killing strategy spreads, until it comes back home. Violence becomes the way to do things—a necessary evil or justifiable expedient. It becomes the world order.

What's wrong with a destructive strategy goes back to its basic assumptions: that doing evil brings good, that destroying someone or something is constructive, or that killing one group preserves another's life.

Granted, at one time or another, we all imagine how much easier things would be if only so-and-so weren't around. We can imagine a World War II made shorter, for instance, if Hitler had only slipped off a rock at Berchtesgaden. Not too long ago, the Pentagon imagined a world made easier without Colonel Qaddafi, which accounted for the bombs deposited on his home in Tripoli.

But according to Adam and Eve's experience, the dualistic premise (the tree of the knowledge of good and evil) brings death. Strategies based on this assumption don't achieve the good they promise. Both winners and losers end up cursed.

To break the pattern of killing, the Commandment's ban applies to all destructive strategies.

There are plenty of examples in economies alone: profiting from war, destroying nations and their economies to control markets, destroying the environment to make sales and to reduce costs, destroying the competition to perpetuate substandard quality, decreasing safety to increase profits, destroying new inventions to reap gains from existing technologies, in short, destroying whoever or whatever gets in our way on the road to more.

The robber barons even boasted about the destructive strategies they used to inflate their fortunes. One of the most famous said he'd pay a man a million dollars, if he'd use such means without qualms:

> [He] must know how to glide over every moral restraint with almost childlike disregard . . . [and have],

besides other positive qualities, no scruples whatsoever, and [be] ready to kill off thousands of victims—without a murmur.[4]

Such expressions of the robber barons' commandment—Destroy, pollute, maim, and ravage, if you can both profit from it and get away with it!—charmed the pants off many journalists and scholars who wrote about them. According to robber-baron apologists, we need their great battleships of capitalism to keep our economies afloat, and we can't expect battleships to shoot flowers and candy at us. Battleships play rough.

Now we're not sure. At the end of one of the most globally violent and inhumane centuries in history, we're finding out that destructive strategies don't work—not in the long run, not even in the short run. Actually, that's why the Commandment bans them. If a strategy isn't in accord with the way of the whole, it's not practical.

For one thing, destructive strategies aren't liberating. They're designed to achieve dominance. In politics, that's obvious. From dirty tricks to defense establishments to all-out world wars, destructive means try to establish who's going to dominate whom. In economies, it's true, too—just a bit more subtle. Driving out competitors, for instance, is a way to control the market. Granted, it's often harder to spot. But sooner or later, we notice that things have changed: there's less freedom to go around. Mysteriously, the market offers fewer options for everyone—consumers and workers alike.

But with less freedom, there's also less growth. Using destructive means to control markets ultimately kills those markets. With their channels for growth either suppressed or controlled, markets stop growing. When enough markets get the robber-baron treatment, economies roll over and die, as they have in many underdeveloped countries.

Which leads to the other problem: the strategies don't do us any real, practical good. The apparent advantage to the dominators is short-lived, because it drains the entire system. To destroy any part lessens the integrity of the whole. That's simply how systems work. The right hand, for instance, can't get more blood to itself by cutting off the left. To try endangers the whole body, putting a cloud over the right hand's future as well.

Thomas Paine applied this grisly analogy to economies in *The Rights of Man*:

> Every kind of destruction or embarrassment serves to lessen the quantity, and it matters but little in what part of the commercial world the reduction begins. Like blood, it cannot be taken from any of the parts, without being taken from the whole mass in circulation, and all partake of the loss. When the ability in any nation to buy is destroyed, it equally involves the seller. Could the government of England destroy the commerce of all other nations, she would most effectually ruin her own.[5]

The second defensive strategy

Statement of Command- ments	Strategy for protecting freedom	Impact on freedom and evolution	Strategy for protecting economies
Not killing	Not resorting to destructive means to achieve good	Doing what's good for the growth of systems pro- tects the rights of each individual to grow and to prosper.	Protecting economies from robber- baron ruth- lessness— making fortunes by destruction

3) *Not adulterating relations*

But if destructive strategies bring only destruction, why resort to them in the first place? Whether we're Hindus or Buddhists, Freudians or Children of Israel, we have a rough idea: we get trapped by the primitive ego, which isn't too careful about the strategies it uses to get what it wants. For the primitive ego lurking in the human psyche, only the self counts; others are expendable. As far as the ego is concerned, we form relationships for the sole purpose of self-gratification.

Needless to say, the Commandments' third defensive strategy doesn't go along with the way the primitive ego manages human affairs. It opposes strategies that use relationships for self-gratification. Moses expresses this third defensive strategy in a way that grabs the imagination of people bored by desert life: "Thou shalt not commit adultery." (20:14)

Adultery is prohibited, not because Moses predates the sexual revolution, but because adulterous strategies make trouble for freedom and growth. They take otherwise constructive relationships and use them for selfish ends. Specifically, adultery takes the male-female relation—which, in the context of true marriage, represents a mutual commitment to the development of both—and uses it to satisfy sexual urges and ego-fantasies. Development isn't protected; it's sacrificed. Worse, it makes adulterers slaves to self-gratification—their own or someone else's.

But adultery is as bad for economies as it is for marriages. Here, adulterous strategies latch on to the relation of exchange, but they don't use it for mutual benefit. It's used to satisfy greed. Whether or not an exchange is good for the other party, good for the community, or good for the earth isn't a factor. Adulterous strategies consider those arrangements best that approximate something for nothing—that gratify one party at the expense of others. The more others lose, the better the transaction is.

What's wrong with adulterous strategies is that they don't build relations; they destroy them. Exchange isn't improved by lopsided benefits. It's damaged. People either stop exchanging, or the relation slides into theft. The lopsidedness gets even more exaggerated, until a few gratify their greed at everyone else's expense. All the blood gets crammed into one toe.

It's no wonder stealing is the very next strategy that the Commandments tackle. Adulterous strategies guarantee that it will be an issue.

The third defensive strategy

Statement of Command-ments	Strategy for protecting freedom	Impact on freedom and evolution	Strategy for protecting economies
Not committing adultery	Not adulterating relations by using them for self-gratification	Defending the integrity of relations frees us to develop them in line with their original purpose.	Protecting exchange for mutual benefit, so that it isn't exploited by greed

4) Not stealing

The Commandments' fourth defensive strategy speaks directly to economies: "Thou shalt not steal." (20:15)

At the core of today's economies lies a mystery: the world contains vast resources and knowledge, as well as billions of people willing to put these to work. Given these riches, why don't modern economies prosper more than they do? Why are economies the hot issue election after election, headline after headline? Why, with all that knowledge and talent, can't we manage things better?

In part, because of the corollary to the robber-baron commandment: Take as much as you can for as long as you can get away with it. If theft is large-scale and spread out, if it looks official, if it's technically legal (or at least not illegal), if it champions a cause, if it can be buried in statistics, if no one knows about it, or if those who do aren't in a position to challenge it, then it will succeed—as we hear reported every night on the news.

Again, what's wrong with stealing starts with its premise: fragmentation. People steal when they think their own fortunes can be separated from the fortunes of the larger system, that is, from the good of everyone else. Assuming fragmentation, thieves use strategies that fragment systems by taking from them.

It doesn't matter whether the stealing occurs to feed an addiction or to build an empire, the effect is the same. The fragmenting strategy drains systems, until there's nothing left to drain. As in Henry Carey's example (Chapter 1, IV), thieves plunder the farmers' valley first as robbers, then as robber barons, then as government policy, until the poor farmers have nothing left. Stealing is parasitic: it consumes the host that supports it.

Because systems operate as wholes, they require symbiotic relations. In economies, that means relations in which both individuals and systems benefit. Neither can afford to prosper at the expense of the other, since each needs the other. The more individuals strengthen and diversify a system, the more the system rewards them and gives them opportunities in return. The relationship is two-way.

This isn't supersophisticated. It's kindergarten stuff: relationships work on give-and-take. Stealing isn't a good strategy, because it's only take. We can't build a system on taking alone, because systems don't work that way. Taking isn't a foundation on which we or our systems can develop, mainly because it's not a foundation that we all find equally agreeable.

Nor is stealing a strategy that liberates. When we're not secure in what's legitimately ours, we can't be free. In Western law, to respect others' property is to respect their freedom.

The opposite—stealing—denies freedom and creates oppression. If a person or an institution (a business tycoon or a spendthrift government) can take from us without giving us equal value in return, we're made slaves to that person or institution. Along with our money, the takers take power over us. We're not free to arrange a different deal.

The fourth defensive strategy

Statement of Command-ments	Strategy for protecting freedom	Impact on freedom and evolution	Strategy for protecting economies
Not stealing	Not fragment-ing systems by stealing from them: taking more than we give	Give-and-take relations evolve stronger systems, which then free everyone to function more creativly within them.	Protecting economies from economic slavery, which stealing creates

5) *Bearing true witness*

Respecting property rights, though, requires a deeper respect for the person, since the property is, at least legally, an extension of the person.

Yet respect for others is precisely what takers don't have. They think they have a right to take, because they're superior to those they take from. To steal and to get away with it demonstrates their superior intelligence.

They agree with Callicles in Plato's *Gorgias*, who tells Socrates, "Nature herself reveals, I think, that it is just for the better to have a greater share than the worse, right for the more powerful to have more than the weak."[6] Those who take, Callicles argues, are better and more powerful. The very act of taking proves it. They're stronger, and they know how to get away with abusing power.

Of course, neither Socrates nor Moses buy the argument. Socrates uses reason and myths to counter Callicles. With the wandering tribes, however, Moses uses the fifth defensive strategy: "Thou shalt not bear false witness against thy neighbour." (20:16)

Distorting other people's actions is the obvious form of bearing false witness. But false witnessing goes deeper. There's a reason we don't give a fair picture of others. As in Callicles' case, it's tied to the image we have of human nature in general.

In our darker moments, we're tempted to characterize humanity as superficial, self-centered, and depraved. In the end, the serpent gets its way: we're just a bunch of fallen sinners. The human race is nothing but a plague of greedy, small-minded vermin. And those are its good points. Among the vermin, the stronger and more aggressive take over, as they should. It's the law of nature: the takers' version of Darwin's theory.

But it's hard to be dark all the time. To cheer up, we talk ourselves into the other extreme: everyone is basically good and intends only the best. Beneath any appearance to the contrary, each person is really a warm, caring human being. If someone seems to be taking more than their fair share, it's only because we don't understand their perspective. We can't imagine anyone being so greedy as to clean us all out. Unfortunately, it's not always easy to convince ourselves of this, especially when we're handed a few sobering surprises.

Neither view, though, bears true witness to human nature. As Socrates argued in the *Phaedo* (see Chapter 2), human nature isn't fixed at one end of the spectrum or the other. It's constantly moving in between. Change and transformation are the stuff of human life. If so, it makes no sense to reduce human nature to one state or another. Forcing a static frame onto something dynamic can't give a fair picture.

Naturally, there are plenty of things people do that are impossible to respect. The news feeds us with behavior that keeps us foaming. But bearing true witness means looking for the development that news flashes don't capture. However things appear, our neighbors are engaged in a process that's ultimately holy, since grace impels universal development. Not that we're all wonderful, and not that we all respond to grace in holy ways. But we all share in a dynamics that comes from the whole.

That's the context that bears true witness. It points to what we're working out together on deeper levels, beneath the surface of individual actions. Even if people choose the hardest and darkest of ways, they're still doing something ultimately worthwhile. According to their own light, as the Quakers say, they're doing what the Buddha and Paul ordered: working out their own salvation.

But is this a practical strategy in economies, especially when we're dealing with "the greedy vermin"? It's a tough question, but there are at least three points to consider.

First, laws don't stop Callicles types, since they always find ways around laws. They're especially good at this when they're the lawmakers, which Callicles recommended. The only real way for the greedy vermin to stop being greedy is to evolve beyond a greedy-vermin philosophy.

As Gandhi reasoned, it's more practical to appeal to an individual's potential for inward growth, which "bearing true witness" does. The strategy leaves everyone free to change. It doesn't fix some people beneath contempt and others high on a pedestal. Instead, it respects everyone's freedom to develop continually and to choose all kinds of paths to do it.

Second, by making us wise to those of Callicles' persuasion, the strategy reminds us to protect ourselves. We shouldn't assume that everyone is wonderful, or that their business methods are beyond reproach. We're much wiser to be wary—"wise as serpents." (Matthew 10:16) We shouldn't play victim if we can help it.

Third, bearing true witness sharpens our economic skills in dealing with people wherever they are along the spectrum. The context of development makes us more sensitive to what our neighbors need. As Smith argued in *The Wealth of Nations*, if we don't render the kind of help people need as they're developing, we're out of business.

The way to protect mutual respect, then, is to avoid strategies that erode it. Just as it's not smart to treat God one-dimensionally (the fifth offensive strategy), it's not smart to treat humanity one-dimensionally, either (the fifth defensive strategy). If we do, we'll have a hard time forming good ties with each other. From one extreme to the other, false witnessing will sabotage the relation.

The fifth defensive strategy

Statement of Command-ments	Strategy for protecting freedom	Impact on freedom and evolution	Strategy for protecting economies
Not bearing false witness against others	Protecting mutual respect by not reducing humanity to static charac-terizations	Bearing witness to our shared devel-opment frees others to keep developing, both individ-ually and collectively.	Protecting economies from Callicles' cynicism, while assist-ing others in their growth

6) Not coveting

But as important as respect for others is, we can overdo it, especially when it turns into a desire to get what others have. Over-respecting others' achievements devalues what we've done ourselves. Cain respected Abel's offering too much. He coveted Abel's goods, because he thought his own didn't measure up. His jealousy made him lose sight of his own worth.

The sixth and final defensive strategy says that it's not enough to respect others; we have to respect ourselves, too. We protect self-respect by avoiding strategies that under-mine it:

> Thou shalt not covet thy neighbour's house, thou shalt not covet thy neighbour's wife, nor his manservant, nor his maidservant, nor his ox, nor his ass, nor any thing that is thy neighbour's. (20:17)

Conventional wisdom regards coveting as the engine of economies. Getting what others have, we're told, is why we get out of bed at six in the morning, brave the traffic, sit in drab offices or labor in factories, brave more traffic, grab a bite and some quality time, do housework, and fall into bed. If we want the houses, cars, clothes, vacations, pensions, health care, not to mention the reputations that others have, we have no choice. Rat race here we come.

There's even a nationalist appeal to make it a bit more palatable: the GNP would plummet if we took the Commandment seriously. Coveting is our patriotic duty. It's what keeps our economies afloat.

Of course, we're not as gullible as conventional wisdom would have us believe (that's hardly possible). We know from experience that coveting is the bait that leads to economic slavery.

To be first-class coveters, we have to subject ourselves to the people or institutions who control what we want. And we have to pay the price to attain the coveted goals. Whatever form of flattery imitation may be, this brand attacks our individuality. If we covet, we're not free to develop our own thoughts and energies as we see fit.

The Commandment's warning against coveting isn't far from the message of the Buddha's four Noble Truths.[7] In a nutshell, the Noble Truths say it's not a good strategy to get attached to wants. If we do, we'll suffer. It's impossible for anyone to get everything he or she wants. Things change, and wants multiply. Even if we get what we want, the fun in having things can fizzle. They get old or worn out. They slip through our fingers. If getting what we want defines happiness, we're likely to be unhappy.

Moreover, the Buddha explains, wants cluster like swarms of gnats, which we then mistake for our identity. We start thinking of ourselves as odd assortments of desires: the more desires we have, the more we're unique. "I want, therefore I am": the shopaholic's claim to being.

But, according to the Noble Truths, the wanting-self is empty; it's a hungry ghost. It doesn't have substance of its own, otherwise it wouldn't want so much. It doesn't have self-respect either, since there's no real self there to respect.

Which raises the real problem with coveting. The strategy obscures the true self (the Atman in Hinduism) or what later schools of Buddhism called the Buddha-nature, the true nature of all. When coveting dominates, we lose sight of what's worthy of respect, namely, the spiritual dimensions of our being.

All this doesn't mean we're forced into a trade-off between getting a new car and getting a new consciousness, a new VCR or a new nature. Because cars and consciousness, VCRs and Buddha-natures aren't on the same level, sacrificing one for the other makes no sense. It's like saying we should sacrifice friendships for apples.

Coveting, however, puts getting cars over evolving consciousness, when, as the Commandment says, the reverse strategy is better. That is, it's more liberating to seek what's true and enduring about ourselves, because then we're grounded on something worthy of respect. With a respect for both others and ourselves, we're free to get whatever we need without enslaving ourselves in the process.

The noncoveting strategy makes economies healthier. Without the burdens that coveting puts on us, we're freer to develop our individual talents. We don't have to fit the mold but can cast a few of our own. That's not bad for economies. As we've seen, greater individuality diversifies economies, which makes them more flexible in adjusting to the unforeseen. It enlarges their creative reservoir, which means they're more equipped to deal with scarcity.

True, boom and bust—mad buying and mad scrambling to pay for it—may become obsolete strategies. But we'd gain instead economies that are more grounded in their true nature: wise, creative, mutually beneficial household management. If constant cycles of fever and chills aren't the mark of healthy systems, we and our economies might just survive without them.

The sixth defensive strategy

Statement of Command-ments	Strategy for protecting freedom	Impact on freedom and evolution	Strategy for protecting economies
Not coveting	Not getting attached to wanting what others have, since this undermines self-respect	Not coveting frees us to develop our individuality, to cast our own mold, to follow the true self.	Protecting economies from boom-and-bust cycles by adhering to individual standards

But even good strategies—offensive and defensive—aren't enough to evolve practical philosophies equal to setting our economies straight. The next step is to put our strategies into practice. General strategies help only if they're turned into specific responses, so that the freedom we've gained is put to good use. But how? That's a question for the Beatitudes.

Strategies for Working Out
Our Relation to God

Statement of Commandments	Strategy for evolving inward freedom	Impact on freedom and evolution	Strategy for evolving economies
1. Coming out of houses of bondage	Being guided by the whole	The whole-context gives us a ticket out of closed worlds.	Not letting jobs turn into houses of bondage
2. Having no other gods before the one God	Not letting lesser contexts supplant the whole-context	A hierarchy of demands frees us to evolve how we meet all demands.	Economic demands don't take over, which means we're free to keep evolving.
3. Not making graven images and not bowing down and serving them	Not treating one stage as if it were the ultimate	We're free to evolve beyond any one stage.	We don't regard house-hold manag-ing as the end of existence.
4. Showing mercy to those who love God and keep the command-ments	Using mis-takes to understand the whole and to be governed by its system	By learning from mis-takes, we're free to evolve beyond them.	We learn from loss and so construct economies that offset loss more effectively.

Statement of Command-ments	Strategy for evolving in-ward freedom	Impact on freedom and evolution	Strategy for evolving economies
5. Not taking the name of the Lord in vain	Not reducing God to empty concepts by using inap-propriate methods	We're free both to use specialized methods and to evolve others as well.	We expand our concept of economies beyond superficial definitions.
6. Remember-ing the Sabbath; laboring six days	Laboring to evolve who we are in light of reality's own creative process	We're free to evolve beyond super-ficial con-cepts of what it's like to be us day to day.	We expand our concept of work beyond merely making money.
7. Not doing any work on the Sabbath	Being open to grace, which is the source of evolution	We don't confine our evolution to present models but are free to be restructured by grace.	We're not dogmatized by how economies are but are open to what they may become.

Strategies for Working Out
Our Relationships with Each Other

Statement of Command-ments	Strategy for protecting freedom	Impact on freedom and evolution	Strategy for protecting economies
1. Honoring parents	Building relations on a respect for law and obli-gations	Making laws and obliga-tions serve growth frees us from obli-gations that hinder it.	Protecting economies from "I am my own law"
2. Not killing	Not resorting to destructive means to achieve good	Doing what's good for the growth of systems pro-tects the rights of each individual to grow and to prosper.	Protecting economies from robber-baron ruth-lessness— making fortunes by destruction
3. Not com-mitting adultery	Not adul-terating relations by using them for self-gratification	Defending the integrity of relations frees us to develop them in line with their original purpose.	Protecting exchange for mutual benefit, so that it isn't exploited for greed

Statement of Commandments	Strategy for protecting freedom	Impact on freedom and evolution	Strategy for protecting economies
4. Not stealing	Not fragmenting systems by stealing from them— not taking more than we give	Give-and-take relations evolve stronger systems, which free everyone to be more creative in them.	Protecting economies from economic slavery, which stealing creates
5. Not bearing false witness against others	Protecting mutual respect by not reducing humanity to static characterizations	Bearing witness to our shared development frees others to keep developing, both individually and collectively.	Protecting economies from Callicles' cynicism, while assisting others in their growth
6. Not coveting	Not getting attached to wanting what others have, since this undermines self-respect	Not coveting frees us to develop our individuality, to cast our own mold, to follow the true self.	Protecting economies from boom-and-bust cycles by adhering to individual standards

Chapter 8

The Beatitudes:
Responses that Empower

🚦🚦🚦🚦🚦🚦🚦

I. What's in our power and what isn't?

W hat's our role in shaping experience? One school of thought claims that we have no control over life. Some larger process—God, heredity, brain chemistry, or the environment—determines our behavior. Others insist that we have complete control, that our minds create everything.

The middle position sees a network of factors, some of which we can change, others not. Epictetus, the Roman Stoic philosopher, summarized this view in his famous opening to *The Enchiridion*: "There are things which are within our power, and there are things which are beyond our power."[1] Distinguishing between the two, Epictetus explained, makes our efforts more efficient. We work on changing what's within our power and don't waste our energies on what's not.

"Within our power," he explained, "are opinion, aim, desire, aversion, and, in a word, whatever affairs are our own."[2] That is, we control what we do with our minds and character. We choose how to pursue knowledge and how to apply it. We choose which qualities to develop in ourselves. Most of all, we choose our philosophies.

That's good news, since our philosophical choices affect everything else. Philosophies orchestrate what's in our power. They guide how we manage all the stuff that's ours to change. In the end, they're our greatest power.

But experience involves more than individual philosophies. Collective factors have an influence. No single world view controls an entire economy. Because many different people and cultures make up economies, all kinds of assumptions, strategies, and responses go into shaping them. While it's within our power to develop our own philosophy, it's beyond our power to do this for anyone else.

In fact, what lies beyond our power includes all kinds of factors: physical and mental, social and cultural, collective and universal. "Beyond our power," Epictetus wrote, "are body, property, reputation, office, and, in a word, whatever are not properly our own affairs."[3] That we have a body, that we share a culture and history, that we live in space and time, that the new fall television lineup doesn't look that great, or that we all have to deal with more or less the same goofy, archetypal consciousness—all these factors lie beyond our power. Ultimately, reality itself lies beyond our power. We can't change God.

Experience and our response to it

How do the two spheres relate? Since what's beyond our power doesn't jump to fit us, we adapt to it. But there are many ways of adapting. Our philosophies help us choose among the options. They set us up to interact with reality one way or another.

How good are our philosophies' choices? Experience gives us a rough idea. It tests the philosophy-reality fit. Different philosophies give rise to different worlds. The character of these worlds shows just what our philosophies are worth—whether they've mapped reality well or badly.

That's where the third philosophical tool comes in. Since philosophies lie within our power to change, we're not stuck with one choice. Whereas experience presents the interface between what's within our power and what's not, how we respond to experience alters the character of that interface.

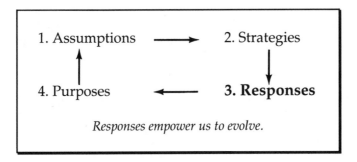

Responses empower us to evolve.

If, for instance, our philosophies are well constructed, responses cash them in and make them practical. They put good philosophies to good use.

If, however, our philosophies aren't working, we can change them. We can rewrite the philosophical scripts that we play out in life. Improving things, then, means not only fixing breakdowns but also changing the philosophies that create them. Through our responses, we have the power to revise both our philosophies and our worlds.

Extending our power

Distinguishing what lies within our power from what lies beyond it is a good start. It channels our efforts to where they have the greatest impact. We don't waste our energies on things that aren't within our power to change.

But the distinction isn't as clear-cut as Epictetus would have us think. He cited body, property, and reputation as lying beyond our power. Yet none of these are entirely beyond our control. If we eat nothing but junk food, the body suffers. If we cut down all the rain forests, we have neither them nor the ecological balance they sustain. If we lie and cheat, no one wants to do business with us. If these things are within our power to harm, they're also within our power to improve.

Physical disciplines (yoga or medicine, for instance) aim to bring the body's condition more within our power. Business skills show how to bring financial matters more under our control. Technology says that it brings nature under our control (though we're having second thoughts about whether this control is better than nature's). Psychiatry and therapy strive to bring our minds and emotions more under our control. Manners and morals bring our relationships more under our control. In general, the advance of civilization extends what's in our power. With development, what once seemed beyond our influence is no longer so.

Because power increases our control over experience, we'd naturally like to extend what's in our power further. But there's a snag. Extending power not through development but as a separate pursuit creates bad responses and worse worlds.

Designing responses only to maximize power disregards the inward growth that's needed to use power wisely. Though we gain power, we don't grasp its responsibilities or the dangers inherent in its misuse.

We have the power to split the atom, for instance, but we're still evolving the philosophy and character needed to use the power wisely. Politicians swim in power, but that's no guarantee they'll exercise it for the public good. Drug lords acquire cash-power by the billions, but the way they use their power, not to mention how they gain it, hasn't made the world a better place. On its own, power lacks the context that makes its use constructive.

Ironically, responses aimed solely at extending power create worlds out of control. That's precisely what we've experienced with the nuclear-weapons world, the political world, and the drug world. The more power we seize, the less we have. The greater our sphere of power, the more we have to fortify it against whatever lies beyond it, so that the balance in our favor isn't threatened. We consume power just trying to keep power. Realizing this, we respond by creating closed systems—fortresses, company towns, monopolies, or blocs of nations—since only within closed systems can we establish certain dominance.

But even there, the dominance-response isn't successful. It ignores the dynamics of evolution, namely, the now-familiar fact that closed systems don't evolve; they run down. We exercise absolute power over something that's dying—what fun. Moreover, what's beyond our power threatens the closed powerdom. In fortresses and company towns, there's always the chance of a siege or a revolt. We can never be certain that something won't happen to restructure the closed system.

Maximizing power without also maximizing spiritual growth forms the dark end of the spectrum of responses. But the response takes us down a road that's not even successful on its own terms. We don't end up empowered.

Spiritual power

Evolution and power, like evolution and freedom, work together. Real power doesn't come without development, and development doesn't occur without empowerment. The power that spiritual evolution brings, though, isn't the same as the kind that can be seized.

Seizable power deals in partial orders. A seize-response works to control a person, group, resource, or market. It seeks power over a specific realm—a family or a constituency, a nation or a conglomerate. It carves out a territory and tries to dominate it. Assuming a fragmented universe and using fragmenting strategies, seize-responses manipulate the fragments to gain power over them.

Spiritual power, though, is something else. It's not seizable, and it doesn't go around seizing. It grows with development. In the first place, spiritual power operates from different premises. It assumes that real power is of the whole, much as power in any system resides in the whole system, not in detached parts of it. Power comes from the same source as evolution: "from above." (John 19:11) "Power belongs to God." (Psalms 62:11, NEB)

In the second place, the strategy for acquiring it is different. It's no use trying to break off bits of the whole's power, since what we'd end up with wouldn't be whole-empowered. It wouldn't carry the same force, because it would be cut off from its origin. A wave cut off from the ocean would only give us a puddle, something a puppy can do.

Instead, the way to grow in spiritual power is to align ourselves with its source—to work at one with the whole. Rather than jockeying to possess power, we can choose responses that invite spiritual growth, so that we blend with reality's workings. We and reality operate as one. Who has how much power ceases to be an issue: the model becomes obsolete. There's just the power of the whole at work, which we get better at working with.

At least, that's roughly how spiritual teachings view power. Taoist philosophy, for instance, differentiates the two types of power. One type is aggressive and seeks to dominate. It works contrary to the Tao (the whole) and fails as a result. The other is achieved by the sage, who acts in harmony with the Tao and so works inconspicuously. The sage doesn't impose a will of his own, yet by working with the whole, all things are accomplished. In the central Taoist text, the *Tao Te Ching*, the book (ching) of the whole (Tao) and its virtue-power (te), states:

> He who assists the ruler with Tao does not dominate the world with force.
> The use of force usually brings requital.
> Wherever armies are stationed, briers and thorns grow . . .
> A good general achieves his purpose and stops.
> But dares not seek to dominate the world. . . .
> Whatever is contrary to Tao will soon perish.[4]

Also:

> Tao is eternal and has no name.
> Though its simplicity seems insignificant, none in the world can master it.
> If kings and barons would hold on to it, all things would submit to them spontaneously.[5]

The Taoist conception of power is also Jesus'. In John's Gospel, for instance, Jesus describes his power not as a private possession but as a result of his unity with God:

> My Father worketh hitherto, and I work. (John 5:17)
> The Son can do nothing of himself, but what he seeth the Father do: for what things soever he doeth, these also doeth the Son likewise. (5:19)
> I can of mine own self do nothing: as I hear, I judge: and my judgment is just; because I seek not mine own will, but the will of the Father which hath sent me. (5:30)

The Beatitudes: choosing spiritual growth

Naturally, spiritual power calls for continual transformation on our part, since we're much more accustomed to muddling through as separate and detached creatures. Seeking the will of the Father or holding to the Tao takes some doing. For example, working at one with the whole requires that we understand how the whole works. It also requires that we restrain the inclination to work any other way.

That's where responses come in. We need responses that keep our transformation going.

The Beatitudes (Matthew 5:3–12) map such responses. Blessed responses are those that support spiritual growth. They choose inward development over power-seeking and so keep us moving toward the end of the spectrum where true power lies. *Choosing spiritual growth* is therefore the first movement of each Beatitude.

Not that the Beatitudes' responses leave us disempowered. They're not advocating a "slave morality" of weakness and submission, as 19th-century philosopher Friedrich Nietzsche claimed. With the Beatitudes, Jesus explains what real power is, what it takes to get it, and how we can tap its source from where we are now.

Empowerment is, in fact, the second movement of each Beatitude—the reward side. Choosing development increases our power to work in harmony with the whole. It also empowers us to break patterns that put us at odds with it. By choosing spiritual growth, we're empowered to develop all the more, which means we're empowered to work more at one with God.

Whole-seeking responses empower us more than any other response could, because they move us into new dimensions of power. With development, we respond to experience from higher levels. Jesus' life, for instance, changed history. The power he exercised gave him mastery over every aspect of life, from healing the sick and stilling storms to finding tax-money in a fish's mouth.

If Jesus' power is real power, and if that's the kind we want to be empowered by, then development is the way to get it. But how? Which responses empower us spiritually? Which invite development?

II. Choosing spiritual growth empowers

1) *Being poor in spirit*

The first Beatitude describes a response that's necessary to begin any development: "Blessed are the poor in spirit: for their's is the kingdom of heaven." (5:3) "Poor in spirit" doesn't mean dimwitted or emotionally wiped out. The phrase translates as "those who feel their spiritual need" (Gspd), "those who sense spiritual poverty" (Ber) and are "humble-minded" (Phi).[6]

The Beatitudes begin with something close to Socrates' response: acknowledging that we don't know. If we're aware of our need for spiritual growth, the first Beatitude says, then we'll be more open to inward change as we go along. We won't feel we have to defend where we are. Instead, we'll be ready to let go of assumptions and strategies that aren't helping us anymore, so that we can evolve beyond them. We'll be "humble-minded" before ultimate reality and before what we can become.

A Zen story illustrates the poor-in-spirit response by contrasting it with the opposite, a mind filled with its own notions:

> Nan-in, a Japanese master during the Meiji era (1868–1912), received a university professor who came to inquire about Zen. Nan-in served tea. He poured his visitor's cup full, and then kept on pouring. The professor watched the overflow until he no longer could restrain himself. "It is overfull. No more will go in!" "Like this cup," Nan-in said, "you are full of your own opinions and speculations. How can I show you Zen unless you first empty your cup?"[7]

The reward for an open response is simple: openness invites growth. By responding with the inward emptiness of Taoist and Buddhist teachings, we use what's in our power to explore the reality that lies beyond our concepts:

"for their's is the kingdom of heaven." Responding with emptiness of mind opens us to possibilities we haven't thought of. It opens us to the universe we don't know. We're rewarded with the power to gain a new vision—to see things in the light of the whole, or at least in a wider perspective.

By contrast, the professor's response robs us of power, because it diminishes our ability to think and to evolve our concepts. If we respond with opinions that aren't open for examination and revision, we stop thinking. The ideas we live by lose their vitality and harden into dogmas. We stuff the pantry with old, dried-out junk.

Worse, the old junk gains power over us. Dogmas maneuver us into worlds that are closed conceptually— where the deft use of terms edges out real thought. Labels ("capitalism," "communism," "liberal," "conservative") and technospeak ("securitization," "indexed arbitrage," or "revenue enhancement") intimidate us into not asking obvious questions. In the kingdoms of label-mongering and official gobbledygook, there's no room for creative thought. In fact, there's not much room for thought at all.

Yet behind all these terms lie very simple, basic issues. A poor-in-spirit response opens us to see them. It empowers us to look beyond the castoff shells of thought (the words and jargon) and to grapple with the deep issues— those that count in the big picture and expose problems at their root.

That's the challenge for economies. Allowing experts to reduce economies to technical definitions hasn't enhanced our power to reshape economic experience. It's made us prisoners to the jargon and to those who are good at tossing it around. A jungle of complicated dogmas obscures the very issues that are in our power to change: issues of philosophy, of development, and of character. We end up feeling helpless before blind, economic forces, when really the helplessness comes from professorial, theory-laden responses.

**1. "Blessed are the poor in spirit:
for their's is the kingdom of heaven."**

Spiritual growth:		*Economies:*	
Responses that empower		*Responses that empower*	
Being open to growth and aware of our need of it	empowers us to think and to evolve our concepts.	Opening economies to the influence of ideas	empowers us to reshape economic experience.

But openness itself is more than a word. To empty the cup, the first Beatitude calls for the second.

2) Mourning

Concepts that are closed aren't just passively dogmatic. They're an outright nuisance. Their limits begin to pinch, until we're finally forced to slough them off. But the process can be traumatic. We mourn the wrenching that separation involves. Fortunately, the Beatitudes promise a reward: "Blessed are they that mourn: for they shall be comforted." (5:4)

Mourning isn't only grief. J. B. Phillips, for example, translates the Greek phrase as "knowing what sorrow means." Mourning occurs when we leave behind patterns of thought or life (beliefs, relations, attitudes, or activities) that, for one reason or another, no longer serve growth.

Why, then, do we mourn them? Because the old ways are familiar, and letting them go means adjusting to something new. We'd rather have both. We'd like to go forward as well as keep everything the same. That's not asking too much, is it?

According to the Buddha, though, having it both ways won't work. The Noble Truths, as we've seen, state that suffering arises from attachment to things that are impermanent. For a time, the attachments help. Forms serve as vehicles for development. But after a while, we need new vehicles. Bonds loosen and shift to reflect the changes going on in us. If we try to keep things the same, we suffer from the wrenching.

It's like the relation between a chick and its shell. At first the shell protects the chick. But as the chick grows, the shell gets too small. If the chick doesn't break the shell, it dies. The very thing that protects the chick's growth will kill it. Not that the shell turns against the chick or becomes evil. Nor does the chick do something wrong that the shell gets in its way. The relation changes because the chick keeps on growing.

Development goes through similar chick-and-shell rhythms: initial attachment to useful shells, followed by growth and gradual separation from them, leading to new attachments and new separations. Knowing the rhythm makes it easier to go with it. Attachment is easy. Detachment—letting go—is trickier.

On one hand, if we try to stay inside shells too long, the attachment causes more pain. The bond tightens and is harder to break. On the other hand, if we drop the shell too soon, we lose its protection while we're still a yolk. Detaching too soon is as dangerous as staying attached too long.

The ideal response lets evolution determine when to let shells help us and when to let them go.

The comfort (the reward) is that we go forward. By choosing spiritual development—by mourning vehicles once they've served their role—we move with evolution, which empowers us to keep evolving. Our power isn't to seize vehicles and to hang on to them. Rather, it's the greater power not to depend on one vehicle or another. Valuing development more than its vehicles, we gain, as Phillips renders it, the "courage and comfort" to go on.

Economies grow through the same rhythm. Economic vehicles—jobs, associates, duties, abilities, and demands—come and go. We can't be sure of staying in one economic arrangement for life. Factors beyond our control mandate change. The more we respond by developing knowledge and talents, the better off we are. We're empowered to move with growth more easily and not to be thrown by changes that aren't in our power to stop.

Industries aren't exempt from the rhythm, either. We all know, for example, that fossil fuels are environmentally costly and that the time to find new energy sources is running out fast. Yet the energy industry's attachments to established forms—from existing technologies and factories and the fortunes made from them to the furnace in the basement and the engine in the car—make it harder for the industry to be enthusiastic about alternatives. So much would have to change. Unfortunately, the longer it postpones transition, the more disruptive the transition will be.

On a broader scale, no single economic theory provides a panacea for solving economic problems. Free markets, taxes, tariffs, interest rates, and control of the money supply—the familiar devices—shape economies in ways that are sometimes useful, sometimes harmful. Several decades ago, for instance, government spending buoyed up lagging economies. Now it threatens to bury them in debt. Different concepts serve as tools in the rhythm of development, without any one of them being the final solution to economic ills.

But the rhythm also touches the evolution of our broad, economic awareness. Chapter 2 traced a progression from matter to energy to information to consciousness. Feudal economies build on matter and energy. They fight wars to see who can own the land and control the resources. But information and consciousness introduce economies with dynamics quite different from the old fight-and-dominate tactics. By letting go of feudal forms, we don't increase our power within feudal models. Instead, we exercise the far greater power to transcend them and to evolve new forms.

**2. "Blessed are they that mourn:
for they shall be comforted."**

Spiritual growth:		*Economies:*	
Responses that empower		*Responses that empower*	
Valuing development more than its vehicles	empowers us not to depend on forms but to keep evolving.	Not getting stuck in one economic form	empowers us to adapt as economies change.

3) Responding with meekness

One reason we avoid letting forms go, though, is that we're afraid of losing our identity. Billiard-ball maps tell us that we're defined by specific roles and functions, specific things. Losing these things means losing a portion of ourselves. When we retire, for instance, we're no longer the lawyer, the teacher, or the vice-president who manages the East Coast division; we're the "retired" person who walks the dog and watches the grandchildren. We've lost something of ourselves, or so we fear.

The third Beatitude, however, treats egos differently: "Blessed are the meek: for they shall inherit the earth." (5:5) The Beatitude doesn't put egos up front, because it doesn't regard egos as who we ultimately are.

Egos aren't static things, like brass hatracks, that we hang experiences on. Self-images are vehicles for moving with the growth process—vehicles that change as the process goes along. They're shells that protect us until, like the chick, we're ready to break through to the next step.

Egos and identity, then, aren't the same. Identity refers to what's constant in life—to what persists throughout change. Egos aren't that. We don't have the same ego at fifty that we had at fifteen (at least we hope we don't). Even day to day, we don't have the same perceptions, aims, and desires. No one does. *Egos* are impermanent vehicles that we use for discovering our *identity*, which comes from our relation to the whole. We use egos to explore our spiritual self—the identity we have from God.

To ground us on something constant while we're doing our higher-self discovering, the third Beatitude places spiritual evolution at the center of experience. What's constant, then, isn't a given self-image but the spiritual development that transcends self-images and transforms them. Day to day, it's not egos but the process of changing egos that persists. The process is the constant that runs throughout experiences.

Meekness opens us to this process. It gauges our responses according to what's happening in spiritual growth. It values self-concepts for what they are, namely, vehicles for action, channels for learning. Responding with meekness puts the process before the images, growth before egos.

The reward is that meekness empowers development. We don't get frozen in one mold—stuck in one shell—but discover more of our true identity: the meek "inherit the earth." The third day of creation used the earth to symbolize the identity we have from the whole. Meekness empowers us to take hold of this identity. It empowers us to "inherit" who we are in the widest possible context.

If, however, responses turn around fixed egos, growth stops. We do things for ego-reasons and work to satisfy ego-desires. We don't master the vehicle that the ego gives us; it masters us. Ego-desires and ego-insecurities run us around. Worse, we lose sight of our ability to be different. We end up laboring under one self-image—living in one shell.

But what about economies? A response of meekness is fine for personal development, but does it work in the marketplace as well? Not if we're to believe the cliches: "Every man for himself," "Look out for number one," or "If you don't defend your interests, nobody else will." As handy as the clichés are—and as inspiring as it is to live by them—they don't tackle the real question: in economies, what response works better than meekness?

The question takes us back to what economies are all about in the first place: they blend specific interests for the betterment of all. Economies give us a chance to develop our talents and to share them with others, so that we can manage our individual and collective households better.

Meekness serves this activity in a way that selfish responses can't. Instead of putting egos first in economic exchange, meekness considers the totality of the situation. It manages the household as a dynamic community of interests. To this end, meekness keeps our attention on the job at hand and away from the egos involved.

If we listen to the clichés, we think only saints use meekness. But it's really how good businesses run all the time. Good entrepreneurs, managers, salespeople, and workers keep their minds not on themselves but on markets, the competition, clients, customers, and the quality of the work or product. There's enough to think about in managing a business or doing a job without getting bogged down in ego-problems.

Responding from egos, by contrast, gums up economies with *extra-economic concerns*—concerns that don't have anything to do with managing the household but only with soothing ego-insecurities or satisfying ego-ambitions. Everything turns around egos.

On an everyday level, responses shift from enhancing efficiency, quality, safety, and service (economic concerns) to gaining clout, flexing power, or increasing salaries, bonuses, status, and perks (ego-concerns). Egos aren't used as vehicles for improving household management; household management becomes a vehicle for gratifying egos.

In the end, ego-responses don't empower us. Using them, we don't inherit earth but Eden—a pleasure garden soured by the passion to become as gods. In fact, ego-responses neutralize what's in our power. They try to satisfy inner needs (which lie within our power) with outer manipulations (which don't).

It doesn't work for either side, inner or outer. Outward gains don't quiet ego-fears or sate their appetites. The scale of anxieties and wants simply goes up.

Economies, on the other hand, need management according to objective, economic criteria. That means making decisions according to what's good not only for ourselves but also for the community and the earth. Extra-economic factors, such as satisfying greed, shift attention away from these objective criteria. Ego-responses deprive economies of the balanced judgment they need to prosper. Neither we nor our economies end up empowered. We're all made lackeys to the damned egos.

3. "Blessed are the meek:
for they shall inherit the earth."

Spiritual growth:		*Economies:*	
Responses that empower		*Responses that empower*	
Using spiritual growth as what's constant	empowers us to inherit who we are from the whole.	Acting according to the community of interests	empowers us to manage economies objectively.

4) Hungering and thirsting after righteousness

But even if our responses fall short of the ideals that openness, nonattachment, and meekness describe, we can always change them. That's the response of the fourth Beatitude: "Blessed are they which do hunger and thirst after righteousness: for they shall be filled." (5:6)

It sounds great. Even if we and our economies goof up, we can just seek righteousness, and we'll have it.

The problem is, we've tried this, and it didn't work. We've tried to do the right thing (if that's what "hungering after righteousness" means), and everything didn't turn out as we hoped (if that's what being filled with it means). Besides, we can't be righteous all day. We have to take care of jobs, children, houses, and, of course, cars.

But that's not what the fourth Beatitude is talking about. Hungering and thirsting after righteousness is a philosophical response that applies to everything we do. It means choosing spiritual growth consistently and using everything to serve that growth.

We don't get nearer righteousness, for example, if we treat spiritual growth like a hobby. It's not like knitting or pedaling on an exercise bike. Revising the philosophies we live by and being transformed by the process is as much a discipline as becoming a chemist, athlete, or artist—even more, since the process doesn't stop with a Ph.D. or a peak performance. It's something that goes throughout life and touches every aspect of it.

Not that our responses always have to be right in order to seek righteousness. We'd be sunk if they did. Rather, hungering and thirsting after righteousness means choosing responses that bring us *nearer* the right.

The first three Beatitudes help us along. If we're open and self-critical, we're more able to recognize mistakes when they occur (the first Beatitude). Then, if we're prepared to let attachments go (the second Beatitude) and humble enough to act in the interests of development (the third Beatitude), we'll be able to correct whatever has gone amiss. Disciplined responses extend our power not to *be* right but to *approximate* the right—to seek righteousness.

Using the Beatitudes' responses consistently, we get a better idea of what righteousness means: "for they shall be filled." The discipline of seeking righteousness extends our power to work with reality. We and reality move more in harmony. One power operates.

But what happens when things don't accord with righteousness, especially if it's someone else goofing up instead of us? Though we're all for righteousness—imagine a television editorial coming out against it—aren't we stuck meeting evil with evil, injustice with injustice? If something bad threatens us, aren't we forced to meet the bad on its own terms—to use bad methods to protect ourselves and to re-establish what's right?

What's wrong with this response is that it negates our power to go forward. We can't seek righteousness in a consistent way, if we're stopping to do a few necessary evils along the way. Fragmented responses don't help solve problems in more whole-seeking ways. They keep us on the same level as the evils we're fighting. By meeting evils with evils, we add to evils.

It's as if everyone who had an auto accident abandoned the rules of the road, because their good driving habits hadn't prevented mishaps. We wouldn't be more safe. So, too, the fact that there's injustice everywhere doesn't disprove the practicality of choosing justice; it underscores the need for it. A plague of injustices isn't a time to despair of hungering and thirsting after righteousness. It's a time to seek it all the more by challenging the responses that create injustices in the first place.

The fourth Beatitude's response is equally important for economies. Choosing growth consistently, instead of responding in fragmented and fragmenting ways, extends our economic power. It empowers economies and everyone in them.

The difference between investment and speculation illustrates. Investment represents a steady, long-term commitment to economic growth. In good times and bad, investors support the development of businesses. In turn, businesses contribute to the economy and create new jobs.

Everyone gains as a result. Investors empower entrepreneurs to put their talents and skills to good use, while the entrepreneurs' successes benefit the investors. By supporting development no matter what, the system of investment extends each individual's power to take part in economies. The discipline strengthens economic exchange, creating a system that empowers everyone both to contribute to the economy and to benefit from it.

By contrast, market speculation does the opposite. By playing markets for super-fast gains, speculators make an already risky endeavor more dangerous. They reap profits that others' long-term commitment to growth made possible. Sooner or later, investors stop investing in a system that's riddled with pirates, while the entrepreneurs, burned or bankrupt, watch their capital dry up. All parties lose the power they could have had if their responses had been consistent in supporting economic growth.

In other words, because economies always function as systems, they need disciplined responses—responses that are shaped not by an unquenchable thirst for more but by the objective demands of economic systems. As in the case of investing, responses committed to stable economic growth make economies prosper and put them on the road to economic justice. We use what's in our power to create systems that enhance everyone's power to develop. That's what economies are for.

4. "Blessed are they which do hunger and thirst after righteousness: for they shall be filled."

Spiritual growth:		*Economies:*	
Responses that empower		*Responses that empower*	
Choosing growth consistently to approximate righteousness	empowers us to unite with power's source.	Consistently supporting genuine economic growth	empowers us to evolve economies that are both prosperous and just.

5) *Responding with mercy*

But it's hard to be completely consistent in choosing growth, whether spiritually or economically. It's hard not to wish we'd done a few things differently.

Odd as it sounds, though, present ills don't come from past indiscretions. At least, they don't come from the indiscretions themselves. Present problems come from responses that allow the past to dominate the present.

Justifying the past, for instance, perpetuates it, multiplying its effects into the future. Ignoring the past is just as bad. The response doesn't allow us to learn from the past, which means we're likely to repeat it.

The fifth Beatitude's response breaks the cycle: "Blessed are the merciful: for they shall obtain mercy." (5:7)

Mercy weighs all experiences according to spiritual growth. What we call successes and failures aren't pluses and minuses written in some cosmic black book. They're episodes in development. The plus-minus labels are stuck on. Experiences themselves relate to growth.

Accordingly, a merciful response values past experiences by using them for development. Instead of holding the past against us, a merciful response empowers us to learn from experiences and to go on. We progress cleanly, without the weight of past errors holding us back.

The response has a thoroughly liberating effect: we "obtain mercy." Mercy brings mercy. It empowers us to do things differently and to leave the past behind.

Economies can use mercy. If we respond to them as if the future were governed by past methods, we make sure that future economies will simply replay those of the past, albeit with a few variations—like tossing around "billions" and "trillions" the way we used to think about "thousands" and "millions." The past becomes an excuse for not changing the methods we use to manage our households.

Not surprisingly, unmerciful philosophies tell us that recessions and depressions, wars and poverty are inevitable. But that's not much help. The responses that such philosophies give us aren't empowering. If we assume that economies can't change, we don't even attempt to manage them differently. We don't use our responses to revise our philosophies of economies. Our power sits there unused, while our economies get stuck in reruns.

That's not good news for the future. Denying ourselves the power to manage economies differently means denying ourselves the power to meet new challenges—the fun stuff we read about everyday: a house-of-cards financial system, an ecological time bomb, or a nuclear technology that makes war not the "solution" it once seemed.

Again, mercy breaks the cycle. It says that the choice to go forward lies in our power. Grace gives us the options; mercy frees us to take them. The fact that we've invested decades, even centuries, in one set way of doing business doesn't mean that we have to devote more time to it once we're ready to go beyond it. Mercy makes the weight of the past inconsequential compared to the promise of development.

As a result, the same mercy that liberates us renews our economies. A merciful response obtains mercy: both we and our economies are empowered to evolve.

5. "Blessed are the merciful: for they shall obtain mercy."

Spiritual growth:		Economies:	
Responses that empower		Responses that empower	
Weighing experiences according to spiritual growth	empowers us to leave the past behind.	Not binding economies to past methods	empowers us to tackle future challenges.

6) Pure in heart

As mercy frees us from past habits, we start afresh. The response purifies us of the baggage we're outgrowing, so that we interact with reality more as it is: "Blessed are the pure in heart: for they shall see God." (5:8)

The heart was once considered the seat of consciousness. "Pure in heart" suggests a consciousness that's bent on understanding the whole—on seeking reality as it ultimately is, beyond how it appears from one perspective or another.

To approximate this ideal, a pure-in-heart response continually rethinks its philosophies. It doesn't push one philosophy as the ultimate. Nor does it make arbitrary judgments about which philosophy is the right one. The response is pure in heart in that it seeks a progressively clearer, more comprehensive understanding of reality unconditionally. It sets its sights on what is, and it isn't picky about what that turns out to be.

The response empowers us to "see God." Seeing God doesn't mean finding the one, absolutely right set of symbols or truths, either. It means evolving our understanding of reality, so that we glimpse reality more as it is wholly instead of only in bits and pieces. Our philosophies develop a clearer picture of the central order, which keeps partial orders in perspective. Cutting through the debris, we see more of what is.

Impure responses, by contrast, prejudge reality's total nature by reducing it to one aspect or fragment. Out of the totality, reductionist responses focus on a narrow band to the exclusion of everything else.

According to materialists, for instance, the observable, measurable world (rocks, insects, bones, and labs) exists; everything else doesn't. That's fine if we want to study rocks, insects, and bones in our laboratories. It's just not so fine as a philosophy of life, since there's more to life than these things.

According to mentalists, reality is the human mind and its perceptions: "I think it, therefore it's true," or "I feel it, therefore it's real." Whatever doesn't enter our minds doesn't count. The private, subjective realm becomes the whole world. For those who practice this kind of reductionism, the inward realm soon becomes a burden. We feel responsible for everything that happens, good or bad, whether it's actually in our power or not.

According to absolutists, whether of religion or science, reality boils down to a few absolute statements: e.g., "All is one," "Jesus is our savior," "Everything is random," or "Chemistry, biology, and engineering explain all of human life and civilization." Whatever fails to conform to these statements has neither meaning nor validity. We lose our power to think intelligently about spheres that don't fit the blanket statements.

These responses aren't pure, because they place hidden agendas between us and reality. Thanks to them, we don't respond to reality as it is but as the agendas describe it. The narrow band receives too much attention, while every other dimension receives too little. Reductionist agendas carve up reality. It's not just that we see only bits and pieces. What's impure is the claim that the partial orders are all there is. We're not allowed to see the whole.

The response disempowers us, because it limits our ability to cope with the totality that we face. Though we gain power over the narrow band, we're powerless to deal intelligently with anything else. Impure responses don't reintegrate their insights with larger worlds, because they don't acknowledge that larger worlds exist. Blind to the whole, reductionist responses use knowledge in ways that are dangerous—destructive to integral systems.

Economies are among the casualties. Reducing economies to self-interest, profits, competition, or resources, for
example, leaves out the larger reasons for economies, as
well as the values that make them work. Both economies
and our responses to them become one-dimensional. This
doesn't mean that self-interest, profits, competition, and
resources aren't important. They simply aren't the only
factors worth considering.

In fact, reducing economies to one factor makes otherwise legitimate concerns impure. The factor's importance
gets warped relative to everything else. Legitimate self-
interest, for example, gets warped into selfishness, profit-
making turns into greed, competition degenerates into
mob methods, while limits on resources become a justi-
fication for jungle law.

We lose power, because impure responses reduce our
power to maximize more than one thing. By trying to
maximize one factor, we minimize everything else, which
throws the system out of balance. In the end, even the one
factor suffers, because it can't stand on its own.

The response that's pure in heart treats economies as
whole systems. It strives to see the whole by balancing *all*
the factors that pertain to it. Instead of pushing one aspect
at the expense of the rest, a comprehensive response deals
with economies more as they are, without reductionist
filters distorting them.

The pure-in-heart response empowers us to reshape
our economies. By understanding more of the factors that
make economies what they are—human systems for meeting human needs within an earth-environment that has
needs and systems of its own—we build economies that
are sound and that benefit the worlds in which they exist.

The result is that our response to economies becomes
more effective—more real—in that we see the totality,

all the factors involved. Seeing the whole, we're less likely to choose responses that do violence to any aspect.

6. "Blessed are the pure in heart: for they shall see God."

Spiritual growth:		Economies:	
Responses that empower		Responses that empower	
Seeking reality as it is, instead of pushing one philosophy	empowers us to see the totality.	Not reducing economies to one factor (money, profits, etc.)	empowers us to maximize all the factors involved.

7) Peacemaking

But how do we deal with violence and conflict—the inevitable fruits of reductionist responses—when they do occur? The seventh Beatitude maps a response: "Blessed are the peacemakers: for they shall be called the children of God." (5:9)

So far, nations—and people, too—have made peace by meeting violence with violence or at least by threatening to do so. Whoever is the stronger keeps the peace by either smashing or threatening to smash anyone who challenges them. That was the role, for instance, of the "Peacekeeper" missiles. Most likely, this isn't the peacemaking that Jesus had in mind.

Whatever peacemaking means—and institutes and colleges now study it as a science—it starts with a response that looks beyond aggression to the philosophies that incite it. We're not aggressive just for the fun of it. It takes too much energy. As psychologists explain, we're aggressive because we're afraid.

This is useful. By tracing aggression back to fears, we can bring the fears out into the open to see if they're legitimate and to find out what we can do about them. To start, we can investigate the philosophies that give rise to the fears.

Fears start on simple levels. We're afraid of not having enough food, of being harmed, or of not being able to live comfortably with those we love. From there, the fears get complicated. We're afraid that our stocks won't perform, that our competitors will take over the market, or that our children won't succeed in the right college or profession. Philosophies jump in to tell us why we're afraid and how we should respond to these fears.

The trouble is, not all philosophies are helpful. Junk philosophies, in trying to show us how to meet one set of fears, add new ones.

A philosophy may tell us, for instance, that everyone is out to get what we've got. The adrenalin starts pumping. Another one will stand the hair up on our necks with the scarcity line: we live in a world of unlimited desires competing for limited resources, creating winners and losers, haves and have-nots. With the adrenalin high and our neck hair poised, we'll be told that being aggressive is the way to defend our interests. With this outlook, it's a wonder there's not more conflict in the world than there is.

If we buy conflict-philosophies, it's pointless to say we shouldn't fight. The philosophies leave us no alternative. We can, though, question the philosophies. If everyone isn't out for what we have, if scarcity isn't the bugbear it seems, and if being aggressive isn't the best way of doing business—after all, we don't have to use brass knuckles to get the groceries—then the fears that push us into conflict are baseless. The conflict-response turns out to be a waste of energy.

We're back to the power of revising philosophies. If we choose not to react to aggression but to revise the philosophies that create it, we're peacemakers on deep levels. The peace-response empowers us to go beyond fears by going beyond the philosophies that generate them. Once we do that, making war or reacting through conflict becomes pointless. It's not worth the trouble.

In the Beatitude's words, the response empowers us to unite as "children of God." Children of God behave as one family, born of one origin. They're not constantly at each other's throats. It's bad for the family's reputation. We're brought together, because we all share the same ultimate context, the ultimate parenthood that is God, and because we're engaged in the same ultimate process of spiritual growth. Instead of fighting over the differences that crop up along the way, it's better to use the differences to keep ourselves and our philosophies evolving.

The Beatitude's response makes peace in economies as well. Plenty of philosophies claim that business is war. Books on war have become best sellers in the business section. Attila's secrets are already out.[8] If the Visigoths and Vikings had tips on raiding and pillaging, they'd probably go to the top of the charts, too. When money is involved, it doesn't take much to get conflict going.

Peacemakers don't wander into the fray with white flag in hand, unless they're ready to be skewered by both sides. Instead, a peacemaking response goes back to the philosophies that say war is the best model for doing business. If the philosophies are wrong—if, for instance, they make false assumptions, use divisive strategies, or impose reductionist agendas—then the economic fears they incite aren't real but philosophy-created. They're not necessary. If the fears aren't necessary, then the conflict-responses aren't, either.

In fact, peacemaking responses empower us to regard economies quite differently. Economies can be powerful allies to peace, because they use differences as a basis for exchange. If we were all the same and possessed the same things, we wouldn't need economies. The fact that we're different makes economies interesting and fun, not to mention prosperous. It's why we have economies—to move our differences around.

Instead of fighting over differences, therefore, we can exchange them and profit from the exchange. Thomas Paine wrote, "Commerce . . . is a pacific system, operating to unite mankind by rendering nations, as well as individuals, useful to each other."[9]

That's the kind of economy that fits the "children of God": an economy that celebrates diversity and uses it to develop a deeper appreciation of unity. We each contribute something unique to an economy that's universal and that values each individual's uniqueness.

7. "Blessed are the peacemakers: for they shall be called the children of God."

Spiritual growth:		*Economies:*	
Responses that empower		*Responses that empower*	
Evolving beyond the philosophies that incite fears	empowers us to unite in spiritual growth.	Evolving beyond the philosophies that turn economies into wars	empowers us to exchange our differences and to use economies as agents of peace.

8) Overcoming persecution

Whereas the first seven Beatitudes map responses that support spiritual growth, the last says it's a good idea to stick to the Beatitudes' responses, no matter what:

> Blessed are they which are persecuted for righteousness' sake: for their's is the kingdom of heaven. Blessed are ye, when men shall revile you, and persecute you, and shall say all manner of evil against you falsely, for my sake. Rejoice, and be exceedingly glad: for great is your reward in heaven: for so persecuted they the prophets which were before you. (5:10–12)

If we could be certain that everyone everywhere would respond with (1) openness, (2) devotion to spiritual development, (3) meekness, (4) consistency in seeking the right, (5) mercy, (6) purity of heart, and (7) peacemaking, then we'd feel safe responding this way, too. But given things as they are, we're not convinced that such responses work.

The eighth Beatitude deals with this troublesome issue under the heading of persecution. Persecution, as we've all discovered, isn't limited to throwing Christians to lions or burning heretics at the stake. Persecution is usually much more subtle. It's whatever obstructs spiritual growth.

In general, persecution obstructs growth by locking us in closed worlds—the recurring threat to spiritual evolution. What closes worlds, though, isn't something physical. Like fears, closed worlds are philosophy-created. They're created by responses that:

1) fix concepts rigidly,

2) bind us to one vehicle of development,

3) make selfish concerns central,

4) thwart our quest for what's right,

5) perpetuate past wrongs,

6) impose hidden, reductionist agendas, and

7) manipulate us with unanalyzed, unquestioned fears.

Thanks to such responses, we feel trapped, frozen where we are. Growth seems impossible.

After a while, we're not even sure what growth means. The responses that the Beatitudes describe get turned upside down.

"Poor in spirit" comes to mean accepting whatever others tell us, especially if they're experts.

"Mourning" means fatalistically allowing the power-hungry to take what they want.

"Meek" means letting domineering egos roll over us.

"Hungering and thirsting after righteousness" means retreating to a cloister to escape the evil world.

"Merciful" means picking up stray dogs and making excuses for someone who's being obnoxious.

"Pure in heart" means at least looking holy, which can grow very tiresome.

But worst of all, "peacemaking" means letting aggressors chew us up and spit us out.

Thanks to persecution, the Beatitudes become exercises in impotence. They're reduced to enfeebling responses—just what Nietzsche claimed they were. We're disempowered, because we can't grow. We're stuck where we are.

The way out is to use the Beatitudes' responses to challenge the philosophies that disempower us. The eighth Beatitude maps a method: we protect growth by not abandoning the responses that bring growth.

This doesn't mean that we should wage war against closed philosophies or closed worlds. That's not what the Beatitudes' responses do. Instead, they simply flow around closed limits. They work like streams that wear away boulders, or grass that breaks through concrete—familiar images in Taoist philosophy. Spiritual growth is irrepressible. The Beatitudes' whole-seeking responses simply keep nudging us forward, until the closed philosophy is behind us, and we're off and on our way.

This eighth response, namely, of sticking with whole-seeking responses, empowers us to enter the "kingdom of heaven." Worlds open. We mutate beyond closed systems. Outwardly, we push back limits. Inwardly, we reclaim what's in our power and use it to evolve. As a result, we live open to reality, which is how the Beatitudes started. The eighth Beatitude leads back to the first. Choosing spiritual growth turns out to be the most powerful and empowering response. It makes the kingdom of heaven— infinite reality—ours to explore.

In economies, we're faced with persecution as well. There, persecution says we can't challenge destructive, shark-eat-shark responses. As long as the sharks infest economies, the Beatitudes' responses can't work. We're stuck with sharking: billiard-ball methods. Even if we'd like to behave differently, the shark school of business intimidates us into using responses that oppose mutually beneficial exchange and development.

But adopting shark-responses only escalates danger. If we have even a toe in the water, we can lose it to Jaws. Instead, the best way to avoid being eaten isn't to join the sharks at all but to get out of the water.

Getting out of the water means evolving our philosophies about economies and changing our responses to them. Persecution works only if we buy the notions that sharking reflects economic reality and that that's the way economies will always be. Once we show this isn't so by actually evolving our philosophies and methods, persecution becomes powerless. Our own evolution makes sharking obsolete.

8. "Blessed are they which are persecuted for righteousness' sake: for their's is the kingdom of heaven."

Spiritual growth:		*Economies:*	
Responses that empower		*Responses that empower*	
Not giving up on choosing spiritual growth	empowers us to break through closed worlds.	Continuing to evolve our philosophy of economies	empowers us to make billiard-ball methods (sharking) obsolete.

Whatever the Beatitudes are, they're *not* utopian. Their power doesn't depend on our having achieved perfection or already living in a perfect world. Jesus gave them for the world as it is. In fact, he gave them in a world even rougher and more brutal than ours.

The reasoning he used is simple: responses aligned to spiritual growth bring growth. Opposite responses make hell on earth. It's in our power to choose.

Choosing spiritual growth turns out to be the only realistic response. Waiting for utopia before we give the Beatitudes' responses a chance only guarantees that it will remain "no place"—etymologically, that's what "utopia" means. If, however, we adopt responses that effect evolution no matter where we are or what our situation is, we use what's in our power to move in a direction that's empowering. We evolve, taking our worlds with us.

With all this evolving, where are we going? What purposes guide our growth?

Responses that Empower

Spiritual growth:		*Economies:*	
Responses that empower		*Responses that empower*	
1. Being open to growth and aware of our need of it	empowers us to think and to evolve our concepts.	Opening economies to the influence of ideas	empowers us to reshape economic experience.
2. Valuing development more than its vehicles	empowers us not to depend on forms but to keep evolving.	Not getting stuck in one economic form	empowers us to adapt as economies change.
3. Using spiritual growth as what's constant	empowers us to inherit who we are from the whole.	Acting according to the community of interests	empowers us to manage economies objectively.
4. Choosing growth consistently to approximate righteousness	empowers us to unite with power's source.	Consistently supporting genuine economic growth	empowers us to evolve economies that are both prosperous and just.

Spiritual growth:		*Economies:*	
Responses that empower		*Responses that empower*	
5. Weighing experiences according to spiritual growth	empowers us to leave the past behind.	Not binding economies to past methods	empowers us to tackle future challenges.
6. Seeking reality as it is, instead of pushing one philosophy	empowers us to see the totality.	Not reducing economies to one factor (money, profits, etc.)	empowers us to maximize all the factors involved.
7. Evolving beyond the philosophies that incite fears	empowers us to unite in spiritual growth.	Evolving beyond the philosophies that turn economies into wars	empowers us to exchange our differences and to use economies as agents of peace.
8. Not giving up on choosing spiritual growth	empowers us to break through closed worlds.	Continuing to evolve our philosophy of economies	empowers us to make billiard-ball methods (sharking) obsolete.

Chapter 9

The Lord's Prayer:
The Purpose to Evolve

🔳🔳🔳🔳🔳🔳🔳

I. What's the purpose of purposes?

T hroughout this century, we've had trouble thinking about purposes. Somehow we couldn't decide where they fit within the grand scheme of things, or what purpose purposes serve. Do we get purposes from God, for instance, or do we make them up on our own? Are our purposes real and compelling, or are they private fictions that keep us busy in the meaningless void?

On one hand, we weren't convinced that God tells certain people to do certain things, such as raise millions of dollars or take hostages. On the other hand, we weren't keen on the notion that purposes are entirely our own creations and that, beyond our own devisings, there is no purpose.

It didn't help that some scientists early in the century decided that the universe has no purpose—something they concluded from studying atoms and stars, plasma and cockroaches. We think about purposes, they said, only because our chemical elements happen to combine in ways that create the illusion. On this view, the purpose of purposes is merely to keep our minds off the cold, hard fact that nothing ultimately matters. If we're tough-minded realists, we'll accept that we're nothing more than "Pigpens" of the "Peanuts" cartoons—moving clouds of aimless dust with only our goals as security blankets.

Purposes link us with reality

Granted, God isn't handing out assignments such as "run for President," "bomb that refugee village," or "beat the competition." But is the other view right, either? Are purposes entirely in our heads? True, we think them. They pass through our minds. But does that make them private fictions that have no relation to reality?

In the first place, because we don't live in a vacuum, the goals we pursue bear the stamp of outside factors. Education and social conditioning influence the aims we choose. If purposes were only subjective, wealth, fame, prestige, and power wouldn't exist as goals; each depends on external relations. In a one-person universe, none of these aims would mean anything.

In the second place, subjective purposes have objective consequences. They don't stay cooped up in our heads but spill over to the worlds around us. Families, businesses, economies, civilizations, even the earth itself feel their effects.

In the third place, reality is what it is. Though we can invent all kinds of purposes, we can't invent how they interact with reality. We can't invent their consequences and outcomes. More factors are involved. Hitler chose a purpose, but factors greater than Hitler saw to it that his goals weren't achieved.

In other words, purposes are neither entirely subjective nor entirely objective but weave the two aspects together. In purposes, the inner and the outer join. Guided by purposes, we develop our relation to the worlds beyond us.

For evolution, that's a help. If purposes were only subjective, we couldn't evaluate them. There wouldn't be any objective grounds for arguing that some purposes are better or worse than others. All aims would be of equal value—the relativist's view.

The relativist's view, though, isn't true to life. It's not what we experience. Not all purposes are great guides. Not all bring peace, health, or prosperity. In fact, some purposes don't link us with the worlds around us but put us in conflict with them. Purposes shaped by greed, fear, or insecurity, for example, put us on a collision course with just about everything that crosses our path. Because purposes link us to what's beyond us, there's something more than our own intentions to evaluate when we think about goals. There's reality to consider—what's on the other end of the link.

As with assumptions, strategies, and responses, then, purposes shape the maps we use to interact with reality. They're the fourth tool that goes into making practical philosophies.

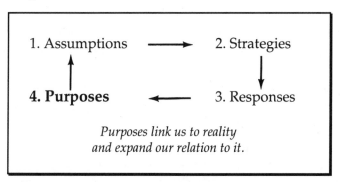

The tool's linking function works many ways. For instance, purposes give us direction. They link us to the future. They give us reasons to keep going and ideals to approximate. With purposes, we take hold of the future.

Without them, the future becomes a blank. Being here is just a matter of killing time.

Which raises another function: purposes not only link us with the future but also focus our energies toward it. They point us in a direction and then guide us there. Just as DNA steers plant and animal growth, purposes steer human development. They channel creativity and make it constructive.

By steering creativity, purposes also restrain behavior dangerous to growth. If we have a purpose, we act consistently with it. Some paths take us forward, others don't. Given a purpose, we can tell the difference. We don't do things that jeopardize our goals.

Most of all, purposes put us in a dynamic relation with what's real. We open a dialogue with reality. With our purposes, we do some talking. With consequences and outcomes, especially long-term, total-picture ones, reality answers back. When things don't turn out the way we hoped, we rethink our goals.

Context and purpose

Where do we get our purposes? Generally, from the reality to which we're linked. As we've seen, though, one reality can appear different according to the different philosophies we bring to it. Contexts, as our philosophies define them, shape our goals. We focus on certain aspects of reality and then design our goals around them.

The context of families, for instance, gives us plenty of goals, especially on weekends, as do the contexts of businesses and governments during the week. For scientists, the physical universe inspires certain purposes, such as understanding nature and working with it creatively. For teachers, a room full of bright, young faces inspires purposes of shaping all that potential—or at least harnessing all that energy. Then there's the context of civilization, which inspires purposes beyond bagging our dinner or curing some skins for our new fall wardrobe. Most broadly, the context of ultimate reality inspires purposes that relate to salvation and enlightenment.

The wider the context, the more interesting and challenging the aims. By linking ourselves to more of reality, we expand our goals.

By contrast, if we draw the context narrowly, we get bored. Narrow contexts limit creativity. We pour energies into narrow ends. There's nothing wrong, for instance, with making or having money. But as our life's aim, it's narrow. Similarly, the fascination with being linked to a body wears thin. Every morning we have to fuss to make it presentable. It gets monotonous.

What's wrong with narrow contexts and goals? For one thing, they're limited to matter, energy, or information. They cut out the wider spheres of consciousness, which is where the greatest challenges begin.

But worse, they shut out growth. When contexts and purposes share the same boundaries, a deathly equilibrium sets in. Each puts a lid on the other, so that neither expands. Fixed contexts restrict the range of goals open to us, while fixed purposes trap us in narrow worlds.

For instance, family needs (a fixed context) require that we make enough money to pay for the kids' food, clothes, and schooling (a fixed goal), while the purpose to make the money traps us in jobs that our hearts aren't in (a context we don't find progressive). The mutually reinforcing limits make for stasis—no growth. At least in this case, kids challenge parents to grow in other ways, until everyone grows up.

Yet neither limited contexts nor narrow goals need be fatal to development. If either expands, the other does, too.

On one hand, an expansive context challenges us to expand our goals. It's as if we've lived on the plains for years, but once we see Mt. Everest, we want to climb it. Once we discover a new dimension to our work, we want to explore it. Or, once we start thinking in terms of global markets, we design ways to restructure our businesses. Widening the context makes us dream wider goals.

Movies use the method all the time. A rich woman finds herself living a poor woman's life; a father finds himself trapped in his son's body; or a banker sees what a town would have been like if he hadn't been born. The character's context changes, giving the person a chance to see things from a completely new perspective. Once this happens, the people are no longer the same. They look for something different in life. Their goals change as well.

On the other hand, expanding our goals makes us seek wider contexts. Even if we haven't seen Mt. Everest, we can imagine it, which gets us going on the quest to find it. Even if we're not trading globally, we can imagine doing so, which gets us thinking in more universal terms.

More basically, even if our goals have been limited to manipulating matter, energy, and information, we can imagine the impact of developing consciousness, which inspires us to seek this dimension. In everyday terms, once we've made enough money and lost enough weight— assuming that both are possible—we start exploring ideas (a wider purpose), which opens us to new worlds (wider contexts). True to the signs in public libraries, exploring the world of ideas (an expansive goal) broadens our horizons (expands our context).

Either way, the very imbalance between contexts and purposes gives evolution a chance. One or the other pulls us out of ruts. The equilibrium is overcome, and we're able to evolve.

Prayer: a threefold movement

Prayer uses the imbalance between context and purpose to keep spiritual evolution going. It sparks a disequilibrium between context and purpose, so that one makes the other expand. There's even a pattern by which prayers do this. It starts by expanding the context.

a) Prayer begins by expanding the context to the whole. The whole transcends all limits. It's not bound by our concepts about it; ultimate reality is, as far as we humans are concerned, unnameable (Judaism and Christianity), Non-being or No-thing (Buddhism and Taoism). Our limits don't fit the infinite. Neither do our symbols or concepts capture the nature of the whole.

If we want a context that won't confine us, the whole is hard to beat. Granted, we may settle into fixed concepts about it. But if we do, we pray only to the fixed concepts. The effect isn't expansive. It's not real prayer.

True prayer seeks the reality beyond all concepts. It throws our assumptions, strategies, responses, and goals into the infinite, so that we have an open framework for evolving them. The context of unlimited reality guarantees that we'll have a context wide enough to keep our purposes evolving—which is the second movement in the pattern of prayer.

b) The whole context inspires whole-seeking purposes. In light of the whole context, we evolve our goals. We rethink our reasons for doing things. Some aims may not make sense within the wider context.

To help us along, prayer gives us an idea of what whole-seeking purposes do. In general, whole-seeking purposes focus us on the purpose to evolve. They point us in the direction of understanding reality's order and of striving to work more in harmony with it. Because God's reality is infinite, whole-seeking purposes aren't ones we're likely to outgrow.

As it happens, such purposes aren't unique to prayer but guide all disciplines. No matter what the discipline, we're in it to develop a better understanding of something, so that we can work with that something (music, law, art, teaching, etc.) more creatively.

In fact, the goals capture the spirit of both religion and science. Both give us the purpose to understand reality more as it is. And both challenge us to transcend ourselves—to evolve our philosophies—in order to see reality's nature more clearly.

c) Expanding both the context and the purpose ensures our growth. When the context widens and our goals expand, we can't stay the same. We're transformed. We live in new worlds with new goals to guide us. Prayer protects this process. It keeps spiritual evolution going: sustaining growth, removing obstacles from the path, and guiding the way.

Through these three phases, prayer puts us in the rhythm of the holomovement. First, the whole context descends. Second, the whole context gives us the purpose to see how we're included in the whole and to evolve purposes that explore what this means. Third, wider contexts and wider goals get us going on the ascent. Through prayer, we take part in reality's universal process.

Prayers often use this threefold pattern: (1) They expand the context, (2) which expands our purpose, (3) so that context and purpose together effect our growth.

A prayer from the *Bhagavad Gita*, for example, illustrates the pattern. First, the prayer turns us toward God, the big "Me":

Fix thy mind on Me. Worship Me and be devoted to Me. Sacrifice to Me, make reverence to Me.

Second, it expands our goals by giving us the aim to unite with God—to "go to God":

> In this way thou shalt go truly to Me, I promise, for thou art dear to Me.

Third, it directs our spiritual growth:

> Abandoning all duties, Take refuge in Me alone. I shall cause thee to be released from all evils. Do not grieve. [Also translated: Fear no more.][1]

In other words, (1) by going to the whole, (2) we receive the expansive purpose to unite with it, (3) which guides our evolution and protects it.

The first and most repeated Sura (or chapter) of the *Qur'an* follows the same movement. It opens by turning us toward God:

> In the Name of God, the Merciful, the Compassionate. Praise belongs to God, the Lord of all Being, the All-Merciful, the All-compassionate.

Next, we're given the aim of adapting ourselves to God's law—of uniting with the central order, so that its order governs our lives:

> The Master of the Day of Doom [judgment]. Thee only we serve.

Finally, the context and purpose together sustain spiritual growth:

> To Thee alone we pray for succour. Guide us in the straight path, the path of those whom Thou has blessed, not of those against whom Thou art wrathful, nor of those who are astray.[2]

The Lord's Prayer (Matthew 6:9–13) shares the pattern. It begins by widening the context to the whole:

> Our Father which art in heaven, Hallowed be thy name. Thy kingdom come.

Second, the whole context inspires us to evolve our purposes, so that our will coincides more closely with the will of God:

> Thy will be done in earth, as it is in heaven.

Third, it shows how the context and purpose together nurture, steer, and protect our development:

> Give us this day our daily bread. And forgive us our debts, as we forgive our debtors. And lead us not into temptation, but deliver us from evil.

The closing doxology, considered to be a later addition, views the entire process as occurring within the whole:

> For thine is the kingdom, and the power, and the glory, for ever. Amen.

But what does it mean to go to the whole? How do we evolve our goals? And how do the context and purpose join to guide spiritual growth?

The seven statements

Figuring out what prayer means isn't easy, since most prayers, the Lord's Prayer included, read like shorthand. That's no surprise, since they're the condensed version, the freeze-dried concentrate, of a comprehensive spiritual philosophy. For instance, from the entire Hebrew law and prophetic writings, the whole Sermon on the Mount and his own life's teaching, Jesus gave just seven phrases—52 words in all—that tell us how to pray.

Saying the phrases over and over fervently doesn't unlock prayer's meaning. The sounds just run together: "OurFatherwhichartinheaven—Hallowedbethyname . . ." What do the words mean?

If prayer's meaning were only subjective—whatever we take it to mean—then there wouldn't be much point in praying. We'd end up with a context no greater than the one we started with and with goals no less narrow. In fact, we'd be tempted to use prayer to fulfill goals we'd already chosen, such as finding someone to marry, having first pick of vacation days, or getting a parking space downtown. We wouldn't be open to letting prayer evolve our goals. Prayer would simply reinforce the limits we bring to it. It wouldn't help us grow beyond them.

If, instead, prayer has an objective meaning and function, how can we approximate it? That's the question that interpretation methods tackle.

In isolation nothing has meaning, since meaning is relational. "Twelve", for instance, doesn't mean anything on its own. It needs a context, a set of relations, to tell us something.

Moreover, the relations that give meaning are formed by categories—categories of grammar as well as categories of perception and categories of thought. "Twelve" needs not just categories of language but categories of arithmetic to mean something. Categories shape the context, which in turn gives words their meaning.

According to the categories we bring to a text, different meanings emerge. With Freudian categories, for instance, we may see in the Lord's Prayer a father dependence. With anthropological categories, we may find the deification of kinship structures. Or, with old-school management categories, we may discover tips for pandering to an autocrat. The question is, which categories are most appropriate for interpreting the Lord's Prayer? Which approximate the meaning originally intended?

That's a tall order, since we're talking about revelation. Even so, we can try to find categories that are roughly in the ballpark. If we want meanings that approximate those Jesus intended, we need categories that approximate those Jesus used—more than those Freud used, for instance. We need categories derived from revelation.

The Bible teachings offer such categories, though they don't necessarily advertise them as such. Within the four-fold category of assumptions, strategies, responses, and aims, each teaching uses a further sevenfold category to arrange its ideas. As it turns out, this pattern—seven ordered elements, plus or minus two[3]—isn't random but pops up in sacred texts from all over the world.

The Bible teachings are good examples of how the sevenfold category works. Given a subject, the sevenfold differentiation highlights the main points. We get an ordered analysis that's more or less complete.

The two contrasting *creation accounts*, for instance, examine the *spectrum of assumptions* about reality (Chapter 6). The seven days and seven parts of Adam and Eve's story don't cover every conceivable assumption. They do, however, highlight those that are most basic to grasping the ultimate order of things. By mapping the spectrum, they show which assumptions make us more creative.

The *Commandments* map *seven offensive and six defensive strategies for advancing freedom and protecting it* (Chapter 7). Many strategies aren't included. The Commandments don't, for instance, put self-help books out of business. They do, though, focus on what's necessary for freedom. If we stick with the Commandments' few, basic strategies, we'll keep moving toward the end of the spectrum where true freedom lies.

The *Beatitudes* map *eight responses that empower us to evolve* (Chapter 8). Not that the Beatitudes say how we should respond when someone cuts us off on the highway or what to do when we make a humiliating gaffe at a dinner party. They don't compete with etiquette counselors. Instead, they map responses that open us to spiritual growth. Using their broad, evolution-oriented responses, we evolve our day-to-day responses. That more or less covers the waterfront. No matter what responses we're using, the Beatitudes show how to evolve them.

Comparing the *Lord's Prayer* to these other teachings gives us a way to read the shorthand. We draw on categories given by revelation to explore revelation's meaning. We interpret the Lord's Prayer according to categories that Jesus both inherited from Hebrew law and used himself in formulating the Beatitudes. In other words, we use the Bible to understand the Bible.

In turn, interpreting the Lord's Prayer this way, we can use it to summarize the content of the other three Bible teachings. The Lord's Prayer pulls together whole-seeking assumptions, strategies, and responses, showing how these tools serve the *whole-seeking goal of spiritual evolution.*

How, then, does the Lord's Prayer give a step-by-step method for expanding our contexts and thereby evolving our goals?

II. Prayer:
Expanding our contexts and goals

1) Going to the whole

The Lord's Prayer opens by turning us towards the whole: "Our Father which art in heaven." (6:9) Whereas the eighth Beatitude raised the problem of persecution—of getting trapped in closed, no-growth worlds—the Lord's Prayer shows the way out. By going to the whole, we bypass the limits that define contexts narrowly—that make worlds closed.

What does going to the whole mean? That's what the first day of creation, first statement of the Commandments, and first Beatitude show. If we assume a primal intelligibility to things—a coherency that stems from the whole ("light")—then we adopt a strategy of looking to that source to liberate ourselves from closed philosophies and closed worlds (coming out of "the house of bondage"). Rather than imposing fixed views on experiences, we respond to experience openly ("poor in spirit"). We don't drag along the philosophical baggage that makes our lives closed to wider perspectives.

By pointing us toward the whole, the first day of creation, Commandment, and Beatitude prepare us for the first statement of the Lord's Prayer. They give us the tools for doing what it says. Through whole-seeking assumptions, strategies, and responses, we seek "our Father in heaven." We look to the whole as the ultimate context that impels our growth. We're more open to reconceiving our lives from its spiritual perspective.

What if we don't pray? In other words, what does it mean not to go to the whole? Simple: we stay in our own philosophies—our own worlds—and don't look beyond them. We assume that a partial order is the whole or an island unto itself. We get stuck in worlds of "mist" and set up housekeeping there (the start of Adam and Eve's story).

The trouble is, mist traps us in our own philosophies, until we forget that they're ours. We get so used to their limits, that we regard them as absolute. Unwittingly, we adopt strategies that lead into "houses of bondage" (Moses talking to desert folk again) and bolt the doors behind us.

The confusion creates well-frogs and summer insects. We know everything about one world but don't know how that world relates to wider contexts. We lose the power to see beyond our own limits. We respond only to a partial order.

That's how we find ourselves in closed worlds. The more we live in them, the more the whole, the Father in heaven, seems remote and irrelevant. God and the spiritual seem off somewhere. No whole context exists.

The closed approach describes what's wrong with economies. Economies don't have to become islands of mist—worlds of ignorance and desires gone mad. They don't have to trap us with fears about money or survival. They don't have to dictate our responses or take away our power to evolve. Economies become dictators only when they're cut off from higher levels.

In the end, economies need prayer. Not that they're so far gone that all we can do is fall on our knees and beg deliverance—though anything is worth a try. Rather, they need to be managed in wider contexts. Economies thrive or fail according to how we conceive of them and the qualities we bring to them. Philosophical factors make the difference. If we ignore these factors, we cut economies off from the dimensions that make them work as whole and healthy systems. We deprive economies of the spiritual resources—the ideas and creativity—they need to prosper.

Breaking out of narrow contexts is what prayer is all about. Prayer puts all our assumptions, strategies, responses, and goals on the table to be revised in the open context of the infinite. Through prayer, we turn to the whole as *our* context, as that which fathers and, for that matter, mothers our development.

a) Expanding our context:

The Lord's Prayer	*Prayer (the process)*	*keeps evolution going,*	*which transforms economies.*
1. Our Father which art in heaven.	Going to the whole	opens us to reconceive life from a wider perspective,	which deposes economies as dictators.

2) Taking the central order as the ultimate

In the context of the whole, many limits aren't as absolute as they seem. Expanding the context introduces alternatives. Whether we take these alternatives seriously depends on what we regard as ultimate. If the limits are ultimate, then there's no point in exploring alternatives. There aren't any—or so narrow philosophies claim.

The second statement of the Lord's Prayer, though, puts alternatives back into the picture by accepting only the whole as ultimate: "Hallowed be thy name" (6:9)—a text which is also translated: "May thy name be held holy" (TCNT), "Thy name be revered" (Mof), and "May your name be honoured" (Phi).

Hallowing God is a guaranteed context-expander. Not that it tells us more about God than the first statement does. Rather, it says something more about how we approach God. If we regard only the ultimate as the ultimate ("hallow God's name"), then we have room to expand our context. No matter which specific contexts catch our interest (families, nations, businesses), we don't lose sight of the whole as something more. We leave the door open to looking beyond them.

Whereas the first statement of the Lord's Prayer invites us to open our philosophies to the whole context, the second statement shows us how to stay open—how to keep lesser contexts from clamping shut on us again.

Revering, honoring, or hallowing God, then, is more than just saying, "Yes, God is something special." Greeting cards say as much. Rather, hallowing God goes back to our philosophies—beginning with what we assume about reality.

According to the second day of creation, it means assuming that there's only one ultimate, God, and that its order (the "firmament") gives the ultimate framework—

a spiritual order of values—for putting everything else in perspective and keeping it there.

But assumptions aren't much use if they don't inform strategies. Hence, honoring God also means having no other gods. Partial orders aren't the same as the central order. It's not a good strategy to "hallow" them as if they were the same, because then they become the whole for us. Their limits—limits that define, for instance, a social life, a career, or a family role—take over, until we're not free to grow beyond them. A fixed context becomes everything (mostly a pain in the neck).

That's why the Beatitudes recommend a response of "mourning"—of letting go of vehicles (our eggshells) once we outgrow them. Knowing what's holy and what's to be hallowed as the ultimate context, we take the lesser contexts for what they are, namely, useful but impermanent vehicles. The response empowers us both to develop our worlds and to develop beyond them.

Not that lesser contexts are denigrated by prayer. Quite the reverse. Hallowing God means letting reality's whole context establish the value of each lesser context within the totality. Hallowing the whole hallows everything that the whole includes. It brings out the true significance of events and happenings, because it shows their role within the big picture.

For instance, prayer shows that there's more involved with having a family, working at a job, or doing everyday things than the conventional and obvious. Through apparently commonplace experiences, we're actually wrestling with universal, spiritual issues—issues of spiritual growth. Through our temporal activities, prayer says, we're engaged in the work of eternity.

By contrast, hallowing specific contexts—people, ideologies or activities—as ultimates (an assumption) makes them small and petty. At first the group or ideology seems super-important. Everything turns around it (a strategy that's easy to fall into). But sooner or later, the limits of a given context begin to show. Hanging on to the context (a response), even when its limits won't allow for growth, only makes things worse. The context becomes even more isolated—more cultish and closed.

How we view economies illustrates prayer's point. Hallowing economies as if they were the ultimate makes a mess of them, because it splits them off into their own worlds. Economies don't take their values from the whole (the "tree of life"). Instead, they adopt dualistic values (the "tree of the knowledge of good and evil"). Win/lose, we/they, profit/loss, have/have-not oppositions fill the economic firmament. As we've seen, though, dualism isn't intrinsic to economies. It's an assumption thrust on them by dualistic philosophies.

The assumption gives rise to strategies of getting as much as possible of duality's upside—wealth or power. But these strategies don't work. From the premise of dualism, both sides follow—good and evil. In fact, we reap more of the downside, since dualism always creates conflict. Dualistic premises persuade us that we've no choice but to use destructive means to gain the good we want. They push us into doing what the Commandments' second defensive strategy warns against: killing to get ahead.

The fear of duality's dark side leads to responses that freeze us where we are. We're not permitted to "mourn" stages we've outgrown. In a world of haves and have-nots, the only stage we're allowed to develop is the stage concerned with money—getting more of it. If we focus on inward-growth stuff, we might do things that jeopardize our economic security. The chuck-the-growth response, however, works against us. Without development on any deeper levels, we bring to economies only our hungry side, when economies themselves are hungry for more.

In the end, hallowing economies—taking them as some kind of ultimate context—creates closed worlds: worlds that we hope will shut in the good and shut out the bad. In practice, though, closed economic worlds shut out the role economies could serve in effecting prosperity and economic security all around. We're left with the narrow contexts we see every night on the news—worlds drowning in conflicts over money.

Prayer provides the ticket out. Hallowing God keeps us from losing ourselves in economies, because it keeps us looking for a "more" that, while valuing economies, is more than just making money.

a) Expanding our context:

The Lord's Prayer	*Prayer (the process)*	*keeps evolution going,*	*which transforms economies.*
2. Hallowed be Thy name.	Taking the whole as the ultimate context	opens us to the "more" that goes beyond any specific context,	which focuses economies on a "more" that's more than money-making.

3) Letting the whole context transform us

Hallowing "the big more" changes us. The open context restructures the closed. The third statement of the Lord's Prayer—"Thy kingdom come" (6:10)—suggests that we not only accept these changes but seek them out.

What kinds of changes are we talking about? Whatever other kingdoms might be coming—a kingdom of alien beings or a new hotel chain, perhaps—from a philosophical perspective, the kingdom that comes from the whole is one that transforms us: emotionally, intellectually, morally, and spiritually.

It starts with our assumptions. Change begins with what we assume about ourselves. According to the third day of creation, our identity comes from the whole (earth). Prayer invites us to accept this identity, beyond the way lesser contexts define us. We're not just mothers or fathers, teachers or students, management or labor, thirtysomething or eightysomething. We're something more. As "Thy kingdom comes"—that is, as the true self appears, like the dry land of the third day—we begin to discover what the "more" is.

As our assumptions change, we move away from strategies that trap us in fixed notions ("graven images") about God, ourselves, or what's wrong with the world. Concepts are tools for philosophical housekeeping, but they don't have to set the furniture in stone to be a help. "Thy kingdom come" brings with it a stream of new insights. That's more or less what we experience. Just when we've got things all figured out, some new idea comes along that restructures our concepts completely.

Given that "Thy kingdom come" brings transformation, then, meekness is the best response. Even though self-concepts provide useful vehicles for growth, we can't afford to get attached to any one self-image. A response of meekness leaves us open to self-transformation. With meekness, we "inherit the earth": we accept new dimensions of our identity.

Change isn't threatening, then, if reality's whole context brings it. To help us along, the Bible teachings show

how to value lesser contexts as servants to the spiritual process. Otherwise, their separate kingdoms come, which puts us back in closed worlds.

Economies also wrestle with kingdoms coming. The question is, whose? The assumption that we exist as separate selves, each building a private pleasure garden ("Eden"), gives rise to strategies that use economies for self-gratification ("adultery"). Responding to experience means putting our own interests first, without worrying about how the pursuit of those interests affects wider contexts. What are the meek for, anyway, if not to elbow when they get in the way?

But the worlds created by such philosophies aren't expansive, just expensive. A parade of private kingdoms come—Rockefeller's or Morgan's, Helmsley's or Trump's, Smith's or Jones'.

What's wrong with private kingdoms coming, besides the fact that everyone else's kingdom comes before ours, is something philosophical. The direction of change is backwards. Instead of the whole context having an expanding impact on household management, household pressures take over: they "come." Money tells us what to do and when to do it. How we make money—and how much money we make—says who we are and what we're worth.

Prayer puts the process right. By continually redefining us and our philosophies in the whole context, the Lord's Prayer changes the soul of economies. "Thy kingdom come" changes who it is that manages information, energy, and resources.

As a result, we and our economies emerge transformed by the whole's descent, which is what the first phase of prayer (expanding the context) sets out to do. Prayer gets us started by giving us a method for widening the context that frames our lives.

a) Expanding our context:

The Lord's Prayer	Prayer (the process)	keeps evolution going,	which transforms economies.
3. Thy kingdom come.	Letting the whole context transform us	evolves who we are—the true self appears—	which changes who it is that manages economies.

4) *Evolving our purposes*

The fourth statement of the Lord's Prayer now shifts the focus from the whole context to *how that context expands our purposes*. If we're changed by prayer, we'll want to do something different with our lives. But the Lord's Prayer doesn't give us just one purpose that counts as spiritual. It gives us the purpose to evolve our purposes—to derive our purposes more from the whole: "Thy will be done in earth, as it is in heaven." (6:10)

How do we do this? By getting our assumptions, strategies, and responses to help out. The more expansive they are, the more natural it is to expand our goals as well.

Evolving our purposes starts with our assumptions. If our assumptions are narrow, we won't seek wider goals. The way to expand our assumptions, the fourth day of creation suggests, is to pattern them on the central order (the sun, moon, and stars giving light on the earth). To paraphrase the Lord's Prayer, the more we evolve assumptions on "earth" that reflect the order of "heaven," the more we can evolve goals that are equally expansive—that link us to the whole and align us with its order.

Having goals that link us to heaven's order doesn't mean much, though, if we lack a strategy for pursuing these goals. To fill in the gap, the Commandments' fourth offensive strategy shows how to approximate "loving God and keeping the commandments." It says we shouldn't give up on expanding our goals just because we make mistakes along the way. We might get caught up in purposes that prove disastrous, or we might simply get rutted in narrow aims.

Whatever the circumstances, evolving more whole-seeking goals doesn't mean we're expected to be perfect overnight. Halos and wings won't sprout; we'll still be normal. Evolving our goals means we'll aim at spiritual growth. Even if we bungle things, there's mercy, since it's the learning process, rather than not making mistakes, that's important.

Evolving our goals needs support from our responses as well. We can't expand our purposes if our day-to-day responses tie us down to fixed aims: e.g., getting 1.5 houses, 2.5 kids, 3.5 cars, and n+1 investments. Instead, the fourth Beatitude suggests, we need responses that "hunger and thirst after righteousness"—that seek the whole consistently. With whole-seeking responses, we're ready to tackle more whole-seeking aims.

Which is what the Lord's Prayer challenges us to do. Rather than binding us to fixed goals, the Lord's Prayer links our will to God's will, our aims to the aim to evolve. If we wonder why we're here day to day, the Lord's Prayer replies that we're here to develop spiritually—to move with the ascending side of the holomovement by evolving the goals that guide us.

This meta-goal—the goal to seek the whole context and to be at one with it: "Thy will be done"—keeps us evolving our goals. Prayer's method is thus unlimited. It inspires us to develop a great diversity of goals, all pointing us toward the whole.

Evolving our goals gives economies a chance to evolve, since our goals shape them. Purposes can fragment economies, or they can lead to prosperity. But whether or not we evolve our economic goals depends entirely on the economic assumptions, strategies, and responses that our philosophies give us.

If we assume, for example, that no unifying principle governs economic life—that economies are fragmented jumbles of desires locked in conflict—then fragmenting strategies follow. Stealing (veiled or blatant, legal or illegal) becomes routine. Insofar as our responses aren't shaped by any economic discipline (criteria of mutually beneficial exchange, for instance), they can be honest or dishonest, fair or exploitive according to advantage.

With a philosophy that shuts out evolution, we're stuck with fixed goals. Specifically, the philosophy thrusts on us goals that pit private interests against public interests, individual good against the common good, in other words, us against others. It says we're here only for the purpose of surviving at everyone else's expense. That's our goal. Evolving wider goals is out of the question.

Of course, we don't buy this philosophy and its screwy goals just to amuse ourselves, the way some people enjoy horror movies, marathon running, or cocktail parties. It's too depressing. We buy it because the philosophy convinces us that we have no choice.

According to the Bible teachings, though, that's not so. We can evolve different and more expansive goals from the ones this philosophy gives us, because we can evolve different and more expansive philosophies.

First, if dualism and fragmentation don't work as ultimate principles ("in heaven"), they're not likely to work for economies, either ("in earth"). It's possible to develop goals on other premises than win/lose.

Second, strategies that encourage us to learn from mistakes—that show "mercy unto thousands of them that love me, and keep my commandments"—free us to develop in spite of mistakes. Instead of perpetuating fragmenting strategies, we can learn from the fragmented worlds they produce and develop different strategies. The fear of mistakes doesn't have to lock us in one way of life.

That means our goals can develop, too. If our goals are limited to things we can do perfectly—things we can win at every time—then not many goals are open to us. But if our strategies don't demand perfection, we're free to explore all sorts of goals—and to learn as we go.

Third, responses that "hunger and thirst after righteousness" inspire goals that are more challenging than the goal to make money. Money isn't hard to get, if it's all we want. For the average person, though, it's not all they want, otherwise people wouldn't choose the careers they do. Making money isn't why people become teachers, policemen, nurses, ecologists, or waste-treatment experts.

Rather, the goals we'd like to evolve are precisely the kind that prayer generates: goals that align us with the whole. We want to be linked to more than some detached, partial order.

In economies, this meta-purpose inspires us to look beyond controlling matter, energy, and information and to explore goals that bring ideas and values to the marketplace. We strive to manage "earth" according to the order of "heaven"—to manage partial orders in line with the central order.

This purpose—the purpose to evolve—keeps us, our goals, and our economies evolving: a process that the last third of the Lord's Prayer protects.

b) Expanding our purpose:

The Lord's Prayer	Prayer (the process)	keeps evolution going,	which transforms economies.
4. Thy will be done in earth, as it is in heaven.	Deriving our purposes from the whole	gives us the meta-purpose to evolve,	which evolves the purposes we bring to economies.

5) Evolving as a way of life

Given the world as it is—given the opposites of the last three statements of the Lord's Prayer: hunger, debts, and temptations—can we take prayer's method seriously? Is the purpose to evolve practical, given things as they are? In the third and last section, the Lord's Prayer suggests that spiritual growth—expanding our context and evolving our goals—is the most practical course. In fact, it's the remedy for all ills.

The Lord's Prayer starts the last section by tackling the bare necessities: "Give us this day our daily bread." (6:11) E. V. Rieu translates: "Give us the bread of life today."

Prayer raises the issue of what sustains our lives. It's not money or food, nice as they are if well earned and well cooked. Rather, spiritual growth sustains us. The more we evolve, the more we're alive. We see more of what's going on around us and what's possible. To stop evolving is to start dying. Spiritual growth is the "bread of life," because it provides the inner resources we need to manage the necessities wisely.

It's not true, then, that people can think about spiritual matters only after they have bread in their mouths. What takes food out of people's mouths is the lack of spiritual growth—greed for money and power, for example. For all the good that relief agencies do—and it's considerable—hunger won't end without the bread of life, that is, without the spiritual growth that exposes economic exploitation and violence and rejects the philosophies that create them.

How do we get life's bread? By conceiving of our lives within the whole context and by evolving our relation to it through a whole-seeking purpose. In other words, we get the bread of life through prayer.

Not that prayer's method is esoteric or other-worldly. It's what works every day. Whether we're talking about squirrels in forests or merchants downtown, life forms depend on their relation to their life-support systems.

In ecology, for instance, plants and creatures depend on whole, living systems within nature. One of the biggest challenges for horticulturalists and zoo keepers is to keep wild plants and animals alive once they're removed from their natural habitat. So, too, with people. Anthropologists discovered early in this century that well-fed, well-clothed "specimens" from "primitive cultures" languished when they were taken away from their homes. Having their physical needs met wasn't enough.

It's not much different in business. Success depends on the relation we have to the people and systems around us. We can move a successful business to a different location and have it flop. It won't succeed until it works out a new relation to the larger systems that make it prosper.

Prayer applies this concept to ultimate matters. Our lives depend on the totality that is God, the whole. If we want a fuller sense of life, the Lord's Prayer says, we get it by evolving our relation to the whole context on which our lives depend.

If, instead, we assume that we're cut off from the whole context—that we're on our own in the void—then we also assume that our lives depend on attaining and maintaining idealized states (becoming "as gods").

Before long, we adopt strategies of maneuvering to gain the ideal condition. If survival is what counts, it's okay to use our neighbors unfairly and even bear false witness against them if it puts us ahead.

We respond to experience as if it were a struggle to establish the states—the perfect house, family, income, dog—states that we can never quite reach or keep. As responses go, it's not the most merciful, because it continually devalues what we have. We're driven by inadequacy.

Once attained, the goals can be empty. They take more from us in the getting than they give back in the having. Pursuing such goals doesn't support growth on deeper levels. Quite the reverse, it cuts us off from the contexts that make life dynamic and rich.

The fifth day of creation, fifth statement of the Commandments, and fifth Beatitude show what brings fullness to life. In the fifth day of creation, fish teem, and birds soar. There aren't any limits to growth if it comes from the whole. The limits that seem final are in fact embedded in our assumptions. To have the bread of life, we don't need a less limited universe; we need less limiting assumptions.

Similarly, not taking God's name in vain bases strategies on less limited methods for understanding what's ultimately real. Instead of narrowing reality to what we can measure or what we think, we challenge such limits. The purpose to evolve sustains us with strategies that make current views and attitudes obsolete. As Shakespeare put it, "There are more things in heaven and earth . . . than are dreamt of in [our] philosophy." (Hamlet I.v.)

"Blessed are the merciful" describes responses that challenge the limits imposed by the past. Neither past wrongs nor past successes determine the future. The more we question limits, the more we use what's in our power to get ourselves out of past ruts, so that we're able to draw on life's source freely. Then, what's ahead of us doesn't have to replay what's behind us.

c) How the purpose to evolve guides:

The Lord's Prayer	Prayer (the process)	keeps evolution going,	which transforms economies.
5. Give us this day our daily bread.	The purpose to go to life's source	unites us with the whole systems on which our lives depend,	which liberates economies to evolve beyond past limits.

Letting go of limits, then, is what keeps evolution going. It's what sustains growth. The prayer to receive daily bread isn't a plea from the helpless to gain supernatural help. It's a method of being open to the whole by letting go of the limits that cut us off from it. This method not only sustains us but also frees us from debts.

6) Evolving consciousness forgives debts

"And forgive us our debts, as we forgive our debtors." (6:12) "Debts" is also translated as "shortcomings," "failed duties," "offenses," or "wrongs done." Debts concern what we owe in life—and not just economically. There's the weight of guilts and regrets—heavy stuff.

How does prayer deal with all the heavy stuff? Not through blame, which only makes things worse. Accusation makes debts weigh on us more, without doing anything to lighten them. It leaves us no way out.

Instead, the purpose to evolve relieves us of debts. Debts aren't absolute values; they come and go with development. The way to cancel them is to keep evolving. As we're transformed by prayer, our debts are forgiven, because we're no longer the person who incurred them. The old weights go, because they don't belong to the new form. If there are outward debts to be paid—things that need to be done to make amends—spiritual evolution enables us to find the best way to repay them.

In fact, growth is how we've escaped trouble all along. We don't so much rectify mistakes as outgrow them. Kids stop pulling wings off insects and taunting small children, for instance, when they outgrow the notion that these things are fun. Parents forgive these little monsters, because they know that in a couple of years the tormenting-insects-and-small-children stage will pass (unless perhaps they grow up to be entomologists or drill sergeants).

In turn, the purpose to evolve enables us to forgive wrongs done to us, because we understand the development involved. We've been there, and we realize that inward growth isn't easy. Any step forward on another's part makes us ready to put past wrongs behind us. Each Christmas, everyone forgives old Scrooge, in spite of how mean and miserly he's been, when he pleads with the Ghost of Christmas Future, "I am not the man I was. I will not be the man I must have been."[4] His transformation evokes spontaneous forgiveness.

If transformation "forgives us our debts," how does it work? The sixth day of creation initiates the process by giving us something to shoot for, namely, our true nature (symbolized by generic man), which reflects the whole (made in the image and likeness of God). In the context of the whole, we find wholeness. The sixth day thereby transforms our assumptions both about our ultimate nature and about what's possible for us. Being a debt-ridden sinner isn't our destiny, not according to the sixth day.

But the assumption poses an ideal. What does it mean practically? The Commandments' sixth offensive strategy provides a method for finding out. "Six days shalt thou labour" focuses labor on evolving to understand what the six days of creation reveal. A life's work isn't first to do outward things—make money or gain status (though we'll take them as they come). It's to wrestle with our own reality and to evolve the ideals that guide us.

As we do, hidden agendas fall away, so that we see reality more as it is: "The pure in heart . . . see God." We respond to experience in ways that make us more open to seeing the whole and to responding in harmony with it.

With spiritual growth, then, our debts are forgiven, as Scrooge's were. By affirming development under all circumstances, the purpose to evolve makes offenses—the heavy stuff—obsolete. We become someone new. Spiritual growth outweighs debts.

Debts are a hot issue for economies, now more than ever. There's the national debt. There are massive corporate debts and trade-imbalance debts. There are third-world debts; countries with an average personal income of $200–500 a year are paying billions of dollars, mostly in interest, to countries with an average personal income of $22,000–24,000. Then there are personal debts: mortgages, credit cards, business loans, car loans, and college loans.

Obviously, the Lord's Prayer doesn't address debt-particulars, such as the relation between lending rates and inflation, or national debts and economic growth—it would take too long to repeat in church, anyway. Instead, it speaks to how we manage debts in general.

Historically, debts don't have a good reputation. What the debt-holder demanded, the debtor couldn't refuse.

Debts came to be used as powerful tools of oppression, holding people in poverty by denying them economic self-determination. Time and again, once debts started, they compounded, making growth beyond them almost impossible. People were lucky to stay even. If they couldn't, they went to debtors' prison, where they were sure never to pay back their debts.

Because of debts, wars have been started, and entire civilizations sacked. To pay back the Doge of Venice, for instance, the Crusaders sacked Constantinople in 1204. Similarly, debts have broken up families, alienated friends, and brought on suicides. They've dominated nations and reduced cultures to a struggle for survival. They've made the powerful despotic and the weak defenseless. They give new meaning to "heavy stuff."

It's no surprise, then, that both Christianity and Islam originally opposed both lending and interest. Money given to those in need was a gift from someone's bounty to be shared freely—without the expectation of repayment, certainly not with interest. The privilege of helping friends and fellows was return enough.

Eventually, though, Christian and Islamic states began to regard lending as a constructive tool for economic growth. Those who have creativity, skills, and vision may not have cash. To put their abilities to work, they need the help of those who do.

Seen this way, lending forms a mutual support system, whereby we affirm each other's potential for creative, economic expression. When the creativity pays off, everyone, including the economy, gains. When misfortune strikes, loans help us get going again.

When debts serve this way—to help people and economies develop—they're easily repaid, because everyone prospers. Development takes care of debts.

Whether debts suppress or support growth depends on the philosophical approach to them, starting with what we assume about the basic nature and aim of humanity.

If, for example, we assume that humanity is cursed with economic slavery and that within this slavery there are superior and inferior people, according to who owns what or whom (Cain's assumption), then our strategies manipulate debts to secure superior positions for ourselves by keeping others dependent and inferior. The desire for superiority makes coveting a way of life.

Moreover, our day-to-day responses use debts to work out hidden and not-so-hidden agendas for gain. Debts become a way for some to render others powerless, or at least to diminish their power, much the way the robber barons managed their company towns. The goal doesn't have anything to do with development. It's to control others by prolonging their indebtedness—to keep them in subordinate positions, so that our position on top is more secure.

By contrast, if we assume, as Augustine did, that we're moving towards the spiritual nature described by the sixth day—that we're perfectible—then we develop strategies that help us go in this direction. Developing higher ideals (laboring six days) guides the right use of economic tools, lending being one of them. We respond to debts by using them to further economic development, no matter which side of the debt we're on. Our responses are pure in heart, in that they're designed to serve the development of whole systems and everyone in them.

Managing debts is constructive, then, when it serves the goal to support growth. This approach wouldn't sacrifice development in order for a debt or the interest on it to be paid. It wouldn't make people slaves to indebtedness. Nor would it extend repayment by imposing usurious interest rates, like those that descended on us in the late '70s.

Such policies violate the purpose of lending, which is to support growth toward economic independence and self-determination.

The Lord's Prayer thereby provides the context and purpose that keeps debt-management constructive. When the purpose to evolve leads, debts aren't an obstacle—spiritually or economically.

c) How the purpose to evolve guides:

The Lord's Prayer	*Prayer (the process)*	*keeps evolution going,*	*which transforms economies.*
6. And forgive us our debts, as we forgive our debtors.	The purpose to evolve our nature	neutralizes debts by rendering them obsolete,	which gives economies a goal that keeps debt-management constructive.

7) *The purpose to evolve protects development*

The seventh and final statement of the Lord's Prayer summarizes the soul of economies. The purpose to evolve delivers us from individual and collective, private and public evils: "And lead us not into temptation, but deliver us from evil." (6:13)

Prayer speaks to two basic fears: one subjective, the other objective. On the subjective side, we're afraid of our own failings. Will our lack of growth ruin things for us? Will we make mistakes so awful that we can't come back from them? Is "temptation" the one thing, as Oscar Wilde suggested, that we can't resist?

But that's only half our problem. On the objective side, we fear what's beyond our control: "evil." Even if we get by personally, will an evil universe—a deranged economy or environment, President or motorist—finally do us in? Is the world already a disaster, from which there's no return?

Both fears suggest an even deeper dread that human life exists outside the whole, separated from God, or cut off from the Good. After all, who would want this world with its history to be any part of God? What perverse being would God have to be? Atheism, nihilism, or dualism seem preferable, if only in deference to God's reputation.

But the fears don't frame the problem rightly. If God is one and infinite, then falling outside the whole and its order just isn't an option. We can, though, misunderstand the order of things; we can get it wrong. It's like mathematics, ecology, or music. We can't get outside the realities with which these disciplines deal. We can, though, be confused about how these fields work. The more confused we are, the more we get bounced checks, dead lakes, shrinking ozone layers, and everyday assaults to the senses. These aren't problems with reality's order; they're our problems.

Our getting things wrong is, in fact, quite likely. Prayer doesn't say there's nothing to fear. Given our stage of evolution, there's tons to fear. We could blow ourselves up. We could ruin the planet with our chemical weapons, whether in the form of bombs or hair sprays. Or, thanks to runaway greed, we could make such a mess of economies that it's hell—economic slavery—to live here anyway.

Instead of glossing over the evils and temptations, the Lord's Prayer challenges us to deal with them. If temptations arise from the limits of our philosophies, then how many evils and temptations we face depends on whether we and our philosophies evolve, both individually and collectively.

If we assume, for example, that the second version of creation is how things really are, then we take oblivion as our end (Cain going into Nod). In a world devoid of all meaning or purpose, our only goal is to survive. Our strategies become those of desperation, and we respond to other people, who may be equally desperate, in aggressive ways. Violence escalates, reinforcing the belief that it's necessary. The cycle generates worlds of enemies and suffering. We face one evil or temptation after another and go from crisis to crisis.

Such worlds aren't created by God; they come from dark-end assumptions, strategies, responses, and goals. They're philosophy-created. Tracing such worlds to their philosophical roots gets both God and us off the hook. If God didn't create them, we're not stuck with them. In other words, if junk philosophies create dark worlds of temptations and evils, we can transform the worlds by evolving the philosophies.

Which is what the Bible teachings are all about. The seventh day of creation shows that we can evolve our assumptions beyond premises of fear and fragmentation: "The heavens and the earth were finished," and "God rested." Everything God creates is good, since spiritual creation is the whole expressed. Because God's creation is complete and perfect, and because we're included in it, existential angst doesn't have to be our premise. ("Angst" is a German word that means "the pits" and then some.) Given the seventh day, we can assume that we have a place within the whole and a purpose that's ours alone.

But the seventh day's assumption doesn't necessarily match how we feel or how things look. We have to evolve strategies that explore what wholeness means for how we live. "Remembering the sabbath day" and "keeping it holy" says that doing this involves grace. We can't mastermind our own evolution. Given the limits that make things a mess, the best strategies are those that open us to reality's descent—to the influx of higher dimensions—which re-structures limits in ways we can't foresee.

Carried to the worlds we face, whole-seeking assumptions and strategies open new ways of responding to conflicts. Instead of accepting polarized states, we can evolve responses that first identify the fears that cause conflicts and then change the philosophies behind those fears. We become peacemakers on both corrective and preventive levels by tackling the deeper reasons for conflicts.

What "leads us not into temptation" and "delivers us from evil," then, is the purpose to evolve. We don't have to fear evils and temptations, not because we don't have to deal with them, but because the method of spiritual growth provides a way out of them. By evolving beyond the philosophies that invite nuisance visitors (war, crime, pollution, hunger, homelessness, and general economic slavery), we can win back our economies. Armed with methods that effect spiritual growth, we're free, as the *Bhagavad Gita* puts it, to "fear no more."

c) How the purpose to evolve guides:

The Lord's Prayer	Prayer (the process)	keeps evolution going,	which transforms economies.
7. And lead us not into temptation but deliver us from evil.	The purpose to evolve our philosophies	gives us the method of spiritual growth that delivers us from temptations and evil,	which empowers us to win back our economies and to send nuisance visitors packing.

The Purpose to Evolve

The Lord's Prayer	Prayer (the process)	keeps evolution going,	which transforms economies.

a) Expanding our context:

1. Our Father which art in heaven.	Going to the whole	opens us to reconceive our lives from a wider perspective,	which deposes economies as dictators.
2. Hallowed be Thy name.	Taking the whole as the ultimate context	opens us to the "more" that goes beyond any specific context,	which focuses economies on a "more" that's more than money-making.
3. Thy kingdom come.	Letting the whole context transform us	evolves who we are—the true self appears—	which changes who it is that manages economies.

b) expands our purpose:

4. Thy will be done in earth, as it is in heaven.	Deriving our purposes from the whole	gives us the meta-purpose to evolve,	which evolves the purposes we bring to economies.

The Lord's Prayer	Prayer (the process)	keeps evolution going,	which transforms economies.

c) so that the purpose to evolve guides our growth:

5. Give us this day our daily bread.	The purpose to go to life's source	unites us with the whole systems on which our lives depend,	which liberates economies to evolve beyond past limits.
6. And forgive us our debts, as we forgive our debtors.	The purpose to evolve our nature	neutralizes debts by rendering them obsolete,	which gives economies a goal that keeps debt-management constructive.
7. And lead us not into temptation but deliver us from evil.	The purpose to evolve our philosophies	gives us the method of spiritual growth that delivers us from temptations and evil,	which em-powers us to win back our economies and to send the nuisance visitors packing.

In Closing

During the 1970s and '80s, we more or less spent our time working on ourselves—our careers, homes, relationships, bodies, and minds. We made self-help a booming business. We discussed, exercised, dieted, recovered, read, and studied—and with a fair degree of success. We're either in better shape or getting there.

At the same time, all this work on ourselves led us to ask deeper questions about our lives: Who are we? What are we here for? Is there a meaning and purpose to our lives? Around all the fixing up, we became interested in questions of religion and philosophy.

We responded by taking courses, joining study groups, getting reborn, listening to gurus, researching the lives of mystics and saints, going into therapy, learning to meditate, contemplating, and praying. We made the New Age common parlance, so that talking to plants or discussing past lives doesn't seem as weird as it once did.

We also revived some old traditions. Television shows went back to discussing ethics and the values of religion. Religious thinkers had more to say, and more people listened. According to Gallup polls, over 90 per cent of us believe in God or a Universal Spirit, while nearly three-fourths of us think that we live on after the body dies.

With the coming of the '90s, though, we're facing new questions: What's the use of fixing ourselves up, if the world goes to pot? How fixed up can we be if we don't have clean air or water, if we plunge into a nuclear night-mare (whether by war or a power-plant accident), or if our economies consume the fixing up we've done by sapping all our energies? How blissful can we charioteers be if our chariot is a wreck?

What we've heard since Plato's time is hitting home: we live in a community, and the community's workings affect us. We can't be healthy if the community is sick, just as the community can't be healthy if we're all sick. The challenges of the '90s concern not just us as individuals but more the political, educational, and economic systems in which we live.

In other words, we're rethinking the households we share. We're putting the deeper questions not just to our-selves but even more to our courts, schools, governments, and of course, our economies: What are these systems all about? What values guide them? And to what ends?

More often than not, we don't like the answers we're getting. In spite of the best experts to help us, our systems are a mess. Political and economic scandals have multi-plied. Washington spins in its own orbit, while Wall Street seesaws with our money. The legal system has more laws than justice. Even the educational system, once the bastion of values, is a threat to national security, not to mention a threat to our children's minds, health, and futures. Gone are the days when dictators and oppressive governments were the big threats in our lives. Now the threats are paid for by our taxes. (Nothing's free anymore.)

Such messes challenge us to apply our fixing-up talents to the community—to work on our governments, schools, and economies the way we've worked on ourselves. Can we improve our shared systems as well?

Too often, experts say no. Or at least, that's what we guess they're saying. They analyze problems in terms so layered with jargon that, if they do suggest something we can do, we don't get it. To make matters worse, documentaries paralyze us with the enormity of problems. We're left with the impression that only big corporations, big agencies, and big governments can fix them, even though big corporations, big agencies, and big governments haven't fixed them yet. That's no surprise, since they're often a big part of the problem.

Other experts claim that the problems can't be fixed in principle. We're stuck with them, because they're part of human nature and the world. The forces that create the problems aren't in our power to change. It's the modern version of predestination, minus the fifty-fifty chance of a happy ending.

Experts, though, become experts by studying parts and specialized fields. Those who seek the whole—thinkers such as Plato, the Buddha, Confucius, Paul, Augustine, and Gandhi—take quite a different view. Their teachings assume that we're perfectible, that we can change. Otherwise, they wouldn't have taught. Things can be improved on the collective scale, just as they can on the individual, because at the root of both lie spiritual challenges. The crises in politics, education, and economies spring from deeper, philosophical crises—things that are in our power to change.

In fact, if they were alive today, Augustine, Confucius, Plato, and like-minded thinkers would probably say we're in a strong position to tackle the collective ills. We have everything we need.

To start, we have the spiritual teachings to give us maps for evolving our maps. We're not stuck with the philosophies that got us into trouble.

With tools for evolving, we have ample resources for developing new maps. We're sitting on an explosion of knowledge *(know-what)*. Plus, we've got more channels for moving ideas and information around than ever before. Communicating is our speciality. It's even what we look for in Presidents these days. Computers, modems, satellite dishes, televisions, radios, books, magazines, and now FAX machines are mushrooming businesses.

Added to these resources, we have an abundance of technical expertise and minds able to put this *know-how* to practical use.

All we have to do, they'd say, is bring these powers together under the umbrella of evolving our philosophies. We can develop not just our know-what and know-how but also our *know-whether* and *know-why*. If our educational, political, and economic messes have their roots in junk philosophies (mostly in bad *-whether)*, we always have the option to change our philosophies.

Which means we're not helpless. If the systems we share reflect the philosophies we live by—individually and collectively—then we can improve the systems by evolving our philosophies. Evolving our philosophies is, in fact, our greatest power.

With good methods for doing this, such as revelations give, we can tap this power and put it to work. If we do, when the new millennium comes, the households we share can bear a promise for the future, instead of a curse from the past.

If we don't, at least then we'll *know-why*, and that's learning, too.

Rethinking Economies
—Resources

🝑🝑🝑🝑🝑🝑🝑

F aced with economic and ecological crises, people around the world are rethinking what economies are, how they work, and whether our philosophies cover the factors we need to manage our economies well.

In this Appendix, we'd like to focus on the works of a few individuals who crossed our path while we were doing our research for this book. These individuals stand out to us because they're all actively committed, first, to rethinking economies, and, second, to taking the process of rethinking to the marketplace, so that "we the people" can participate in the dialogue.

This Appendix is by no means exhaustive. Rather, it's a place for readers to start. We've included it—incomplete as it is—because we were so encouraged to see even a part of what's being accomplished on personal, local, national, and international scales. Making economies serve us and the earth isn't just talk: it's what more and more people are working for today.

One such person is **Hazel Henderson,** who began her public career as a housewife with no special education in economics. Although her unconventional approach was resisted decades ago (imagine someone saying in the late 1960s that New York City's air shouldn't be yellowish-brown and putrid), her advice is now sought by governments worldwide. We caught her between trips to Germany and China, just after her work in Venezuela with the South Commission, involving political leaders from Latin America, Asia, and Africa.

Ms. Henderson isn't convinced that traditional economic theories can help clean up the global messes we're facing. In her view, those factors most important to our future simply don't appear in traditional economics. If they did, we wouldn't be facing such universal ecological crises. For this reason, she's spreading the new economic doctrine of "Mutual Development," which embraces a wider range of economic factors and seeks development for all nations interacting in the world economy.

In addition to articles in over two hundred magazines and journals, she has written:

Creating Alternative Futures: The End of Economics (Putnam, 1978) and

The Politics of the Solar Age (Doubleday, 1981; reissued in a new edition by Knowledge Systems, 7777 West Morris Street, Indianapolis, IN 46231, (800) 999-8517).

Just to show the international scope of her work, both her books are available in German, Swedish, Dutch, Japanese, and Chinese.

In England, **Paul Ekins** takes a similar approach. He's the director of *The Other Economic Summit (TOES)*, "a broadly based, independent international forum, seeking to bring economics into line with late twentieth-century realities." Those realities include more than balance sheets and stockholders' profit statements. His book,

The Living Economy: A New Economics in the Making (Routledge, 1986), includes articles from the many economists participating in *TOES*. Their task is to rethink economics "as if people, society, and the earth mattered," to borrow the familiar phrase of E. F. Schumacher's. In conjunction with *TOES*, Mr. Ekins has founded:

The Living Economy Network (42 Warriner Gardens, London, SW11 4DU, England, (71) 498-8180),

which brings together the work of over 300 scholars and businesspeople from 41 countries.

In the American academic community, socially responsible economic behavior is the subject of many works. One that stands out is the recent book by **Amitai Etzioni** of George Washington University:

The Moral Dimension: Toward a New Economics (The Free Press, Macmillan, 1988).

Professor Etzioni explores paradigms for integrating the "I" and the "We," so that the activity of one doesn't destroy the good of the other. He's also the founder of:

The Society for the Advancement of Socio-Economics (714H Gelman Library, 2130 H Street, N.W., Washington, D.C. 20052, (202) 994-8167).

The Society is an international group of academic thinkers, businesspeople, and policy analysts working to develop a more encompassing model of economic behavior, including societal, historical, philosophical, and ethical factors.

Another force in rethinking economies is economist **Ravi Batra** of Southern Methodist University in Dallas. His two bestsellers—

The Great Depression of 1990 (Simon & Schuster, revised edition, 1987) and
Surviving the Great Depression of 1990 (Simon & Schuster, 1988)

—have made him familiar to readers worried about the future of the world economy, not to mention national and local economies. What's special about his work is not only that he's uncannily accurate in his predictions, but more that he weds economics to social, religious, and historical patterns of development. He predicts that we're ready to outgrow the acquisitive model of economic behavior that has dominated the West for centuries. If we don't, we're in trouble, because the acquisitive model lacks the vision to make economies good servants to human life. His new edition of

> *The Downfall of Capitalism and Communism: Can Capitalism Be Saved?* (Venus Books, 5518 Dyer Street, Suite 3, Dallas, TX 75206, 1990)

analyzes economies in the broader context of development, both the development of civilizations East and West and individual development. To support the step to new forms of economies, Professor Batra has founded:

> *S.A.D.* (*Stop Another Depression*, P.O. Box 741806, Dallas, TX 75374, (214) 699-3838).

Central to rethinking economies is the issue of economic justice: what does it mean, and how can we approximate it? Many books wrestle with this issue. One that's especially helpful is **Frances Moore Lappé's**

> *Rediscovering America's Values* (Ballantine Books, 1989).

Rediscovering America's Values relates democratic values to economic and political action. Using a dialogue format, the book explores the basic values needed to turn the economy in more prosperous, humane, and just directions. Applying the issue of economic justice to the most practical level, Ms. Lappé has authored several books that address how to end world hunger, including the popular *Diet for a Small Planet*. The book she coauthored with **Joseph Collins,**

> *World Hunger: Twelve Myths* (Grove Press, 1986),

shows that hunger isn't an economic necessity at all but a function of the economic choices we make in a political world. What creates hunger and perpetuates it in a global economy of food surpluses are the myths we hold about hunger's necessity. An activist as well as an author, Ms. Lappé has cofounded:

> *The Institute for Food and Development Policy/Food First*
> (145 Ninth Street, San Francisco, CA 94103, (415) 864-8555).

Another independent, economic rethinker is **John Robbins**, who first came to the public's attention when, as heir to the Baskin-Robbins Ice Cream fortune, he turned away from that industry to concern himself with the way Americans live and eat. His book,

> *Diet for a New America: How Your Food Choices Affect Your Health, Happiness, and the Future of Life on Earth* (Stillpoint Press, 1987),

was nominated for a Pulitzer Prize and has focused attention on the practical, economic value of a vegetarian diet. The implications are more far-reaching than they may appear at first glance. The book is a genuine eye-opener, whether one intends to be a vegetarian or not. Mr. Robbins has also started:

> *EarthSave* (706 Frederick Street, Santa Cruz, CA 95062,
> (408) 423-4069),

an organization devoted to rethinking how our personal dietary choices affect our environment and our future.

Someone who's been rethinking economies as part of a larger development of human consciousness for a long time is **Willis Harman**. His latest book,

> *Global Mind Change: The Promise of the Last Years of the Twentieth Century* (Knowledge Systems, 1988),

discusses the power of consciousness to transform every sphere of life, economies included. Once we evolve our concept of economic reality, he argues, our economies will naturally follow. Dr. Harman is President of:

The Institute for Noetic Sciences (475 Gate Five Road,
Suite 300, Sausalito, CA 94965, (800) 525-7985),

a nonprofit organization devoted to exploring the role of consciousness in evolving more peaceful, harmonious patterns of life on the planet.

Another singular person rethinking economies is **Dr. Brian P. Hall**, an Episcopalian priest. His book,

The Genesis Effect: Personal and Organizational Transformations (Paulist Press, 1986),

shows "how human, spiritual, and institutional growth are interconnected and form a dynamic whole." In quite specific ways, Dr. Hall discusses how the dynamics of inner, spiritual development affects change in what seem like immovable corporate systems.

From a theological perspective, **M. Douglas Meeks** rethinks economies in his book,

God the Economist: The Doctrine of God and Political Economy (Fortress Press, 1989).

Challenging the dominator model so prevalent in economic and political life, he explains how a nonauthoritarian God-concept can create a democratic, just economy.

Similarly, a fresh look at the relation of theology to economics has come from theologian **John B. Cobb, Jr.** and economist **Herman Daly** in:

For the Common Good: Redirecting the Economy toward Community, the Environment, and a Sustainable Future (Beacon Press, 1989).

Using the theological concern for community, they propose broadening the traditional economic focus to include both present and future, human and nonhuman communities, thus providing a new model for everything from trade and land use to taxes and national security.

Of course, rethinking economies goes on everyday in business, and business writers are quick to notice the changes. Few people in business don't know the works of consultant **Tom Peters,** businessman **John Diebold,** or management guru **Peter Drucker.** But the rethinking isn't limited to these heavyweights. There's a groundswell of rethinking occurring in management. Information changes so quickly in business that the decision-making can't be limited to a handful of all-powerful higher-ups. The role of autocrat is being replaced by the role of team-leaders in businesses where everyone takes part in shaping the company's future. Bookstores are filled with titles that discuss this change and its implications for how we do business.

One excellent book that set the stage for "participation management" in American corporations is **Rosabeth Moss Kanter's**

The Change Masters: Innovation for Productivity in the American Corporation (Simon & Schuster, 1983).

Her vision is that any future, corporate renaissance will depend on making full use of the new ideas generated by people within the corporation. She believes that encouraging people to act on their ideas taps the innovative potential that each of us brings to our work.

Max DePree's popular and readable book,

Leadership Is an Art (Doubleday, 1989),

defines the qualities and skills that managers need to do precisely what Rosabeth Moss Kanter recommends, as does **Peter B. Vail's:**

Managing as a Performing Art (Jossey-Bass, 1989).

Taking a comprehensive view of business in society, **Robert Theobald,** in

The Rapids of Change: Social Entrepreneurship in Turbulent Times (Knowledge Systems, 1987),

describes the expanding contexts that frame business decisions today. Mr. Theobald shows how we can refocus our economic decisions, so that our economies affirm both human and environmental wholeness.

One aspect of economics that's being rethought in particular is the model of business as win-lose games. As we argued in Chapter 2, this notion is more and more seen as dinosaur thinking. It doesn't work in making better companies or better industries, much less better worlds. **Ross R. Reck** and **Brian G. Long** discuss alternatives in:

> *The Win-Win Negotiator* (Simon & Schuster, 1985),

as do **Lucy Beale** and **Rick Fields** in:

> *The Win/Win Way: The New Approach Transforming Business and Life* (Harcourt Brace Jovanovich, 1988).

Business ethics is also playing a big role in rethinking economies. To mention just a few of the many books available, there are:

R. Eric Reidenbach and Donald P. Robin's
> *Business Ethics: Where Profits Meet Value Systems* (Prentice Hall, 1989),

Laurence Shames'
> *The Hunger for More: Searching for Values in an Age of Greed* (Times/Random House, 1989),

Gerard I. Nierenberg's
> *Workable Ethics: What You Need to Succeed in Business and Life* (1987, available from Nierenberg and Zieff Publishers, 230 Park Avenue, New York, NY 10169),

Tad Tuleja's
> *Beyond the Bottom Line* (Penguin, 1985), and

Robert C. Solomon and Kristine Hanson's
> *It's Good Business* (Harper & Row, 1985).

These books argue that doing business according to ethical principles enhances a company's bottom line, because it builds the foundation of trust that's so essential to a good and prosperous business.

On a personal and everyday level, we experience economies through our work. But our work doesn't have to be unsatisfying. If it is, chances are we're either doing the wrong thing or going about the right thing in the wrong way. That's what **Nancy Anderson** argues in:

> *Work With Passion: How To Do What You Love For A Living* (New World Library, copublished with Carroll and Graf, 1984).

It's also the subject of **Marsha Sinetar's**

> *Do What You Love, The Money Will Follow: Discovering Your Right Livelihood* (Dell, 1989),

and **Linda Mark's**

> *Living With Vision: Reclaiming the Power of the Heart* (Knowledge Systems, 1988).

But how do we pull it off? Not everything is lovable in business. That's where creativity comes in. **Michael Ray** and **Rochelle Myers** give a range of tools for expanding the creativity we bring to our work in:

> *Creativity in Business* (Doubleday, 1986).

One of the most enjoyable writers to rethink how we do business day to day is **Paul Hawken**. He's had plenty of experience starting businesses himself and interviewing other creative entrepreneurs. The two books we can't keep around the house because we keep giving them away are:

> *The Next Economy: What To Do With Your Money And Your Life in the Coming Decade* (Ballantine Books, 1984), and

> *Growing a Business* (Simon & Schuster, 1987). This book is a companion to a public television series showing how small businesses become successful.

There's a growing number of organizations devoted to nurturing businesses that adhere to more whole-seeking methods. At one point, we thought of doing an appendix listing these organizations. Then we discovered that entire books were devoted to doing just that. A noteworthy example is **Susan Meeker-Lowry's**:

Economics as If the Earth Really Mattered: A Catalyst Guide to Socially Conscious Investing (New Society Publishers, 1988).

Ms. Meeker-Lowry has cofounded the *Institute for Gaean Economics*, which explores the possibilities for a Gaean or Earth-based economy. She also edits *Catalyst*, a newsletter for those interested in "putting their money where their heart is." *Catalyst* draws attention to small, environmentally conscious businesses and investing opportunities here and around the world working to make economies more respectful of people and the earth. The address for both *Catalyst* and the *Institute for Gaean Economics* is:

64 Main Street, 2nd Floor, Montpelier, VT 05602.

Another major source of information about businesses and organizations working to rethink economies is **Co-op America**, which, in their own words, works:

- to bring together individuals and organizations to build a marketplace based on social and environmental responsibility and a spirit of cooperation in the workplace;
- to affirm the importance of considering how products and services are made and delivered;
- to emphasize economic democracy, worker participation, responsiveness to members, and customers; and to demonstrate that business can be done in an ethical manner; and
- to help existing progressive businesses and organizations emerge and succeed.

These objectives are taken from Co-op America's quarterly publication, which is packed with business information:

Building Economic Alternatives (2100 M Street N.W., Suite 403, Washington, D.C. 20063, (800) 424-"COOP" or (202) 872-5307).

Building Economic Alternatives is great reading, because it shows how many people are working creatively to reclaim our economies. It also gives small businesspeople ideas about how to run their businesses in more environmentally and socially responsible ways. And it alerts readers to businesses that still think they can get away with persisting in the old exploitive patterns. Co-op America also has a fine catalogue of products that are earth-safe:

Co-op America Order Service, 2100 M Street N.W., Suite 403, Washington, D.C. 20063, (202) 223-1881.

Other books that provide good references to organizations and businesses working to rethink how we manage our household include:

Jeffrey Hollender's *How to Make the World a Better Place: A Guide to Doing Good* (William Morrow, 1990). Mr. Hollender started the *Seventh Generation* catalogue for recycled and earth-safe products (Colchester, VT 05446, (802) 655-3116);

The Council on Economic Priorities' *Shopping For a Better World* (1989, CEP, 30 Irving Place, New York, NY 10003, (212) 420-1133);

The Earth Works Group's *50 Simple Things You Can Do to Save the Earth* (Earthworks Press, 1989, Box 25, 1400 Shattuck Avenue, Berkeley, CA 94709, (415) 841-5866);

Paul Ekins' *The Living Economy,* which we mention again for the many addresses that he includes in his Appendix 2.

Another excellent place to find books and materials on rethinking economies is the:

Guidebook for the '90s: Resources for Effecting Personal and Social Change (Knowledge Systems, Inc., 7777 West Morris Street, Indianapolis, IN 46231, (800) 999-8517).

Knowledge Systems offers many books that speak to the economic and global challenges of the '90s. Rethinking economies is very much their business.

Finally, every economy has businesspeople who put into practice whole-seeking methods in a natural way. We've been most fortunate to have had these exemplars of mutually beneficial exchange all around us as we wrote.

One such person is **Helen Woodhull**, one of New York's most creative and classic jewelry designers. Ms. Woodhull brings to her work precisely the kind of whole-seeking qualities and strategies that we've outlined. Her work is of the very highest quality, and her service is both friendly and professional. Added to that, she dedicates part of her business to championing artistic and social causes, combining these in ways that demonstrate how businesses can be integrated into the larger community. That she can achieve what she does in the heady world of Fifth Avenue designers shows what's possible.

But Ms. Woodhull is just one example. Professionals and entrepreneurs devoted to true economies all over the world form the backbone of local, national, and global businesses. They keep our economies afloat in spite of the assaults of the confused, billiard-ball-model practitioners that make so much noise on the news.

Again, we emphasize how incomplete this Appendix is. We can't begin to reference all that's going on. What these books, periodicals, organizations, and businesses tell us is that "we the people" are back in the economic game. In fact, we've never really been out of it. The more we realize this, the more we can reclaim our power to evolve what's closest to home: ourselves and our economies.

Surveys of
the World's Religions

🔲🔲🔲🔲🔲🔲🔲

W e're often asked to suggest books that give general readers a basic understanding of the world's religions. There are many good introductions. One we always recommend is **Huston Smith's:**

The Religions of Man (Harper & Row, 1958).

The book was originally a series of radio talks. As a result, Professor Smith's approach is tirelessly practical. He relates the ideas, concepts, and practices of the religions, especially the Eastern ones, to things we in the West can understand. What comes through is a deep respect for the religions, showing why they changed history and why they've been honored for millennia. We've assigned *The Religions of Man* in our university classes for nearly two decades, and we know we're not alone: a new edition came out in 1989.

Professor Smith discusses themes and concepts that recur in the religions, exploring how they all add up, in:

Forgotten Truth: The Primordial Tradition (Harper & Row, 1976).

Another good survey of the world's religions is **David A. Rausch and Carl Hermann Voss':**

World Religions: Our Quest for Meaning (Fortress Press, 1989).

Like Professor Smith, the authors aim to make sense of the world's religions, ending their book with an appeal for people in the various religions to understand each other's teachings and traditions. Professors Rausch and Voss also list readings for each religion, providing excellent bibliographical guidance for those who wish to study a specific religion more deeply.

A major source for historical, cultural, and sociological information is **David S. Noss** and the late **John B. Noss'**:

Man's Religions (Macmillan, 1984).

This is often used as a college text, because it's so packed with information. Unfortunately, this feature leaves less space for the conceptual, that is, for making sense of the religions the way Huston Smith, David Rausch, and Carl Voss do. But the book has its own conceptual approach, and it's helpful, if less captivating than the other books.

A similar text—full of information, maps, and photographs—is **Ninian Smart's**:

The Religious Experience of Mankind (Scribner's, 1969).

Writing from a distinctly Christian perspective, **Denise Carmody** and **John Carmody** have applied the world's spiritual teachings to two leading social issues in:

Peace and Justice in the Scriptures of the World Religions (Paulist Press, 1988).

For comparing the myths and teachings of one religion with another—especially those in the Bible with other religions—there are fine selections in:

Roger Eastman, *The Ways of Religion* (Canfield Press, Harper & Row, 1975) and

Ninian Smart and **Richard D. Hecht,** *Sacred Texts of the World: A Universal Anthology* (Crossroad Publishing, 1982).

The actual sacred texts and teachings of the world's religions need no recommendation. The ones we've used throughout the book—the *Bible*, the *Qur'an* (also spelled *Koran* or *Kur'an*), the Sufi texts, the *Tao Te Ching*, the *Four Books* of Confucianism (the *Analects of Confucius*, the *Great Learning*, the *Doctrine of the Mean*, and *Mencius*), the *Vedas*, the *Bhagavad Gita*, the *Upanishads*, and the *Buddhist Sutras*—have been translated hundreds of times (this year alone, we noticed five new translations of the *Tao Te Ching* at our local bookstore).

For those on the go, a convenient and direct way to get acquainted with these texts is through audio tapes that give readings of the texts themselves. **Jacob Needleman**, who has been introducing the public to spiritual ideas from the world's religions for decades, is now the general editor of:

> *Spiritual Classics on Cassette* (Audio Literature Inc.,
> 325 Corey Way, Suite 112, South San Francisco, CA 94080,
> (800) 446-7695).

Related writings from the world religions, though, can be less easy to find. Fortunately, a few publishers are starting series that translate and reprint the spiritual treasures of the world.

One publisher that stands out for making the great works of Western spirituality available is **Paulist Press**:

> 997 Macarthur Boulevard, Mahwah, NJ 07430,
> (201) 825-7300, FAX: (201) 825-8345.

Paulist has two outstanding series of translations:

> *Ancient Christian Writers:* a series of nearly fifty volumes of original works of major Christian writers, and

> *The Classics of Western Spirituality:* a series of sixty volumes of original works by Jewish, Christian, Muslim, Sufi, and Native American thinkers, including many women (those

few women in history, that is, whose names weren't "Anonymous").

Another excellent source on spirituality is a projected 25-volume series, entitled *World Spirituality: An Encyclopedic History of the Religious Quest* (1985–). Twenty-four volumes have been completed to date. The articles aren't translations of original texts but are written to explore the spiritual dimensions of religion as an eternal quest. The series is obtainable from:

Crossroad/Continuum Publishing Group,
370 Lexington Avenue, New York, NY 10017,
(800) 242-7737, FAX: (212) 532-4922.

A publisher devoted to making the sacred texts of Buddhism available to the public is **Wisdom Books**. Their catalogue offers 1500 books of their own and eighty other publishers on Buddhism. Their addresses are:

361 Newbury Street, Boston, MA 02115, USA,
(800) 272-4050, (617) 536-3358, FAX: (617) 536-1897;

402 Hoe Street, London E17 9AA, England,
(71) 520-5588, FAX: (71) 520-0932; and

P.O. Box 1326, Chatswood, NSW 2067, Australia,
(02) 922-6338.

Today, it's much easier to find books on the world's religions than it was even ten or twenty years ago. Perhaps the best approach to exploring the spiritual teachings of the world is the old advice to start browsing in a library, bookstore, or good catalogue and to let one book lead to another. Sooner or later, the ones that open new worlds find their ways into our hands.

Interpreting Symbols and Revelations

🔲🔲🔲🔲🔲🔲🔲

How we've used the Bible represents one interpretation of it. We don't think it's the only interpretation—not even remotely. Gnostic scholar, **Elaine Pagels**, for example, underscores the latitude for interpreting the Bible in:

Adam, Eve, and the Serpent (Random House, 1988).

She explains that the opening chapters of Genesis have been interpreted by the Church since the fourth century as speaking to sin and human sexuality. But she contrasts this interpretation with earlier Gnostic interpretations, which found in Genesis something more liberating, namely, a path of spiritual self-discovery.

Another interesting (and equally controversial) writer, **Andrew M. Greeley**, sociologist and Catholic priest, takes a very different look at the Bible in his book,

Myths of Religion (Warner Books, 1989),

which combines in one volume three earlier books, *The Jesus Myth* (1971), *The Sinai Myth* (1972), and *The Mary Myth* (1977). *Myths of Religion* deals with more traditional questions of Roman Catholic doctrine and practice in challenging ways.

Interpreting the Bible as myth doesn't take away from its spiritual meaning. If anything, it enhances it by making its universal message more accessible to us every day. As Father Greeley explains in his Introduction, "myth" means "not fairy tale or legend, not make-believe or fiction, but rather a story that points beyond itself and gives meaning, purpose, and direction to life."

In this book, we focused the Bible in yet a different way. We wanted to explore methods for evolving the philosophies we live by, so that our economies can be better guided. The more we considered the Bible in this light, the more it was clear that it could speak to these issues as well.

But using the Bible to think through an issue—and inevitably interpreting the text along the way—raises the question of how to interpret revelations and their symbols. What is a text's revealed meaning, and how do we know whether we're on the right track in the meaning we're attributing to revelation?

It's a tough question, one that's occupied the minds of many thinkers. For example, the great Jewish thinker, **Philo of Alexandria** (20 BC–50 AD), wrote on the method of interpreting the Bible, as did the Christian Alexandrian philosopher, **Origen** (185–254 AD). In the fourth century, the African Christian writer, **Tyconius**, wrote *The Book of Rules*, which gives seven rules for interpreting the Bible. During the Renaissance, the Italian humanist philosopher, **Pico della Mirandola** (1463–94), wrote the *Heptaplus*, a volume on the spiritual structure of the seven days of creation and the method of interpreting them. Later, **Benedict Spinoza** (1632–77), the Dutch lens maker and philosopher, wrote about methods of interpreting the Bible—as have countless others in history, many of whose works are lost to us. (The works are cited by ancient writers but no copy remains.)

The list of contemporary thinkers tackling the subject is as innumerable. The writers we'd like to mention are those who interpret revelations in a universal but also practical way. They try to find a meaning that both includes and transcends time and culture, so that works of revelation mean something for us all.

One of the best known writers is **Mircea Eliade**, the Romanian-born scholar who studied in both Bucharest and Calcutta and then lived in an ashram in Rishikesh, Himalaya. Later, he taught at the University of Bucharest, the Sorbonne, and the University of Chicago. In his last years, he was editor-in-chief of Macmillan's 16-volume *Encyclopedia of Religion*, published in 1987, a year after he died. Among his many writings, the most immediately relevant would be:

Myth and Reality (Harper & Row, 1963) and

Patterns in Comparative Religion (World Publishing Company, 1963).

The first discusses myths and their meanings in general terms, while the second gives the specific meanings of nature symbols—the sun, moon, stars, stones, water, etc.—in different cultures. A slightly more academic but very informative work is his:

A History of Religious Ideas, three volumes (University of Chicago Press, 1978, 1982, 1985).

Rituals represent another language that the Bible uses to convey its message. A highly respected scholar in both myth and ritual interpretation is **Theodor Gaster**, whose works focus on Near Eastern rituals and Biblical symbols:

Thespis: Ritual, Myth, and Drama in the Ancient Near East (Harper & Row, 1950) and

Myth, Legend, and Custom in the Old Testament, two volumes (Harper & Row, 1969).

For comparative studies of creation myths in particular, the best we know is **Charles Long's:**

Alpha: The Myths of Creation (Collier-Macmillan,
Toronto, 1963).

Of course, there's **Joseph Campbell's** Jungian perspective for interpreting myths. His books, tapes, and videotapes have exploded onto the market since his death in 1988. Professor Campbell accentuated the universal structure of myths. For example, his first book, published over forty years ago, analyzes the pattern underlying hero tales from all over the world. The book is aptly titled:

The Hero With A Thousand Faces (World Publishing
Company, 1949).

Some of his other books include:

The Masks of God, four volumes (Viking Press): Primitive
Mythology (1959, 1969), Oriental Mythology (1962),
Occidental Mythology (1964), Creative Mythology (1968), and

The Power of Myth (Doubleday, 1988), which is based on
Bill Moyers' interviews with Professor Campbell for public
television. The videotapes of the program are available
and well worth watching.

One of the most practical and accessible discussions of myths is given by **Carol Pearson**, who applies universal patterns or "archetypes" of myths to themes of personal development. Her book,

The Hero Within: Six Archetypes We Live By
(Harper & Row, 1986),

shows how myths speak to where we are—whether we're an Innocent, Orphan, Wanderer, Warrior, Martyr, or Magician—and help us develop our innate wholeness.

Looking for deeper levels of spiritual meaning in the Bible—for themes, patterns, and structures that bring out revelation's universal and timeless message—was British thinker **John W. Doorly's** approach. He's no longer well-known, and his books are hard to find, but his work is unique in cutting through often obscure ancient symbols to the Bible's spiritual message. For a year, he was president of the Christian Science Church, but he parted company with that organization during World War II. He continued his research independently and had planned to compare his studies on the Bible with the teachings of the world's religions, but he died in 1950. He gave several series of lectures on the Bible, published as:

> *Talks on the Science of the Bible*, nine volumes (The Foundational Book Company, 1947–50),
>
> *Talks at the Oxford Summer School, 1948*, two volumes (The Foundational Book Company, 1948), and
>
> *Talks at the Oxford Summer School, 1949*, two volumes (The Foundational Book Company, 1949).

Though his language and examples reflect his Christian Science background, John Doorly's interpretations are accessible to general readers and express a fresh insight into the Bible's universal meaning. His books are distributed by:

> Rare Book Company, P. O. Box 957, Freehold, NJ 07728, (201) 780-1393 and
>
> D. & J. Andreae, 9 Olicana Park, Middleton, Ilkley, West Yorkshire LS29 OAW, England, (943) 602-686.

Finally, we'd like to mention the work of archaeologist and historian **John Romer**. He's not exactly an interpreter of sacred symbols, but his research on the ancient Near East and ancient Egypt gives an excellent background for understanding the everyday world of the Bible and the big movements of people and culture that shaped it. His book on the Bible,

> *Testament: The Bible and History* (Henry Holt, 1988),

was also the basis for an outstanding television series and is available on videotape. He recounts history and the evolving study of the Bible like a detective cracking a case. But more than history, he sketches the quest for cosmic order and meaning that the Bible represents.

As all of these scholars and thinkers point out, when we read the Bible or any other sacred text, we come away with some meaning from what we've read. But if that meaning were the whole of what the text has to say, it wouldn't be much of a revelation. People would have figured out the meaning long ago and gone on to something more challenging.

But that's not what happens. If we read the Dalai Lama, for instance, he's constantly rethinking and reinterpreting Buddhist teachings. Rethinking the Bible is the story of Judaism and Christianity. It's what happens in Islam with the Qur'an, and it's also the history of Hindu, Confucian, and Taoist philosophy. The more we evolve, the more we discover new dimensions of what a sacred text says. Interpretation turns out to be a many layered and continually evolving process. That being so, the methods we use for interpreting revelations remain very much an issue.

Notes

Preface

1. Louis Fischer, *The Essential Gandhi: An Anthology of His Writings on His Life, Work and Ideas* (New York: Random House, 1962, Vintage Books Edition, 1983), 88–91.

CHAPTER 1:
The Crises that Came To Dinner

1. Aside from watching *Murder, She Wrote*, we learned about the relation between crime and money from criminal justice consultant Fred Ward, who directs all interested readers to the quarterly, *Criminal Justice Abstracts*, Richard S. Allinson, ed. (Criminal Justice Press, P. O. Box 249, Monsey, NY 10952). Its index for the last 17 years of issues has recently been published.

2. Plato, *Phaedo*, 66c. Hugh Tredennick, trans., *Plato: The Last Days of Socrates* (London: Penguin Books, 1954), 111.

3. Paul Kennedy, *The Rise and Fall of the Great Powers: Economic Change and Military Conflict from 1500 to 2000* (New York: Random House, 1987).

4. *Katha Upanishad*, Part 3. Juan Mascaro, trans., *The Upanishads* (London: Penguin Books, 1965), 60–61. "Upanishad," by the way, means "to sit down near a teacher." The *Upanishads* are a vast collection of sacred and revealed Hindu reform teachings, the oldest of which dates to 800 B.C.

5. Richard Conniff, "A Deal That Might Save a Sierra Gem," *Time Magazine* (3 April 1989), 10.

6. "Practical Enlightenment, An Interview with Charles T. Tart," *The Sun* (Issue 150, May 1988), 7.

7. Ibid.

8. Peter Riga, Interview in "Trouble in the Banking Business," *MacNeil/Lehrer NewsHour* (WNET/Thirteen, Box 1335, New York, NY 10101, January 6, 1988), transcript p. 11.

9. Thomas I. White, *Right and Wrong: A Brief Guide to Understanding Ethics* (Englewood Cliffs, NJ: Prentice Hall, 1988), 88.

10. Ibid.

11. Ibid., 89.

12. Viktor Frankl, *Man's Search for Meaning* (New York: Pocket Books, Washington Square Press, 1959, 1984). The book was first published in Austria, 1946 under the title *Ein Psycholog erlebt das Konzentrationslager.*

13. Brand Blanshard, *Reason and Belief* (New Haven: Yale University Press, 1975), 434.

14. Werner Heisenberg, *Physics and Beyond* (New York: Harper & Row, 1971), 214.

15. St. Gregory of Nyssa, *The Lord's Prayer, The Beatitudes*, Hilda C. Graef, trans., *Ancient Christian Writers*, No. 18, Johannes Quasten and Joseph C. Plumpe, eds. (New York and Ramsey, NJ: Newman Press/Paulist Press, 1954), 87-88.

16. Riane Eisler, *The Chalice and the Blade* (New York: Harper & Row, 1987). Ashley Montagu calls this work "the most important book since Darwin's *Origin of the Species.*"

17. Zarathustra's life is tricky, since so little is known about it. Nonetheless there are useful books on it, for instance: Mary Boyce, *Zoroastrians: Their Religious Beliefs and Practices* (London: Routledge & Kegan Paul, 1979); A. B. Williams Jackson, *Zoroaster, The Prophet of Ancient Iran* (New York: Columbia University Press, 1898 and 1926); R. C. Zaehner, *The Dawn and Twilight of Zoroastrianism* (New York: G. P. Putnam's Sons, 1961); Rustom Masani, *Zoroastrianism: The Religion of the Good Life* (New York: The Macmillan Company, 1968).

18. N. A. Nikam and Richard McKeon, eds. and trans., *The Edicts of Asoka* (Chicago and London: University of Chicago Press, 1959), 44.

19. Fazlur Rahman, *Islam* (Chicago and London: University of Chicago Press, 1966, second edition, 1979), 12.

20. Ibid.

21. T. B. Irving (Al-Hajj Ta'lim 'Ali), trans., *The Qur'an: The First American Version* (Brattleboro, VT: Amana Books, 1985), 393.

22. See John H. Mundy and Peter Riesenberg, *The Medieval Town* (Huntington, NY: Robert E. Krieger Publishing Company, 1958, reprint 1979), 28-29; and P. Boissonnade, *Life and Work in Medieval Europe: Fifth to Fifteenth Centuries*, Eileen Power, trans. (New York: Dorset Press, 1987), 154–158.

23. Philip B. Kurland and Ralph Lerner, eds., *The Founders' Constitution* (Chicago and London: University of Chicago Press, 1987), Vol. I, 429.

24. Henry C. Carey, *The Past, the Present and the Future* (New York: Augustus M. Kelley, reprint 1967, first ed. 1847), 83–86. Augustus M. Kelley, Publishers, (300 Fairfield Road, Fairfield, NJ 07006; (212) 685-7202) is a great source for economic classics.

CHAPTER 2:
Who's Driving the Chariot?

1. Ravi Batra's books include *The Great Depression of 1990* (New York: Simon & Schuster, revised, 1987), *Surviving the Great Depression of 1990* (New York: Simon & Schuster, 1988) and *The Downfall of Capitalism and Communism: Can Capitalism Be Saved?* (Dallas TX: Venus Books, 1990, first ed. London: Macmillan, 1978). Professor Batra's approach relates economic conditions to stages of spiritual development and argues that we need to emerge from the acquisitive stage of the last few centuries.

Pitirim A. Sorokin (1889–1968) was a Russian sociologist expelled from Russia in the 1920s for his anti-Bolshevism. He emigrated to America and in 1930 founded the department of sociology at Harvard University. He wrote many volumes explaining how a few basic philosophical mindsets shape civilization and culture. His most popular book is *The Crisis of Our Age: The Social and Cultural Outlook* (New York: E. P. Dutton,

1941). He argued that creative, altruistic love must be understood and practiced as a science to avert worldwide chaos.

Christopher Wood is the New York-based reporter for *The Economist*. In *Boom and Bust* (New York: Atheneum, 1989), he argues that someday soon we'll have to liquidate the mega-debts of the '80s, and that when we do, we'll have some rough sailing.

2. Paul Hawken, *Growing a Business* (New York: Simon & Schuster, 1987), 33, 35.

3. Kenneth Boulding, *Evolutionary Economics* (Beverly Hills and London: Sage Publications, 1981), 45.

4. Bill Moyers, *A World of Ideas* (New York: Doubleday, 1989), 182.

5. Adam Smith, *An Inquiry into the Nature and Causes of the Wealth of Nations* (reprint, New York: The Modern Library, 1937), 13, 16.

6. The win-win model is gaining acceptance in the literature appearing on business in bookstores and libraries. For instance, there's Ross R. Reck and Brian G. Long's *Win-Win Negotiator* (NY: Simon & Schuster, 1985) as well as Lucy Beale and Rick Fields' *The Win/Win Way* (NY: Harcourt Brace Jovanovich, 1987). In *The Strategy of the Dolphin* (NY: William Morrow, 1988), Dudley Lynch and Paul L. Kordis buy win-win as the basic goal but warn that the win-win can't be achieved superficially, otherwise neither side benefits. But then, that's not real win-win.

7. Porphyry, *Porphyry's Letter to His Wife Marcella Concerning the Life of Philosophy and the Ascent to the Gods*, Alice Zimmern, trans. (Grand Rapids: Phanes Press, 1986), 55–56.

8. Plato, *Phaedo*, 89d–90a. Tredennick, 144.

9. Sarvepalli Radhakrishnan, *Religion and Society* (London: Allen & Unwin, 1947), 137.

10. Smith, *Wealth of Nations*, 14.

11. When competition isn't practiced within the framework of cooperation, it means only win-lose. One party gets the prize; the other doesn't. This conflict-model of competition has been challenged in studies conducted by Robert Helmreich and the University of Minnesota's David and Roger Johnson. It's also been criticized in works such as Alfie Kohn's *No Contest: The Case*

Against Competition (Houghton Mifflin, 1986). These studies indicate that competitive situations stifle individual creativity.

For understanding how economies work, however, we're not sure we can do away with competition altogether. After decades of experimenting with a noncompetitive model, Eastern Europe is now concluding that the free-market system of economic competition works better. A lack of competition leads to domination by one or two powerful factions, as the West has discovered with its own monopolies. True, people will likely evolve other models for noncompetitive economies that might prove more successful. But for now, the remedy for the negative effects of competition may lie simply in finding a context that makes the competitive response constructive. The context of cooperation seems to fit the bill. Cooperation makes room for both parties competing. In such a context, competition serves as a tool for increasing economic diversity and spurring the pursuit of excellence, all of which makes economies better as a result.

12. Smith, *Wealth of Nations*, 99.

13. Quoted by Charles Sanford, "Alumni Viewpoint: Some Suggestions for Planning Your Career," *Wharton Alumni Magazine* (Fall, 1987): 15.

14. Desiderius Erasmus, *The Education of a Christian Prince*, Lester K. Born, trans. (New York: Octagon Books, 1987), 212. Erasmus' work was originally printed in 1516.

15. Plato, *Gorgias*, 494c., R. E. Allen, *The Dialogues of Plato*, Vol. I (New Haven and London: Yale University Press, 1984), 281.

16. Boethius, *The Consolation of Philosophy*, S. J. Tester, trans., Book V:II (Cambridge, Massachusetts: Harvard University Press and London: William Heinemann, Loeb Classical Library, 1973), 393.

17. One of the philosophers most noted for arguing that scientific work is never value-free is Michael Polanyi. His works include *Personal Knowledge* (New York: Harper & Row, 1964) and *Knowing and Being*, Marjorie Grene, ed. (Chicago: University of Chicago Press, 1969).

18. Plato, *Apology*, 38a. Tredennick, 71–72.

19. Henry Carey, *The Unity of Law* (Philadelphia: Henry Carey Baird, Industrial Publisher, 1872; reprint, New York: Augustus M. Kelley, 1967), xvii–xix, 1–2.

20. Charles Dickens, "A Christmas Carol," *Charles Dickens' Best Stories*, Morton Dauwen Zabel, ed. (Garden City, NY: Hanover House, 1959), 106.

21. Kenneth Boulding, *Evolutionary Economics*, 132.

CHAPTER 4:
What's Forward and What's Not?

1. Thomas S. Kuhn, *The Structure of Scientific Revolutions* (Chicago: University of Chicago Press, 1962, second ed. 1970).

2. Rupert Sheldrake, *A New Science of Life: The Hypothesis of Formative Causation* (Los Angeles: J. P. Tarcher, 1981).

3. Marsilio Ficino, *The Book of Life*, Charles Boer, trans. (Dallas: Spring Publications, 1980), 191.

4. Chuang Tzu, *Chuang Tzu: Basic Writings*, Burton Watson, trans. (New York: Columbia University Press, 1964), 97.

5. Kenneth Boulding, *Evolutionary Economics*, 67–68.

6. Chuang Tzu, *Chuang Tzu: Basic Writings*, 99.

7. Lao Tzu, *The Way of Lao Tzu (Tao-te ching)*, Chapter 71, Wing-Tsit Chan, trans. (Indianapolis and New York: The Bobbs-Merrill Company, The Library of Liberal Arts, 1963), 225.

8. Kenneth Boulding, *Human Betterment* (Beverly Hills, London and New Delhi: Sage Publications, 1985), 65.

9. Fragment 195 in the translation by G. S. Kirk, J. E. Raven and M. Schofield, *The Presocratic Philosophers*, Second Edition (Cambridge, London, New York, New Rochelle, Melbourne and Syndey: Cambridge University Press, 1987), 187; Fragment 2 in the translation by T. M. Robinson, *Heraclitus: Fragments* (Toronto, Buffalo, London: University of Toronto Press, 1987) and Fragment 2 in the translation by G. S. Kirk, *Heraclitus: The Cosmic Fragments* (Cambridge: Cambridge University Press, 1954), 57-64.

10. Quoted in Ninian Smart and Richard D. Hecht, eds., *Sacred Texts of the World: A Universal Anthology* (New York: Crossroad Publishing Company, 1986), 296.

11. Kenneth Boulding, *Human Betterment*, 62, 69, 102-108. Boulding analyzes the knowing necessary for economies into "know-what," "know-how," and "know-whether." We've put them into the order given here to make them consistent with our four-stage model of how philosophies evolve. We also added the fourth kind of knowing: know-why.

12. Tommaso Campanella, *The City of the Sun: A Poetical Dialogue*, Daniel J. Donno, trans. (Berkeley, Los Angeles and London: University of California Press, 1981), 47.

CHAPTER 5:
The Ups and Downs of Evolution

1. *The Upanishads*, Juan Mascaro, trans., (New York and Harmondsworth, Middlesex, England: Penguin Books, 1965), 65.

2. Colm Luibheid and Paul Rorem, trans., *Pseudo-Dionysius: The Complete Works* (New York and Mahwah, NJ: Paulist Press, *The Classics of Western Spirituality*, 1987), 79. Scholars refer to this unknown writer as "Pseudo-Dionysius," because his—or her— writings were mistakenly attributed to Paul's student, Dionysius the Areopagite (see Acts 17:34). Throughout the book, however, we prefer to refer to the writer only as "Dionysius."

3. Alexander Hamilton, "The Farmer Refuted," Feb. 1775, Kurland and Lerner, *The Founders' Constitution*, Vol. 1, 91. Hamilton expresses a theological viewpoint at least as old as Plato, Philo of Alexandria, Augustine, and Boethius. Not only Hamilton's later economic work but also his interest in the relation of religion to politics—evidenced in his never-completed project (thanks to Aaron Burr) of tracing the history of religion's influence on government—makes his rendition particularly relevant.

4. Quoted in *Pseudo-Dionysius: The Complete Works*, 145.

5. Ibid., 119.

6. Ibid., 84.

7. James A. Wiseman, O.S.B., trans., *John Ruusbroec: The Spiritual Espousals and Other Works* (New York, Toronto and

Mahwah, NJ: Paulist Press, *The Classics of Western Spirituality*, 1985), 120.

   8. *The Four Books: Confucian Analects, The Great Learning, The Doctrine of the Mean, and the Works of Mencius,* James Legge, trans. (Shanghai, 1923, reprint, New York: Paragon Book Reprint Corporation, 1966), 358.

   9. David Bohm, *Unfolding Meaning* (London and New York: Routledge & Kegan Paul, 1985, Ark Paperbacks, 1987), 11.

   10. David Bohm,*Wholeness and the Implicate Order* (London and New York: Routledge & Kegan Paul, 1980, Ark Paperbacks, 1983), 185–186.

   11. Bohm, *Wholeness and the Implicate Order*, 209.

   12. The rendering here of the eightfold path is a composite of different translations. See Radhakrishnan and Moore, eds., *A Source Book in Indian Philosophy* (Princeton, NJ: Princeton University Press, 1957), 275, 277–278.

   13. Except for the second group of Commandments, we derive the structure of these Bible teachings and the method of category-interpretation from John W. Doorly (1878–1950), who studied the Bible extensively and investigated its spiritual structure. See: *Talks on the Science of the Bible*, Volumes I-IX (London: Foundational Book Company, 1979) and *Talks at the Oxford Summer School, 1948: A Verbatim Report*, Volume II, *Matthew and Revelation* (London: Foundational Book Company, 1949). The application of the Bible teachings to evolving both philosophies and economies is ours.

CHAPTER 6:
The Days of Creation:
Assumptions that Make Us Creative

   1. William Butler Yeats, "The Second Coming," *Immortal Poems of the English Language*, Oscar Williams, ed. (New York: Pocket Books, Cardinal Edition, 1952), 489.

   2. See Socrates' discussion with Polus in Plato's *Gorgias*.

   3. Robert Bellah, Richard Madsen, William M. Sullivan, Ann Swidler and Steven M. Tipton, *Habits of the Heart: Individualism*

and Commitment in American Life (New York: Harper & Row, 1985, Perennial Library edition, 1986).

4. Thorstein Veblen, *The Vested Interests and the Common Man* (New York: Augustus M. Kelley, Reprints of Economic Classics, 1964, first published 1919), 93.

5. Ibid., 92.

6. Luibheid and Rorem, *Pseudo-Dionysius*, 84.

7. *How Can One Sell The Air: The Manifesto of an Indian Chief* (Summertown, TN: Book Publishing Company, first published in the Netherlands: Ekologische Uitgeverij Amsterdam & Aktie Strohalm, Oudegracht 42, Utrecht, 1980). The book's pages aren't numbered.

8. Governments have sometimes confused Cainsian economics with the government-spending economic theories of British economist John Maynard Keynes (1883-1946), known, of course, as Keynesian economics.

9. Adam Smith, *The Theory of Moral Sentiments*, III.3.11, D. D. Raphael and A. L. Macfie, eds. (Oxford: Oxford University Press, 1976, first published 1759), 140–141.

10. Lao Tzu, *The Way of Lao Tzu (Tao-te ching)*, Chapter 44, Chan, trans., 179.

11. Ibid., Chapter 46, 181.

12. Ibid., Chapter 33, 159.

CHAPTER 7:
The Commandments: Strategies that Liberate

1. Those who thought having ten Commandments was a nice round number may not be too happy with us. Building on John Doorly's analysis of them (see Chapter 5, note 13), we've drawn out the two tablets to explore the strategies implied for evolving our relation both to God and to each other. As it turns out, several of the Commandments, especially from the first tablet, have more than one thing to say about liberating strategies. When we come to the statements of the Commandments themselves, then, we'll discuss seven statements from the first tablet and six from the second. That's only 13—not too bad.

2. See Paul Carus, *The Gospel of Buddha* (La Salle, Illinois: Open Court, 1973), 247; and Walpola Rahula, *What the Buddha Taught* (New York: Grove Press, 1959, second edition, 1974), 137.

3. The story of the historical Buddha's life can be found in any good book on Buddhism. Paul Carus' compilation is readily available, as is Ananda Coomaraswamy's *Buddha and the Gospel of Buddhism* (Secaucus, New Jersey: Citadel Press, 1988, originally published 1964).

4. Quoted in Robert C. Solomon and Kristine Hanson, *It's Good Business* (New York: Harper & Row, Perennial Library, 1985), 16–17.

5. Thomas Paine, *Rights of Man*, Part II, Chapter V, *Basic Writings of Thomas Paine* (New York: Willey Book Company, 1942), 211.

6. Plato, *Gorgias*, 483d. Allen, *Dialogues of Plato*, Vol. I, 271.

7. The four Noble Truths form the core of Buddhism. Rahula's *What the Buddha Taught* gives a good summary in Chapters II–V, but any book on Buddhism must include them. They're what the Buddha taught his entire teaching life.

CHAPTER 8:
The Beatitudes: Responses that Empower

1. Epictetus, *The Enchiridion*, Thomas W. Higginson, trans. (Indianapolis: Bobbs-Merrill Educational Publishing, The Library of Liberal Arts, 1955), 17. "Enchiridion" means "manual," and *The Enchiridion* has long been regarded as the "soldier's manual" for Stoics in the discipline of self-mastery.

2. Ibid.

3. Ibid.

4. Lao Tzu, *The Way of Lao Tzu (Tao-te ching)*, Chapter 30, Chan, trans., 152.

5. Ibid., Chapter 32, 157.

6. For these translations—Goodspeed (Gspd), the Berkeley New Testament (Ber) in *The New Testament from 26 Translations* and J. B. Phillips' translation (Phi)—see the end of these Notes:

"Bible Translations." All translations that aren't from the King James Version will refer to the abbreviations given there.

7. Paul Reps, comp., *Zen Flesh, Zen Bones: A Collection of Zen and Pre-Zen Writings* (Garden City, NY: Doubleday & Company, Anchor Books, n.d.), 5.

8. We're referring to Wess Roberts' amusing self-help book, *Leadership Secrets of Attila the Hun* (New York: Warner Books, 1988). Though Mr. Roberts argues that Attila's life holds insights for how to succeed in modern economies, we have qualms about emulating someone who spent his time slaughtering innocent people, razing cities, and murdering his brother. But worse, he's described by historians as "irritable." That did it for us.

9. Thomas Paine, *The Rights of Man*, Part II, Chapter V, *Basic Writings of Thomas Paine*, 210.

CHAPTER 9:
The Lord's Prayer: The Purpose To Evolve

1. See both *The Bhagavad-Gita* 18:65–66, Juan Mascaro, trans., 121, and *The Bhagavad-Gita*, XVIII:65–66, R. C. Zaehner, trans. (London, Oxford, New York: Oxford University Press, 1969), 108.

2. A. J. Arberry, trans., *The Koran Interpreted* (New York: The Macmillan Company, 1976), 29; see also *The Meaning of the Glorious Koran*, Mohammed Marmaduke Pickthall, trans. (New York: New American Library, Mentor Books, 1958), 31.

3. George A. Miller discusses the role of this category in human perception in *The Psychology of Communication* (New York: Basic Books, 1967), 3–44, which includes his chapter, "The Magical Number Seven, Plus or Minus Two: Some Limits on Our Capacity for Processing Information." This entertaining chapter argues that the reason the number seven appears so universally is that it's the maximum number of random things that we can easily process in our heads and remember. In other words, the magic about it relates to our own ability to retain information.

4. Charles Dickens, "A Christmas Carol," *Charles Dickens' Best Stories*, 137.

Bible Translations
(with abbreviations)

The Holy Bible from Ancient Eastern Manuscripts, Containing the Old and New Testaments Translated from the Peshitta, the Authorized Bible of the Church of the East. George M. Lamsa, trans. Philadelphia: A. J. Holman Company, 1957. **Abbreviation:** *Lamsa*

The Jerusalem Bible, Reader's Edition. General Editor, Alexander Jones. Garden City, NY: Doubleday & Company, 1968. **Abbreviation:** *Jer*

The New English Bible with The Apocrypha. New York and London: Oxford University Press, 1971. **Abbreviation:** *NEB*

The New Testament from 26 Translations. General Editor, Curtis Vaughan. Grand Rapids, MI: Zondervan Publishing House, 1967.

> *The Berkeley Version of the New Testament,* Gerrit Verkuyl, trans. **Abbreviation:** *Ber*

> *The New Testament: An American Translation,* Edgar J. Goodspeed, trans. **Abbreviation:** *Gspd*

> *The New Testament: A New Translation,* James Moffatt, trans. **Abbreviation:** *Mof*

> *The Twentieth Century New Testament.* **Abbreviation:** *TCNT*

> *The Four Gospels,* E. V. Rieu, trans. **Abbreviation:** *Rieu*

The New Testament in Modern English. J. B. Phillips, trans. New York: The Macmillan Company, 1962. **Abbreviation:** *Phi*

Acknowledgments

M any people took time from busy schedules to help us write and produce this book, and we're more grateful than we can express.

The authors who read the manuscript and offered comments represent a diverse group: economist Ravi Batra, theologian John B. Cobb, Jr., economist Paul Ekins, socio-economist Amitai Etzioni, futurist Hazel Henderson, activist Frances Moore Lappé, religious scholars Louis Dupré, Huston Smith, and Rabbi Steven Shaw, and psychologist Charles T. Tart. These people are in constant demand, and we deeply appreciate their time and contributions.

We're also most grateful to historian Hilary Conroy and his son, philosopher Fran Conroy, for reading the manuscript and writing a Foreword to it. They aided and abetted us all along. We also thank the scholars in the Cosmic History Seminar at the University of Pennsylvania, which the Conroys have nurtured for seven years now, for stimulating our thinking.

We've also had the advantage of having readers from very different professional backgrounds: chemist Jeannine Baden, tool designer Mike Baden, inventor Ernie Breton, lawyer Victor Bridgman, businesswoman Carole Chinman, artist Betty Collins, editor Barbara Fleischman, poetess Janet Hickman, activist and mother-extraordinaire Anne Kendall, herbalist Liz Largent, planner Bob Largent, media activist Kathleen Lynch, "sludge lady" Ruth Newman, "herb-lady" Mickey Robertaccio, teacher and super-mother Mary Rice, ad executive Charles Roth, and physician Danton Spivey. For all their valuable comments and suggestions, we're thoroughly indebted.

Our own editorial and proofreading staff have made the job of proofing infinitely easier. In this country, we benefited from the excellent work of Claudia Ballou, Mary Joy Breton, Lois Ann Crouse, and Susan Gerry, who saw the book through various stylistic, comma, and semicolon crises. From England, we gained the fine and thorough editing help of Joyce and Derek Andreae, and Hilda and Cecil Colson, who kept our Americanisms from becoming too outrageous and made their suggestions with wit and good humor. If, to British eyes, offenses remain—not to mention offences—it's simply because we're stubborn, not because they didn't try. For the monumental job of indexing, we're indebted to Mary Joy Breton again, who did the job the good, old-fashioned way.

For the book's layout and cover, we thank Claudia Ballou, whose impeccable artistic talents are obvious, as well as Pam Finkelman of Peyton Associates. We're also indebted to coin collector David Ganz, who helped locate the right coin to fit Claudia's cover. For text layout, we benefited from Susan Gerry's skills in tackling the Macintosh. For book production, we're grateful to Vivian Curl and Kim Eder at BookCrafters, whose patience and tireless efforts were above and beyond the call of business duty.

During the years we worked on the book, we had the encouragement of many people, including Dr. Frank Dilley and Mary Imperatore, who keep the Philosophy Department at the University of Delaware in good philosophical and administrative order; Mike Davis, who first suggested that we read Adam Smith's *Wealth of Nations* (all 900 pages of it); and our friends Edith Beck, Ellen Bergis, Alice Bigler,

Jule Bingham, Peggy Brook, Jim and Judy Clapp, Cedric Davenport, Jan Hoffman, and Louise Gordon. We were also greatly helped by the expertise of business consultant Glenn Sherk, the enthusiasm of the National Audubon Society's Chris Palmer, the knowledge of criminal justice consultant Fred Ward, and most of all, the unfailing support of our business partner and friend, Mary Joy Breton.

We want to offer a very special thanks to the staff of Longwood Gardens, Kennett Square, Pennsylvania, for their friendship and warmth. And our gratitude to Will Cuppy and P. G. Wodehouse, wherever they are, for all the fun and laughs.

Behind this book is the conviction that people everywhere are approaching businesses in creative, innovative, and whole-seeking ways. In our own experience, we've known and interacted with many businesspeople who exemplify what this book is all about. We're grateful to them all for showing us what economies can be.

We also gratefully acknowledge permission to reprint the following material:

Excerpt from David Bohm, WHOLENESS AND THE IMPLICATE ORDER, Copyright © 1980 by David Bohm, Routledge & Kegan Paul. Reprinted by permission of the publisher.

Kenneth Boulding, EVOLUTIONARY ECONOMICS, pp. 45, 132, 67-68. Copyright © 1981 by Kenneth Boulding. Reprinted by permission of Sage Publications, Inc.

Kenneth Boulding, HUMAN BETTERMENT, pp. 62, 65, 69, 102-108. Copyright © 1985 by Kenneth Boulding. Reprinted by permission of Sage Publications, Inc.

Excerpt from UNFOLDING MEANING: A WEEKEND OF DIALOGUE WITH DAVID BOHM, Copyright © 1985 by David Bohm, Routledge & Kegan Paul. Reprinted by permission of the publisher.

PSEUDO-DIONYSIUS: THE COMPLETE WORKS, trans. by Colm Luibheid, trans. collaboration by Paul Rorem. © 1987 by Colm Luibheid. Used by permission of Paulist Press.

David L. Ganz, THE WORLD OF COINS AND COIN COLLECTING, p. 15, the photo of the Syracuse dekadrachm featured on the cover. Copyright © 1980, 1985 by David L. Ganz. Reproduced by permission of David L. Ganz.

ST. GREGORY OF NYSSA: THE LORD'S PRAYER, THE BEATITUDES, trans. by Hilda C. Graef. © 1954 by Rev. Johannes Quasten and Rev. Joseph C. Plumpe. Used by permission of Paulist Press.

Paul Hawken, GROWING A BUSINESS, Copyright © 1987 by Paul Hawken, reprinted by permission of Simon & Schuster, Inc.

Excerpt from HOW CAN ONE SELL THE AIR?, Book Publishing Company, Summertown, Tenn.

Werner Heisenberg, trans. by Arnold J. Pomerans, PHYSICS AND BEYOND: ENCOUNTERS AND CONVERSATIONS. Planned and edited by Ruth Nanda Anshen. Copyright © 1971 by Harper & Row, Publishers, Inc. Reprinted by permission of the publisher.

Excerpt from "Trouble in the Banking Business," *MacNeil/Lehrer News-Hour*, an interview with Peter Riga, January 6, 1988, reprinted courtesy of *MacNeil/Lehrer NewsHour* © 1988.

PORPHYRY'S LETTER TO HIS WIFE MARCELLA CONCERNING THE LIFE OF PHILOSOPHY AND THE ASCENT TO THE GODS, trans. by Alice Zimmern. © 1986 by Phanes Press. Used by permission of Phanes Press.

JOHN RUUSBROEC: THE SPIRITUAL ESPOUSALS AND OTHER WORKS, trans. by James A. Wiseman, O.S.B. © 1985 by James A. Wiseman, O.S.B. Used by permission of Paulist Press.

Charles Tart, CREDO OF SCIENTISM, Copyright © 1983 by Charles Tart, reproduced with his permission.

Thomas I. White, RIGHT & WRONG: A BRIEF GUIDE TO UNDER-STANDING ETHICS, © 1988, pp. 88, 89. Prentice Hall, Englewood Cliffs, New Jersey. Used by permission of Prentice Hall.

Index

About the Authors

Denise Breton and Christopher Largent, working as a husband-wife team, split their time between teaching and writing.

They teach for the Philosophy Department of the University of Delaware—courses on ethics, logic, the Bible, and most frequently, Eastern and Western religions. They are also in demand at lifelong education programs and churches of various denominations. In addition, they've taught seminars on philosophy and religion on the East and West coasts of the United States, in Canada as well as in England.

Their writing includes both fiction and nonfiction. They're working on two historical novels, one set just after the death of Plato, inspired by the Pythagorean-Platonic schools in ancient Greece and Egypt, and the other set in the time of William the Conqueror, inspired by the Bayeux Tapestry in Bayeux, France.

Following THE SOUL OF ECONOMIES, the second volume in their series on applied philosophy and practical spirituality will focus on politics.

About Idea House

I dea House books are printed on *permanent (acid-free)*, high-quality *recycled* paper with large type for ease of reading. Hardcover editions are Smythe sewn and have library-quality covers. Paperback editions are also sewn for durability.

Recycled paper is usually only 50 per cent recycled. Moreover, the quality of recycled paper acceptable to libraries and bookstores now comes from industry scraps, which have never been inked, and not from post-consumer sources, which require de-inking. Fortunately, this is changing rapidly as the demand for recycled paper increases. The quality of post-consumer recycled paper is getting better all the time, and the ink is getting less toxic.

To compensate for the 50 per cent new paper, Idea House, joining with a growing number of publishers, makes contributions to *Global ReLeaf* (The American Forestry Association, P.O. Box 2000, Washington, DC 20013, (202) 667-3300) proportionate to the number of trees used for editions and reprints.

Idea House is a member of COSMEP—The International Association of Independent Publishers, PMA—Publishers Marketing Association, New Age Publishing and Retailing Alliance, and the Mid-America Publishers Association. It is also an associate member of the American Booksellers Association and a special member of the American Library Association.

Idea House Publishing Company

Editorial address: SAN: 297-228X
2019 Delaware Avenue, Wilmington, DE 19806
(302) 571-9570   FAX: (302) 571-9615

Orders address: SAN: 630-3463
c/o Maxway Data Corporation
225 West 34th Street, New York, NY 10122
(212) 947-6100   FAX: (212) 563-5703
          Toll-free: (800) 447-8862

T he most important thing is practice in daily life; then you can know gradually the true value of religion. Doctrine is not meant for mere knowledge but for the improvement of our minds. In order to do that, it must be part of our life. If you put religious doctrine in a building and when you leave the building depart from the practices, you cannot gain its value.

The Dalai Lama